AGRICULTURAL PROGRESS
IN THE COTTON BELT
SINCE 1920

Agricultural Progress in The Cotton Belt Since 1920

By

JOHN LEONARD FULMER

THE UNIVERSITY OF NORTH CAROLINA PRESS
CHAPEL HILL

Copyright 1950
THE UNIVERSITY OF NORTH CAROLINA PRESS

MANUFACTURED IN THE UNITED STATES OF AMERICA

To My Parents

Preface

BUSINESS CONCERNS TAKE a complete annual inventory in order to determine growth and progress. Similarly, there is need for stock-taking in the different segments of the economy at intervals, not only to gauge progress but also to determine reasons for trends and their interrelationships. Such stock-taking is especially needed in Southern agriculture at present. For several decades now the professional agricultural workers have been struggling with its many complex and multiple problems. Progress has seemed slow, and at times it has not seemed to exist. But a careful examination of the facts indicates that real improvement has occurred. The character of Southern agriculture today is greatly different from what it was a quarter century or more ago. It is better balanced, farms are larger, incomes are higher and trending higher; but what is more important, the ground work has been laid for even greater and more rapid progress.

It is especially fitting that trends in Southern agriculture be analyzed at this time because, as a result of recent adjustments in the national economy and the 1948 bumper crop of cotton, the issues of production control and marketing quotas are again arising. To promote clear thinking in the present situation and during the next few years, data on historical trends may be helpful. Unfortunately, forecasting in economic science is still a hazardous guessing game, but past trends are a fair indication of the direction future economic winds may blow, and often a good forecast of such changes. If this study provides some help along these lines, it will have been justified. It is also hoped that some of the findings herein will give encouragement and provide new enthusiasm to that great host of agricultural workers in the South who over a long period have battled faithfully and against heavy odds in the interest of a more efficient agriculture and hence a more prosperous South.

In this analysis, heavy reliance has been placed on graphic methods. The manner in which census data have been used with this method to establish relationships is unorthodox and quite crude. Although the results are often obviously of low reliability and many others, if subjected to formal statistical techniques, would be found lacking in significance in the event one had grounds for applying such tests in the first place, it is believed that valuable information *about* relationship, and even relationships, has been established. And a framework has been in part constructed for reasoning about the agricultural economy of the region, although in certain cases perhaps only hypotheses have been suggested.

This study is not the result of a research grant or other financial subsidy, but is rather an outgrowth of the author's course work and incidental research on Southern agriculture. In performing the tedious calculations and their checking, he gratefully acknowledges the help of two former graduate students, Messrs. Cecil N. Smith and Gilbert W. Biggs, who, despite their inability to find time to work at it systematically and regularly, rendered valuable clerical assistance. Both held service fellowships and were assigned from the School of Rural Social Economics for this work and I am grateful to Dr. Wilson Gee, the School's head, for thus making their time available; I appreciate also the helpful advice which he gave relative to various aspects of the study and other aid in getting the manuscript published.

The Research Council of the Richmond Area University Center is the sponsor of this book and provided a substantial subsidy for its publication. Without this aid the manuscript probably would have encountered difficulties and delays to appearing in printed form. A grant was also provided by it for drafting the graphs to the specifications of the printer. I sincerely appreciate the interest of this research group and am grateful for its support.

I am deeply indebted to the following persons, who

kindly read the manuscript and offered many excellent suggestions and criticisms: Dr. Lorin A. Thompson, Director, Bureau of Population and Economic Research, University of Virginia, Charlottesville, Va.; Mr. Russell W. Bierman, Agricultural Economist, and Dr. E. A. Kincaid, Vice-president, both of the Federal Reserve Bank of Richmond, Virginia; and Dr. Joseph S. Davis, Director, Food Research Institute, Stanford University, California. The manuscript reflects many of their recommendations and its quality has been thereby improved; however, not all are included, either because of a difference in point of view or because of the lack of research funds necessary for working them out.

I wish especially to acknowledge the aid of the Institute for Research in the Social Sciences of the University of Virginia which provided for the typing of the many revisions of the manuscript. I am greatly indebted to its secretary, Miss Ruth Ritchie, who patiently and carefully typed the manuscript repeatedly. My wife, Mrs. Adelaide Wise Fulmer, helped with the study in numerous ways and I take this opportunity to acknowledge her contribution and to express my appreciation.

Most of the work on the manuscript was completed in the two-year period prior to the fall of 1948; however, certain minor revisions were made in May and June, 1949, after it had been accepted for publication, in order to reflect additional interesting and important data.

University of Virginia   J. L. F.
June, 1949

Contents

	PAGE
Preface	vii
I. Trends in the Cotton Belt	3
II. Regional Trends	24
III. Farm Organizational Changes	47
IV. Mechanization	60
V. The Mechanical Harvesting of Cotton	82
VI. Urbanization and Agriculture	107
VII. Other Dynamic Factors Influencing Southern Agriculture	135
VIII. Income Shifts	149
IX. Summary and Conclusions	169
Statistical Appendix	193
Selected Bibliography	215
Index	229

List of Figures

NUMBER	PAGE
1. Trends in Acreage, Yield, and Production of Cotton in Ten Cotton Belt States, 1910-48.	6
2. Trends in Acreage Harvested of Specified Crops in Ten Cotton Belt States, by Census Years.	8
3. Number of All Cattle, Milk Cows, Hogs, and Chickens on Farms January 1 in Ten Cotton States, 1910-48.	13
4. Sources of Gross Farm Income in the Cotton Belt, 1924 to 1947.	19
5. Major Cotton-producing Areas in the United States.	25
6. Trends in Cotton Production in Major Producing Areas Since 1928.	26
7. Trends in Acreage Harvested of Important Crops in Different Regions of the Cotton Belt, by Census Years.	29
8. Trends in Average Farm Organization in Different Regions of Ten Cotton States, by Census Years.	49
9. Percentage of Cropland Harvested Occupied by Major Categories of Crops in Different Regions, By Census Years.	50
10. Relation of Tractors on Farms to Number of Other (Non-Cotton) Farms, by Census Years.	73
11. Relationship of Price of Cotton Received by Farmers in U. S. Preceding October to April Wage Rate Per Day Without Board for Farm Labor in South Carolina, 1923 to 1941.	77
12. Combined Effect of Selling Price of Cotton and Average Yield Per Acre on the Economic Advantage of Using the Mechanical Cotton Picker.	96

List of Figures

NUMBER		PAGE
13.	Important Urban Counties in the Cotton Belt, 1940	111
14.	Relative Rate of Growth of Important Urban Counties in the Cotton Belt Between 1930 and 1940	112
15.	Projection of Population Trends by Major Categories for Ten Cotton States	120
16.	Trends in Relative Population Distribution by Areas	122
17.	Relation of Nonfarm Population to Milk Sold, by Census Dates	126
18.	Relation of Nonfarm Population to Vegetables Harvested for Sale, by Census Dates	127
19.	Relation of Total Population to Eggs Produced, by Census Dates	128
20.	Relation of Number of Other Farms to Number of Cotton Farms, by Census Years	137
21.	Trends in Cotton Acreage Harvested and Bales Produced Per Farm Reporting Cotton, by Periods	138
22.	Relation of Farms Growing Cotton to Total Farm Population, by Census Years	140
23.	Relation of Number of Cotton Farms to the Number of Horses and Mules on Farms	142
24.	Trends in Gross Farm Production Per Worker by Geographic Divisions, 1919-46	155
25.	Per Capita Incomes of the Eastern, Delta, and Oklahoma-Texas Cotton Producing Regions Expressed as a Percentage of Per Capita Income of the 38 Other States Plus the District of Columbia, 1929-47	160
26.	Total Population and Total Income Payments in Different Regions of the Cotton Belt Expressed as Percentage of 38 Other States Plus the District of Columbia, 1929 to 1947	162

AGRICULTURAL PROGRESS IN THE COTTON BELT SINCE 1920

CHAPTER I

Trends in the Cotton Belt[1]

FROM THE EARLY agricultural societies late in the 18th century to the present day, Southern agriculturalists have crusaded for independence from the bondage of a one-crop system. In the early decades this agitation did not progress much beyond the society debates and editorial comment in the newspapers of the time and it was not until 1862 that positive national action came with the enactment of the Morrill Land Grant Act, which established agricultural instruction in state institutions on a broad and firm basis. Continued agitation for agricultural betterment produced the Hatch Act of 1887, the Smith-Lever Act of 1914, the Smith-Hughes Act of 1917, which established respectively the agricultural experiment stations, extension work in agriculture and home economics, and vocational agricultural education in the public schools. These acts made it possible to put science to work for the farmer and teach him how to apply it. But the mass of farmers were still inaccessible to its well-intentioned benefits because of their intellectual backwardness.

From 1920 on, a succession of events did more to force diversification on farmers than all previous legislation combined. They were the advent of the boll weevil, the depression of the 1930's, the Agricultural Adjustment Act of 1933, the Soil Conservation and Domestic Allotment Act of 1936, the Agricultural Adjustment Act of 1938, and World War II.

The boll weevil increased the difficulties of growing the crop successfully and made risk of financial failure much greater. To grow the crop at all for a time required adop-

[1] Includes North Carolina, South Carolina, Georgia, Alabama, Tennessee, Mississippi, Louisiana, Arkansas, Oklahoma and Texas.

tion of scientific control measures which the mass of farmers mastered slowly and some never efficiently. The shrinkage of income and credit forced the production of certain food and feed crops. Some idea of the effect of the boll weevil on cotton acreage can be gathered by what happened to Alabama. Heavy infestation first appeared in 1915 when 3,138,000 acres were harvested. By 1917 only 2,033,000 acres were harvested and acreage harvested remained below 3,000,000 acres until 1923, after which considerable recovery occurred. In the meantime considerable progress toward diversification had been made. Coffee County, Alabama, regarded the weevil with such favor that a monument was erected in recognition of the progress which had been forced upon agriculture by this insect.

The depression caused a renewed emphasis on food and feed crops because the returns from cotton were so low that little was left, after taxes and debt service, for the necessities of life.

The various government programs, beginning with the A.A.A. of 1933, touched all farmers, and, partly through compulsion and partly through subsidy, cotton was reduced, leaving land that had to be used for feed crops or allowed to remain idle. The incentive payments introduced some farmers to practices they had carelessly neglected. Perhaps the process has had its educational aspects and some of the benefits will remain.

World War II removed the surplus labor,[2] and the draft, coupled with migration to defense jobs and other types of city employment, caused a labor deficit in some areas, or at least forced farmers to make an economic use of a factor of production once superabundant but suddenly in scarce supply. A more extensive agriculture was the only alternative. Increased city wages afforded a larger outlet for meats and other livestock products and vegetables, and, since there was not as much surplus of them as of cotton, the price relationships favored an expansion.

[2] As a result of the end of the war in 1945 and the subsequent demobilization, there was a net back-to-the-farm movement of population in 1945 and 1946, but normal trends in migration were resumed in 1947 and are continuing.

TRENDS IN CROPS

Cotton

Estimates of acreage, yield, and production of cotton issued by the United States Department of Agriculture are shown in Figure 1 for the period from 1910-48. The turning point in both acreage and production was reached in 1926 when 43.5 million acres and 17.3 million bales were harvested in the ten Cotton Belt states included in this analysis. A near record crop (17.2 million bales) was again harvested in 1937 on about 12 million acres less, but it cannot be considered the turning point in production, as is clearly shown by the chart. Acreage harvested declined steadily after the 1926 crop, decreasing about 1.4 million acres annually, reaching a low of 16.2 million acres in 1945, a decrease of 27.3 million acres or 63 per cent. While the turning point in acreage can be regarded as having been reached in 1926, the sharp declines in acreage did not begin until 1931. It was not until after this date that acreage harvested definitely moved to a lower level. World War II established some new lows in acreage in recent decades. In 1945 acreage harvested was the lowest since 1882. Since 1946 acreage has expanded each year, but the October, 1948, estimate of acreage for harvest is still 1.3 million acres short of the 1939 acreage of these ten states.

While the trend in production since 1926 has likewise been downward, it has contracted much less rapidly than acreage. From 1925-29 to 1943-46 production declined 47 per cent, although the drop to 1947-48 was only 25 per cent. The 1945 production of 7.4 million bales was the smallest crop since 1895. The 1947 crop, 10.3 million bales in these ten states, was 0.4 million bales above the 1940-46 average. It resulted from very favorable yields, for acreage was not yet back to prewar levels. However, the October, 1948, estimate shows another bumper crop, one of those cyclical crops which the Southern farmer has dumped on him every so often.[3] It, like the crops of 1931 and 1937, is likely to give Southern agriculture the drug of a surplus, a carryover of 5 to 6 million bales. If this large crop, along with

[3] J. L. Fulmer, "Relationship of the Cycle in Yields of Cotton and Apples to Solar and Sky Radiation," *Quarterly Journal of Economics*, May, 1942.

similar large crops in other United States staple crops, does not, through reduced farmer purchasing power, touch off the long-expected depression, the favorable factors in

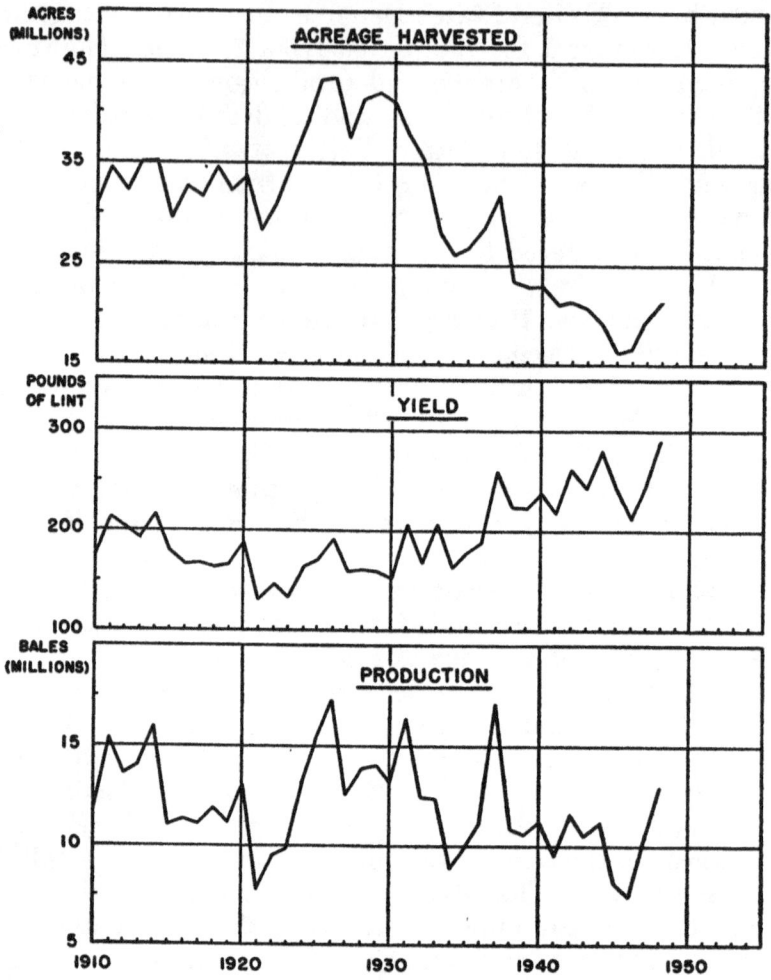

FIGURE 1. TRENDS IN ACREAGE, YIELD, AND PRODUCTION OF COTTON IN TEN COTTON BELT STATES, 1910-48

The large crops of 1925 and 1926 marked the turning point, after which both acreage harvested and production declined continuously with irregular recoveries to successively lower levels. However, because of the upward trend in yields, production declined much less rapidly than acreage.

The increase in acreage and very favorable yields in 1947 and 1948 restored production to the prewar level. The year 1948 is a cyclical yield year and such a high level is not expected to persist, but may be expected to occur in another five or six years.

the Cotton Belt's agriculture—fewer farms, larger farms, more diversification, etc.—should not be disturbed greatly. However, if these large crops and the possible chain effects produce a first-class depression and city unemployment, then a back-to-the-land movement can be expected. Nothing could be worse for Southern agriculture, for it has for decades labored under heavy population pressure. World War II relieved some of that pressure but more relief is needed. If city unemployment adds more to that pressure, the situation may become as bad as it was in the early 1930's.

The downward trend in production has been retarded relative to acreage harvested because of great improvement in yields. Average yield increased 74 pounds from 1925-29 to 1940-46, or 44 per cent, while the annual increase in yield from 1926 to 1948 is computed as 4.6 pounds. Many causes might be given for the increase in yields but the most important are improvement in land quality, increased fertilizer per acre, more systematic crop rotation, introduction of higher yielding varieties, and more favorable weather than in the 1920's.

Other Crops

In the Eastern cotton states[4] tobacco is a very important cash crop. It is hardly grown in the other cotton states considered in this study, but its importance is exerted in income figures for the Cotton Belt as a whole. No important changes in acreage occurred from 1929 to 1944. But although there was a small decrease in acreage harvested in 1944 as compared to 1929, production had expanded from 732 million pounds to 1,002 million, or 37 per cent. This, along with the tendency of tobacco prices to remain high relative to other farm products and the greater increase in tobacco prices during the war period, has led to a considerable gain in the position of tobacco in the income stream, not only in the Eastern cotton states but for the Cotton Belt as a whole. From the six-year period, 1924-29, to the five-year period, 1941-45, the percentage of the total receipts from farm marketings contributed by tobacco increased from 13.7 to 24.5 per cent in the five

[4] North Carolina, South Carolina, Georgia, Alabama, and Tennessee.

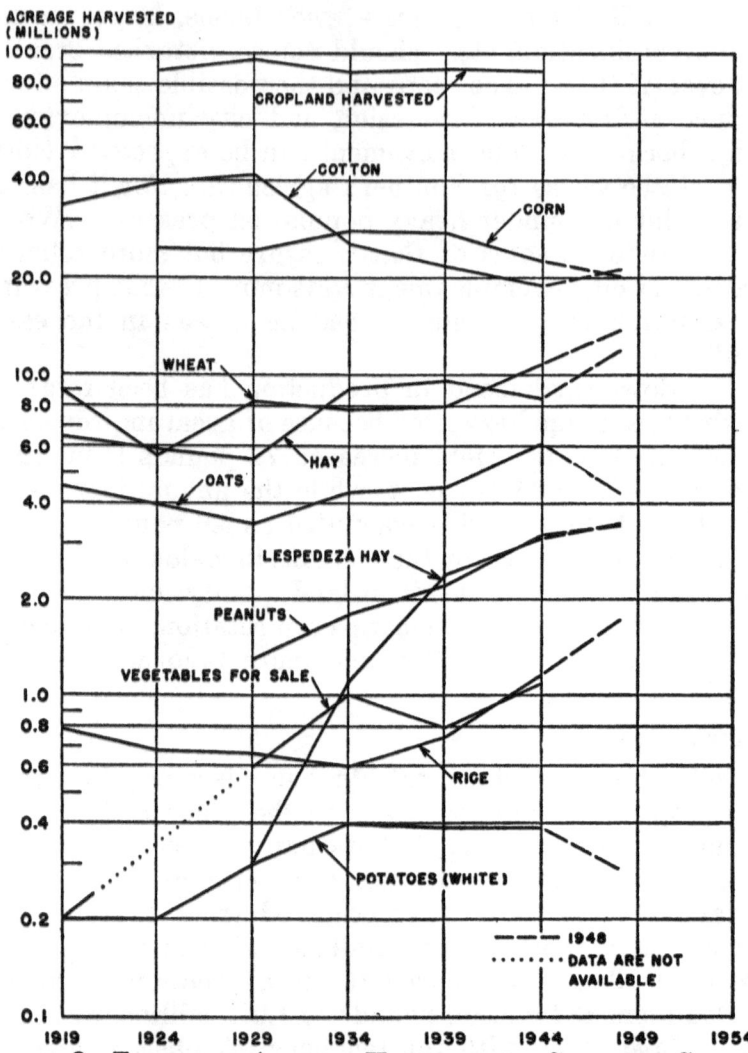

FIGURE 2. TRENDS IN ACREAGE HARVESTED OF SPECIFIED CROPS IN TEN COTTON BELT STATES, BY CENSUS YEARS

The sharp decline in cotton acreage after 1929 was followed by increases in most other crops but Lespedeza hay, peanuts, vegetables for sale, and grain sorghums led the way with the largest and most sustained increases.

Eastern cotton states;[5] and from 4.9 to 9.8 per cent in the ten Cotton Belt states.[6] Thus tobacco gained in emphasis 80 per cent in the former and 100 per cent in the latter.

[5] Cf. below, Chapter II, Table 8. [6] See Table 4, this chapter.

Figure 2 shows the acreage of other important Southern crops along with cotton on a semi-logarithmic scale by census years. Accordingly, the trends in the lines are directly comparable. Irrespective of the year we may take to make our comparisons, it is seen that Lespedeza hay, peanuts, vegetables for sale, grain sorghums, and oats, in that order, show the largest relative increases in acreage harvested. Corn is an important crop which fell off in acreage after 1939; however, estimates of the Crop Reporting Board, United States Department of Agriculture, indicate that corn acreage harvested reached a peak in 1938 at 28.5 million acres. Therefore, the acreage of corn of 22.7 million in 1944 represents a decrease of nearly 6.0 million acres, or 20 per cent, in the six-year period in the second most important soil-depleting crop in the Cotton Belt. However, the net decrease of corn acreage harvested for the fifteen-year period is not nearly so much, being only 2 million acres. Acreage and percentage increases in other crops from 1929 to 1944 are shown in Table 1.

TABLE 1
INCREASE IN ACREAGE HARVESTED OF SPECIFIED CROPS IN TEN COTTON BELT STATES, 1929-44
(In thousand acres)

Crop	1929 acreage harvested	1944 acreage harvested	Increase from 1929 to 1944	
			Acres harvested	Per cent
Sorghum*..................	5,306	10,489	5,183	98
All hay....................	5,465	8,473	3,008	55
Lespedeza hay.............	323†	3,157	2,834	877
Oats......................	3,376	6,192	2,816	83
Wheat.....................	8,289	10,800	2,511	30
Peanuts‡..................	1,284	3,254	1,970	153
Soybeans and cowpeas§.....	997	2,573	1,576	158
Rice......................	657	1,162	505	77
Vegetables for sale.........	623	1,099	476	76
White potatoes.............	299	388	89	30
Sweet potatoes.............	517	558	41	8
Total‡................	26,813	44,988	18,175	68

* For all purposes other than syrup.
† Includes sweet clover.
‡ Grown alone for all purposes.
§ Grown alone.
‡ Exclusive of Lespedeza hay which is included in all hay.
Source: Census Reports of Agriculture.

The composite increase of the eleven crops shown in Table 1 is 18.2 million acres, or 68 per cent. If all hay, which to a considerable extent is double cropped, is omitted, the increase is 15.2 million acres. But the additional land available equals the decrease of 24 million in cotton acreage plus 2 million acres in corn, which totals 26 million acres. Deducting 7 million acres for the total cropland decrease, plus 15.2 million acres for the net increase of other crops, leaves close to 4 million acres unaccounted for, which are available for miscellaneous crops, meadows, etc.[7]

Vegetables harvested for sale, rice, and peanuts represent increases in cash crops, while the other crops except wheat are additions to the feed supply. As a matter of fact the effective increase in the feed supply is even greater than is indicated by the above figures. Since horses and mules decreased 1,776 thousand head, or 31 per cent during the period, an important feed requirement was thus released for feeding salable livestock and other livestock on Southern farms.

The 1948 data for most of the crops discussed above are plotted in Figure 2 for comparison with census data. In general the majority of the trends established from 1929 to 1944 have continued with important exceptions in the acreages of cotton, grain sorghums, oats, vegetables harvested for sale, and Irish potatoes. In the case of cotton the recovery in acreage from the lows in 1945 and 1946 appears to restore the enterprise to the 1939 level, but this would be an erroneous conclusion since the census data are not strictly comparable to Crop Reporting Board estimates. See Figure 1 where it is shown, for the ten cotton states under consideration, that the October, 1948, estimate of acreage harvested is 1.3 million acres below the 1939 acreage harvested.

Pasture

The change in pasture acreage in the ten cotton states during the last fifteen years is one of the major developments in Southern agriculture. From 1929 to 1944 the total acreage in pasture in these states increased from 131.5

---

[7] Not shown in idle and fallow land, however, since this class decreased from 11.9 million acres in 1929 to 11.1 million acres in 1944.

to 168.6 million acres, an increase of 37 million acres or 28 per cent. Since woodland not pastured increased only 3.2 million acres, a large part of the pasture increase comes from the expansion in total farm land, which amounted to 27 million acres during the period. This leaves about 13 million acres, coming very largely from cropland and idle and/or fallow land, which showed decreases of 7 million acres and 0.8 million acres respectively from 1929 to 1944. A considerable proportion of the remaining 5 million acres probably comes from waste land and other miscellaneous classes of farm land.

From the standpoint of the livestock development in the South, the type of pasture represented by the increase is of more significance. The data indicate that the bulk of the increase in pasture area was confined to plowable pasture and other land in pasture not classed as woodland, the expansion in the area of these classes being 32.7 million acres, or 88 per cent of the total pasture increase. In 1944, 78 per cent of all pasture in the ten cotton states was in types of pasture other than woodland; however, woodland constituted 43 per cent of the pasture area in the Eastern cotton states and 41 per cent in the Delta states (Mississippi, Louisiana, and Arkansas), but only 16 per cent in Oklahoma and Texas. During the fifteen-year period the greatest relative increase in pasture area occurred in the Delta states and the least in the Eastern cotton states. Oklahoma and Texas, however, had the greatest absolute increase, 26.2 million acres, or 71 per cent of the total in all three regions.

LIVESTOCK TRENDS

The measurement of trends in livestock numbers, especially of cattle and hogs, is complicated by two factors. The census inventory dates and definitions of livestock classes differ greatly from census to census. Since adjustments are not practical because of technical and other difficulties, the census data are not of much use in such comparisons. Another complication is the cycle in the numbers of cattle and hogs. The cattle cycle runs from eleven to sixteen years and the hog cycle from four to seven years, which renders year-to-year comparisons difficult and subject to great error. To be valid the trend comparisons must consider the general changes over several cycles. Fortunately, the Crop Reporting Board of the United States Department of Agriculture has released estimates by years, based on sample studies and adjusted census data.[8] The yearly numbers on farms as of January 1 for all cattle, cows milked, hogs, and chickens, the first three from 1910 to 1947 and chickens from 1925 to 1947, are shown in Figure 3. A trend line was fitted by the method of least squares to the number of all cattle from 1910 to 1947; and to the number of hogs from 1926 to 1947. It is apparent that hog numbers moved to a much lower level quite rapidly from 1919 to 1926, after which there was a gradual recovery, the annual rate of increase being 186,000 head annually. However, in spite of a very strong recovery during the war years, the *trend value* for 1947 was still nearly 3 million head below the 1919 level. Only in 1944 did the number of hogs exceed the number in 1919, by 250,000 head, both years being peaks in the respective war periods. The 1944 figure is not in accordance with census figures and it is probable that when hog estimates are revised this high figure may be reduced considerably.

The number of all cattle on farms is running at a very high level currently. Part of this high level is due to the cycle, but the trend line shows that the enterprise is definitely expanding, the rate of increase from 1910 to 1947 being 132,000 head annually.

Milk cows showed a very gradual expansion from 1910 to 1932, then moved rapidly to a new level in numbers which was maintained until the war period when some further expansion occurred. The peak in number of milk cows was reached in 1945, with considerable decline thereafter, the January 1, 1948, number (5,397,000 head) being about equal to that for January 1, 1939. A notable feature of the number of milk cows on Southern farms is the absence of the characteristic eleven- to sixteen-year cattle cycle. Conse-

---

[8] *Livestock on Farms, January 1, 1867-1935, by States; Crops and Markets,* Vol. 19, No. 2, pp. 33 and 40; *Farm Production and Disposition of Chickens and Eggs, 1925-1937—Chickens on Farms, January 1, 1925-1938, by States; and Livestock and Poultry on Farms, January 1, Number, Value per Head, and Total Value, 1940-1945, by States.*

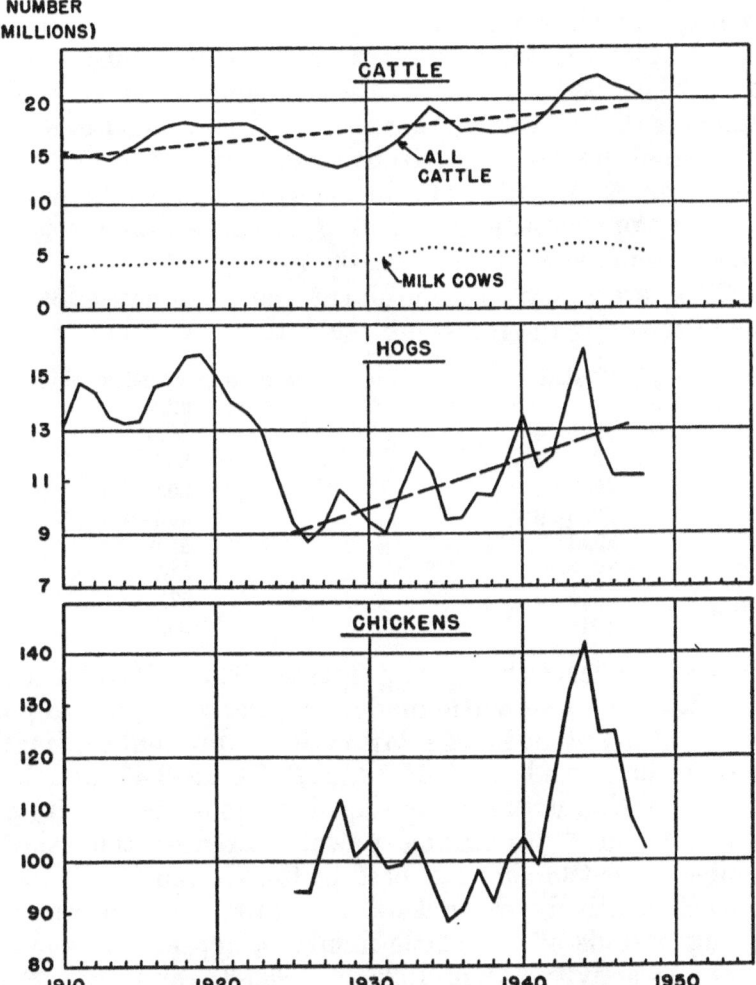

FIGURE 3. NUMBER OF ALL CATTLE, MILK COWS, HOGS, AND CHICKENS ON FARMS JANUARY 1 IN TEN COTTON STATES, 1910-48

The cyclical movements, in numbers of all cattle and hogs on farms, of eleven to sixteen years and four to seven years respectively constitute the most interesting characteristic of these two enterprises since 1910. The trend in all cattle and milk cows was upward during the entire period but much accelerated after 1928. Milk cows show a gradual upward trend although apparently somewhat less rapid for the entire period than other cattle and without the characteristic cycle in numbers of other cattle. Hogs had an upward trend after 1926 but except in 1944 have not yet reached the general level of 1910-19. The number of chickens on farms fluctuated around 95 to 100 million head with a slight downward trend until 1941, after which there was an increase of about 40 per cent in three years, probably induced by the unprecedented war demand and meat rationing; since 1944 they have decreased each year, reaching in 1948 a point in numbers below the 1939 level.

quently, the enterprise tends to maintain itself on an even keel despite the fairly violent changes in numbers of all cattle which occur at comparatively regular intervals. This indicates that all cattle other than milk cows tend to occupy a residual position, apparently absorbing the culls and other classes of cattle not selected or otherwise not suitable for dairy purposes, and including, of course, the strict beef breeds which appear to be on the increase.

The percentage which milk cows is of all cattle by periods is shown in the following tabulation:

Period	Percentage of cattle which were milk cows
1910-14	27.5
1915-19	25.2
1920-24	25.5
1925-29	30.7
1930-32	31.5
1933-39	31.1
1940-46	27.1
1948	25.9

The data indicate that except during 1925 to 1939 the ratio of milk cows to all cattle made practically no gain in position. On the other hand a low ratio is apparent during the prosperous periods of 1915-19, 1920-24, 1940-46, and 1948. The conclusion is that a high level of economic activity and high consumer purchasing power increases the relative number of cattle sold for beef in the Cotton Belt and decreases relatively those kept for milk, and contrariwise during periods of low cattle numbers, depression, and low economic activity, as in 1925-29, 1930-32, and 1933-39 respectively. Apparently, the comparatively greater inflexibility of the price of milk, the longer period involved in developing a milking herd, and the cyclical movements in number of all cattle are important factors bearing on this alternating tendency.

The number of chickens on farms January 1 remained fairly constant from 1925 to 1941, although there is evidence of certain minor diverse trends. From 1928 to 1935 there was a slight downward trend, after which there was considerable recovery until the outbreak of the war, then unprecedented increases until the record level of 142 million head was reached in 1944, an increase of 43 per cent above the number in 1941.

The averages by significant periods for all cattle, milk cows, hogs, and chickens are given in Table 2, below, which also contains recently available 1948 figures.

In general, all cattle and hogs held up well with the previously established trends, if we take into account that both enterprises are in the contracting phases of their respective cycles. Milk cows, however, dropped off inordinately. Likewise, chickens showed a sharp drop in 1948 from the 1940-46 level. In 1948 both milk cows and chickens were back to the 1939 level.

TABLE 2
AVERAGE NUMBER OF SPECIFIED CLASSES OF LIVESTOCK IN THE COTTON BELT BY PERIODS SINCE 1910

Period or year	Million head January 1			
	All cattle	Milk cows	Hogs	Chickens
1910-14	14.66	4.0	13.76	......
1915-19	17.07	4.3	14.84	......
1920-24	17.14	4.4	13.32	......
1925-29	14.12	4.3	9.63	100.95
1930-32	15.20	4.8	9.67	100.65
1933-39	17.52	5.4	10.75	95.52
1940-46	19.96	5.8	13.00	120.27
1948	19.84	5.4	11.19	102.43

Source: *Ibid.*, footnote 8.

LIVESTOCK PRODUCTS

While comparisons can be made primarily by census years, it appears that the increases in livestock products[9] as a whole were more sustained during the period from 1919 to 1947, and in the case of poultry products and eggs were undoubtedly more significant than the change in numbers of the three livestock enterprises discussed above.

The percentage changes from 1919 to 1944, from 1929 to 1944, and from 1944 to 1947, are shown in the following tabulation:

[9] Census data relative to the production of livestock products are not subject to the same errors as the livestock inventories, since the entire year's production is reported, although for the year previous to the date when the censuses were enumerated.

	From 1919 to 1944	Percentage increase From 1929 to 1944	From 1944 to 1947
Chickens raised	75	52	-24
Chicken eggs produced	111	31	15
Milk produced	80	17	5
Whole milk sold	731	128	12

The greater relative increases in livestock products over livestock is accounted for in part by the increase in efficiency of livestock farming, estimated by the Bureau of Agricultural Economics to equal 35 per cent per animal since 1920 for the United States as a whole.[10] This report also estimates that milk per cow has increased 25 per cent, eggs per hen and hogs per sow 40 per cent each during this period. The large increases in whole milk sold are due to the increase in city population and shifts in diets toward more milk consumption per capita.

Note the heavy decline in chickens raised from 1944 to 1947, which is in line with previously noted sharp retrenchments in chickens on farms in all regions of the Cotton Belt since the end of the war.

FARM PRACTICES

Not only have the shifts in the Cotton Belt's agriculture moved it in the direction of a better balance, but they have been accompanied by improved practices which spell a more efficient agriculture. Lime expanded from 460 thousand tons in 1929 to 4,327 thousands tons in 1944, an increase of 840 per cent. Although fertilizer decreased 34 per cent from 1929 to 1934, the recovery was rapid and total applications were 5,575 thousand tons in 1944, representing an increase of 33 per cent over the 1929 level; from 1944 to 1948 there was a further increase of 15 per cent.[11] On the basis of 1944 consumption, all classes of farmers in the Cotton Belt were applying 4 tons of lime for every 5 tons of fertilizer. This is still far from the correct ratio, but it does represent tremendous progress in the short space of fifteen years. Lime applications have been stimulated very greatly by the A.A.A. incentive payments to farmers

---

[10] Sherman E. Johnson, *Changes in Farming*, U. S. Dept. of Agri., Bur. of Agri. Econ., F. M. 58, Revised, June, 1948, pp. 73, 100, and 101.

[11] Based on tag sales.

for liming, which is true also to a considerable extent of the expansion in leguminous crops. In the case of increased fertilizer applications, the factors responsible are higher prices for cotton and increased farm incomes.

MECHANICAL POWER

In mechanical power the Cotton Belt states also came to the forefront; the number of tractors on farms increased by 264 per cent from 1930 to 1945; and 82 per cent in the last five years. However, these increases were insufficient to bring the Cotton Belt abreast of the remainder of the country, for in 1945 there were still only 4.6 tractors per thousand acres harvested in the Cotton Belt as compared to 7.6 tractors per thousand acres harvested in the rest of the United States.

A recent report released by the Bureau of Agricultural Economics[12] indicates that the number of tractors on farms increased 19 per cent in the South[13] from January 1, 1945 to January 1, 1947; and a further increase of 19 per cent from January 1, 1947 to May 1, 1948 occurred. It is interesting and highly significant that the latter increase, occurring in sixteen months, equaled that of a two-year period, which may indicate either an acceleration of demand for tractors on Southern farms or dissipation of accumulated demand in the postwar period, but it is more likely to be largely the latter.

In 1945, 349 thousand motor trucks were reported on farms in the Cotton Belt, which was an increase of 55 per cent from 1940; 703 thousand farms, or 31 per cent, reported electricity as compared to only 3.4 per cent of all farms in 1930.

FARM POPULATION

From 1930 to 1945 the ten Cotton Belt states considered in this report lost 3.6 million persons from farms,[14] or 28

[12] *Farm Machinery*, U. S. Dept. of Agri., Bur. of Agri. Econ. (mimeo.), March 15, 1949, p. 2.

[13] The South as here defined includes the Southeast plus Oklahoma and Texas, or the four states of Virginia, West Virginia, Kentucky and Florida added to our ten cotton states. The relative changes are, therefore, only roughly comparable.

[14] Experts in the Bureau of Agricultural Economics have expressed a belief that farm population was undercounted in the 1945 Census, which indicates that the actual decrease may not have been as much as here shown.

per cent, practically all of this decrease occurring from 1940 to 1945. Since there was a back-to-the-farm movement during the period from 1930 to 1933, the decrease in population from 1933 through 1940 was somewhat greater.

Although there appears to be a well-defined long-run tendency for farm population to decrease in the Cotton Belt, much of the decrease in the period 1940 to 1945 was associated with the war (service in the armed forces and migration to war factories in the South and elsewhere). Recent farm population estimates of the B.A.E. show the extent of the back-to-the-farm movement from war service, etc. Data for the three geographic regions, South Atlantic, East South Central, and West South Central, which are roughly comparable to the ten Cotton Belt states, indicate that nearly one-half of the war loss in farm population had been regained by January 1, 1947; on the other hand, beginning in 1947, farm migration resumed its normal farm-to-city direction.[15] However, despite the reversal of farm migration in 1945 and the return, in 1946, of such a high proportion of the wartime migrants, the loss in farm population from 1940 to 1948 was considerable, amounting to 11 per cent. Farm population experts in the B.A.E. point out that because of the acute housing shortage there has been a heavy movement to farms solely for residence purposes, which indicates that the effective number of bona fide farm residents is much lower than the actual figures show.[16]

For many years agricultural economists have recognized that the number of people on farms is in excess of available resources; therefore, a movement of population out of agriculture is regarded as helpful to the cotton problem. Even if only the movement to 1948 can be retained, which is likely because of the pace of industrialization in the South, the gain to the Cotton Belt will be significant because of the effects of such a movement on size of farms and mechanization. Accompanying the 1930 to 1945 decrease in population, but not necessarily entirely due to it, was a large decrease in the number of farms. In this

[15] *Farm Population Estimates, January, 1948*, U. S. Dept. of Agri., Bur. of Agri. Econ., June, 1948.
[16] *The Agricultural Situation*, July, 1948, p. 5.

fifteen-year period, the number of farms in the Cotton Belt decreased from 2,612 thousand to 2,260 thousand, or 13 per cent; and farms growing cotton decreased from 1,931 thousand to 1,180 thousand, or 39 per cent, with decreases of 5 per cent and 24 per cent respectively occurring during 1940 to 1945. Significantly, this decrease in number of farms was largely the cause of an increase of 26 per cent in the average farm size (acreage of land per farm).

Data on the change in number of farms from 1945 to 1948 are not available, but presumably there was considerable increase in line with the back-to-the-farm migration during 1945 and 1946.

SHIFTS IN GROSS INCOME AND CASH RECEIPTS

Figure 4 shows that phenomenal shifts occurred in the agricultural income of the ten Cotton Belt states from 1924

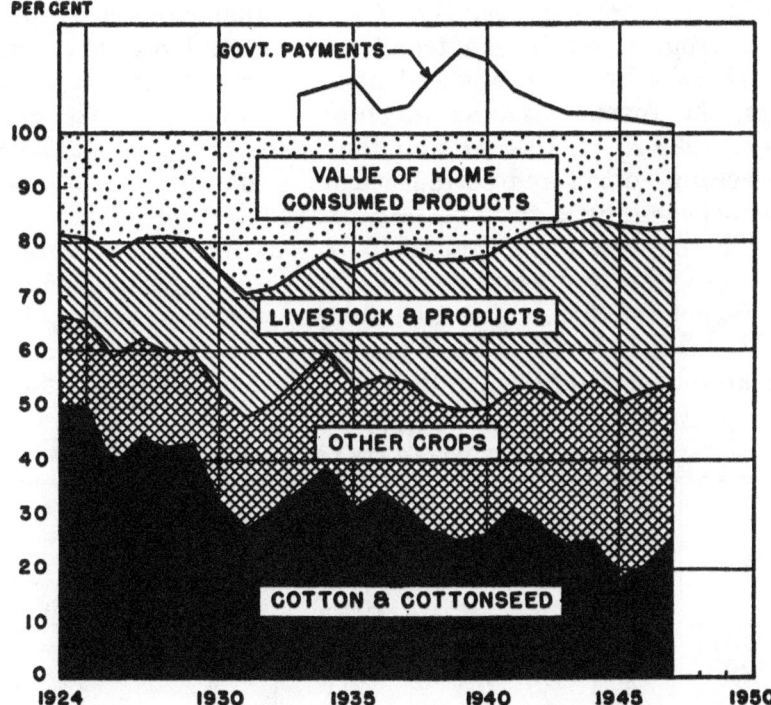

FIGURE 4. SOURCES OF GROSS FARM INCOME IN THE COTTON BELT, 1924 to 1947

Note the declining importance of cotton and cottonseed and the increasing importance of other crops and livestock and livestock products.

to 1947. In this time cotton and cottonseed lost one-half the crop's relative position in the farm income stream, dropping from 50 per cent in 1924 to about 25 per cent. As cotton and cottonseed declined in importance, livestock and livestock products and all other crops gained in importance. These shifts had brought the gross income stream to the point in 1947 where each of the latter exceeded cotton and cottonseed as a source of gross income.

The trend in the relative importance of various sources of income by periods is shown in Table 3. These periods have been selected on the basis of important economic factors. The period 1924-29 represents the postwar boom and speculative era; 1930-32, the depression period; 1933-39, trial and error in agricultural relief; 1941-45, World War II; and 1946-47, postwar reconversion. It should be noted that cotton gained some emphasis in the 1933-39 period, but not significantly. On the other hand there was no retrogression in the trend toward an increasing emphasis of all other crops and livestock and livestock products, the former gaining in emphasis about 75 per cent from 1924-29 to 1946-47 and the latter 64 per cent, both exceeding cotton and cottonseed as a contributor to gross farm income by a good margin in 1946-47.

The depression period, 1930-32, was hard on everyone. Because of city unemployment, there was a net movement to farms in 1932. The unemployed were searching for food. This increase in food production along with the comparatively smaller decline in farm prices of home-consumed

TABLE 3
GROSS FARM INCOME DISTRIBUTION IN TEN COTTON BELT STATES BY PERIODS

Period	Percentage of gross farm income from:				
	Cotton and cottonseed	All other crops	Livestock and livestock products	Value of home consumption	Government payments
1924-29...	44.9	17.2	17.9	20.0	...
1930-32...	30.9	19.5	22.1	27.5	...
1933-39...	31.5	22.3	22.9	23.2	8.3
1941-45...	25.0	27.4	30.5	17.2	4.3
1946-47...	23.3	30.0	29.3	17.4	1.5

Source: Compiled from data published in *The Cotton Situation*, Bureau of Agricultural Economics, CS-113, September, 1946, p. 19; and from *The Farm Income Situation*, FIS-99, June-July, 1948, pp. 12-19.

products resulted in a large increase in the relative importance in the income stream of farm products consumed at home. These products were exceeded in this respect only by cotton and cottonseed and then not greatly. With the improvement in business conditions and agriculture after 1932, the pressure on agriculture was relieved somewhat by a reversal of the back-to-farm population movement, resuming the normal farm-to-city migration of farm population. This caused a decline in subsistence farming and the value of home-consumed products lost emphasis rapidly as other products gained in emphasis. In the World War II period this part of the income stream was less important than at any time in the period.

Sources of cash farm receipts are shown in Table 4. It is seen that our conclusion regarding the decline of cotton and cottonseed in the gross farm income stream is equally true for cash farm receipts. From the period 1924-29 to 1941-45, the crop almost, but not quite, lost one-half of its position in total cash farm receipts.

The relative receipts from several common crop and livestock enterprises are also shown in Table 4. Practically all increased in emphasis from 1924-29 to 1941-45, the trends being carried through the 1935-39 period. The following enterprises *increased in emphasis* 100 per cent or over from 1924-29 to 1941-45: tobacco, truck crops, peanuts, pecans, and hogs; while cattle and calves, dairy products, chickens, and eggs increased in emphasis from 40 to 70 per cent. Compositely, livestock and livestock products have gained in importance as sources of cash farm receipts at the expense of crops, the livestock and livestock products being 64 per cent more important in 1941-45 than in 1924-25. In 1947, an important postwar year, the enterprises tended to retain the 1941-45 balance with only a few important exceptions. Wheat more than doubled in emphasis from 1941-45 to 1947, almost entirely in Oklahoma and Texas; cattle and calves also became more important as a source of cash receipts, again in Oklahoma and Texas very largely; but the enterprise showed some increase in importance in all ten states with surprisingly large receipts being attributed to this enterprise in the Delta states. Only truck crops,

TABLE 4

RELATIVE AND QUANTITATIVE SHIFTS IN SOURCES OF RECEIPTS FROM FARM MARKETINGS IN TEN COTTON BELT STATES BY SELECTED PERIODS, 1924 TO 1947

Source	Average percentage				Average cash receipts by source 1941-45 (000,000)	Percentage of change in total cash receipts		
	1924-1929	1935-1939	1941-1945	1947		1924-1929 to 1941-1945	1935-1939 to 1941-1945	1924-1929 to 1947
Cotton and cottonseed	56.2	38.8	30.1	30.5	$1,103.4	−24	61	34
Tobacco	4.9	9.7	9.8	9.4	359.4	182	109	368
Rice	1.3	1.6	2.2	2.2	82.1	153	188	333
Wheat	3.2	3.2	3.3	6.7	119.5	43	110	412
Truck crops	2.2	2.8	5.4	2.2	195.9	246	301	149
Peaches	0.8	0.7	0.9	0.5	31.9	63	145	71
Peanuts	0.9	1.6	3.0	2.7	109.1	343	276	612
Pecans	0.3	0.2	0.6	0.4	20.2	173	405	241
White potatoes	0.7	0.8	0.8	0.5	30.1	68	118	77
Sweet potatoes	0.6	0.8	0.8	0.6	28.3	84	97	138
Total crops	77.6	68.4	63.1	65.2	2,311.6	15	91	107
Cattle and calves	7.0	10.5	11.7	13.9	428.0	138	131	391
Dairy products	5.2	8.1	7.6	6.6	279.7	106	96	210
Hogs	3.1	4.6	6.3	5.9	231.8	185	183	366
Eggs (chicken)	3.6	3.5	5.0	3.7	183.5	99	194	157
Chickens	1.8	1.8	3.1	2.6	114.3	145	269	257
Total livestock and livestock products	22.4	31.6	36.8	34.8	1,346.7	133	141	283
Total receipts from farm marketings	100.0	100.0	100.0	100.0	3,658.3	41	107	146
Government payments	0.0	11.0	5.2	1.4	189.9	...	...	...

Source: 1. *Cotton:* Hearings before the Subcommittee of the Committee on Agriculture, House of Representatives, Seventy-Eighth Congress, Second Session, Dec. 4 to 9, 1944, pp. 600-7.
2. *Cash Receipts from Marketings by States and Commodities, Calendar Years, 1924-44*, U. S. Dept. of Agri., Bur. of Agri. Econ., Washington, D. C., January, 1946, pp. 83-121.
3. *The Farm Income Situation*, U. S. Dept. of Agri., Bur. of Agri. Econ., current issues.
4. *Agricultural Statistics, 1946*, U. S. Dept. of Agri.

chickens, and eggs showed significant losses in relative position from 1941-45 to 1947. An interesting shift appears in dairy products beginning during 1935-39, the enterprise tending to decline in emphasis through 1947. It is not believed that this is due to any shrinkage in volume, which all evidence indicates has increased very significantly, but is more due to price inflexibilities. The prices of dairy products show less response to inflation and deflation than most other agricultural products. Prices of processed milk products, which determine the price paid for the raw milk component, are set by the large manufacturers. Furthermore, local buying prices of whole milk for sale in bottles, etc., are administratively determined by the local milk authority—milk board, commission, or farmer's cooperative. All these agencies are slow-moving in making decisions and consequently are generally out of step with the flexibilities of supply and demand.

CHAPTER II

Regional Trends

COTTON

FROM 1925-29 TO 1940-46, the average annual total production of cotton declined nearly one-half in Oklahoma and Texas, just over one-fourth in the Eastern states,[1] and one-eighth in the Delta states.[2] Oklahoma and Texas led in the decrease in cotton production between the two periods because this region had the *greatest* acreage decrease and *lowest* yield increase of the three regions, acreage slumping off nearly three-fifths and yield increasing close to one-fourth. The Delta states had the lowest decline in production because they had the smallest decrease in acreage and a yield increase practically the same as the Eastern states, acreage decreasing two-fifths and yield increasing one-half. The Eastern states were between the other two regions in the production change with a decline of just over one-fourth, or 27 per cent, caused by a decline in acreage harvested of just over one-half and an increase in yield of nearly one-half.

Within the regions as here defined certain tendencies toward concentration of cotton production in some limited areas is worthy of note. The detailed production areas in the Cotton Belt are shown in Figure 5. According to data prepared by Langsford of the Bureau of Agricultural Economics and released in 1944,[3] the areas which have gained in production relative to the other areas, are the Delta, Eastern Hilly, Irrigated, and High Plains areas (Figure 6). From 1928-32 to 1941-43 a gain in relative acreage occurred in these areas but the big jump in relative production was

[1] North Carolina, South Carolina, Georgia, Alabama, and Tennessee.
[2] Mississippi, Arkansas, and Louisiana.
[3] E. L. Langsford, *Changes in Cotton Production in War and Peace*, U. S. Dept. of Agri., Bur. of Agri. Econ., F. M. 45, Dec., 1944, pp. 9, 14, and 29-33.

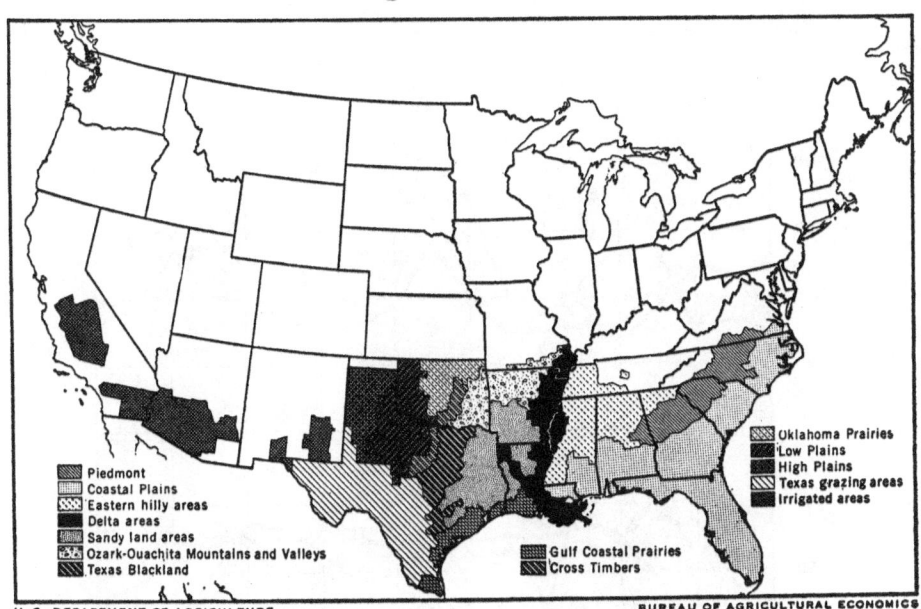

FIGURE 5. MAJOR COTTON-PRODUCING AREAS IN THE UNITED STATES

due to the rapid improvement in yields. Important areas showing a loss between these periods are the Low Plains, Coastal Plains, Piedmont, Texas Blackland (very large drop), Sandy Lands (quite large), Oklahoma Prairie, and Cross Timbers. These declines in importance have occurred despite the tendency for yields to rise above the 1928-32 level, but yields have generally risen less than in the four areas which have gained in importance.[4] All these later areas showed a relative decline in acreage between the two periods. In an era when cotton acreage was being contracted under A.A.A. programs in all areas except the irrigated, this means that the greatest shrinkage in acreage occurred in the areas which over the long run were losing out in cotton production.

Of particular interest is the tendency of cotton production to shift to the irrigated areas—New Mexico, Arizona, and California. These states have been gaining in emphasis relative to the rest of the United States Cotton Belt since 1920. The 1937-46 yields, Table 5, are from 67 to 132

[4] Langsford, *op. cit.*, p. 20.

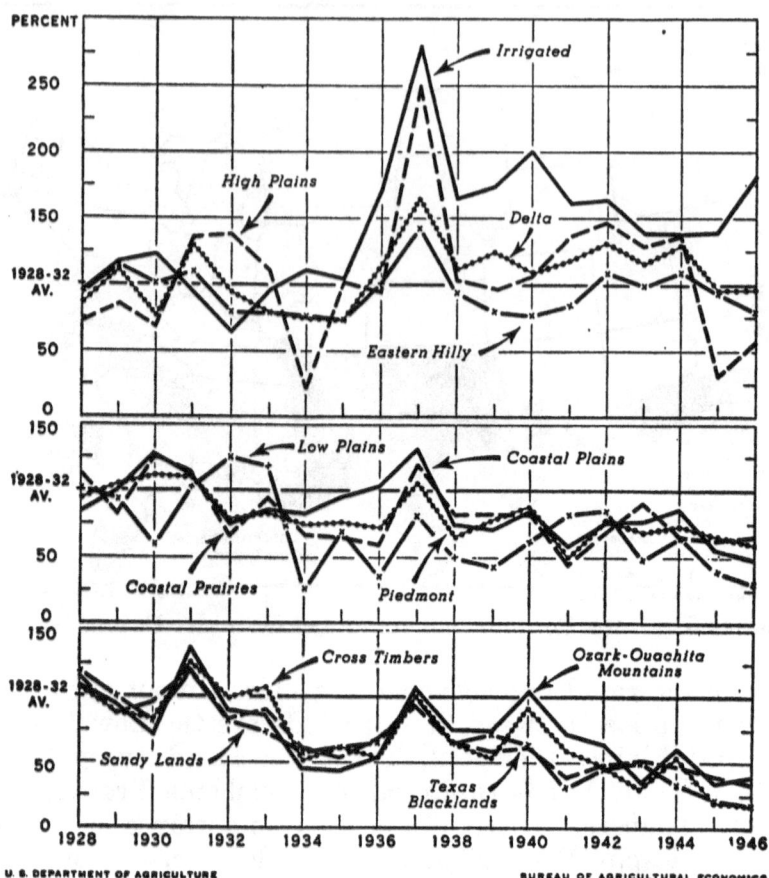

FIGURE 6. TRENDS IN COTTON PRODUCTION IN MAJOR PRODUCING AREAS SINCE 1928

Since 1928-32 the Delta, Eastern Hilly, High Plains and Irrigated areas have gained in relative production. All other areas have lost importance as producing areas, but the Cross Timbers, Ozark-Ouachita Mountains, Sandy Lands, and Texas Blackland areas had the largest relative declines.

per cent above the United States average yield and from 32 to 82 per cent above the yield of Mississippi, the highest yielding cotton state outside the irrigated areas. Irrigation is favorable to intensive farming and due to the control of the water supply yields are much less variable, but according to Langsford, the areas for further expansion of the enterprise are limited and must largely occur at the expense of competing enterprises, which depend upon price

TABLE 5
THE 1937-46 AVERAGE YIELD AND 1948 PROSPECTIVE YIELD OF COTTON IN SELECTED STATES COMPARED TO YIELD OF IRRIGATED STATES

State or area	Average yield (lbs. of lint)		Per cent of U. S. average	
	1937-46	1948	1937-46	1948
Georgia...........	238	286	94	92
Mississippi........	324	430	127	138
Texas.............	170	173	67	56
Irrigated States:				
Arizona........	424	543	167	175
New Mexico....	489	550	192	177
California......	589	567	232	182
U. S..............	254.2	310.3	100	100

Source: *Cotton Production*, Crop Reporting Board, U. S. Dept. of Agri., October 8, 1948.

relationships.[5] The price relationships must have been favorable to displacing competing crops by cotton in these states during 1947 and 1948 because very large increases in both acreage and production occurred. This is shown by the fact that California moved from a rank of eleventh place among the cotton states for the period 1937-1946 to fifth place in 1948.

OTHER CROPS

A comparison of the decreases in cotton acreage with corresponding increases in other crops by regions from 1929 to 1944 is shown in Table 6. Only in Oklahoma and Texas was there a decrease in a second large crop, corn decreasing 2 million acres, or 28 per cent in the fifteen-year period. The table indicates that crops other than cotton and corn expanded relatively the most in the Delta states and the least in Oklahoma and Texas, 171 per cent and 56 per cent respectively. It is noteworthy that the increases in these crops are in excess of or nearly equal to the decline in the acreage of cotton in the Eastern states and the Delta states. On the other hand, in Oklahoma and Texas the acreage of all crops other than cotton and corn increased to the extent of only 75 per cent of the cotton acreage which became available, and only 65 per cent of the combined cotton acreage and corn acreage reduction.

Figure 7 shows acreages of major crops in the different

[5] *Ibid.*, p. 20.

TABLE 6
CHANGE IN ACREAGE HARVESTED OF SPECIFIED CROPS FROM 1929 TO 1944 BY REGIONS

Region and crop	Acreage harvested in 1929 (thousand acres)	Change from 1929 to 1944	
		Thousand acres	Per cent
Eastern			
Cotton	11,632	− 6,584	− 57
Corn	12,261	− 36	..
Wheat	734	532	72
Oats	996	1,156	116
All hay	2,862	1,228	43
Lespedeza hay	179	1,816	1,015
Soybeans and cowpeas grown alone	654	697	107
Peanuts grown alone	917	1,412	154
Irish potatoes	155	54	35
Sweet potatoes and yams	314	− 6	− 2
Vegetables for sale	287	115	40
Total, excluding cotton and corn	7,098	7,004	99
Delta			
Cotton	9,401	− 4,527	− 48
Corn	5,054	72	1
Wheat	17	45	265
Oats	141	815	578
All hay	1,115	1,377	123
Lespedeza hay	135	960	711
Soybeans and cowpeas grown alone	214	686	321
Irish potatoes	66	48	73
Sweet potatoes and yams	142	25	18
Rice	549	268	49
Vegetables for sale	120	61	51
Total, excluding cotton and corn	2,499	4,285	171
Oklahoma-Texas			
Cotton	20,962	−12,892	− 62
Corn	7,320	− 2,015	− 28
Wheat	7,538	1,934	26
Oats	2,239	846	38
Barley	265	323	122
All hay	1,488	403	27
Sorghums for all purposes	5,131	5,082	99
Peanuts grown alone	312	556	178
Irish potatoes	78	− 12	− 15
Sweet potatoes and yams	61	21	34
Rice	106	239	225
Vegetables for sale	216	300	139
Total, excluding cotton and corn	17,434	9,692	56

Source: Census Reports of Agriculture.

regions by census dates since 1919. Despite trends of such force as to reduce cotton acreage from 50 to 60 per cent from 1929 to 1944, it still remains as the second most important crop in the Eastern and Delta cotton states and the third most important crop in Oklahoma and Texas, being exceeded at present by corn in the former two regions and wheat and sorghums in the latter. From 1930 to 1945 the

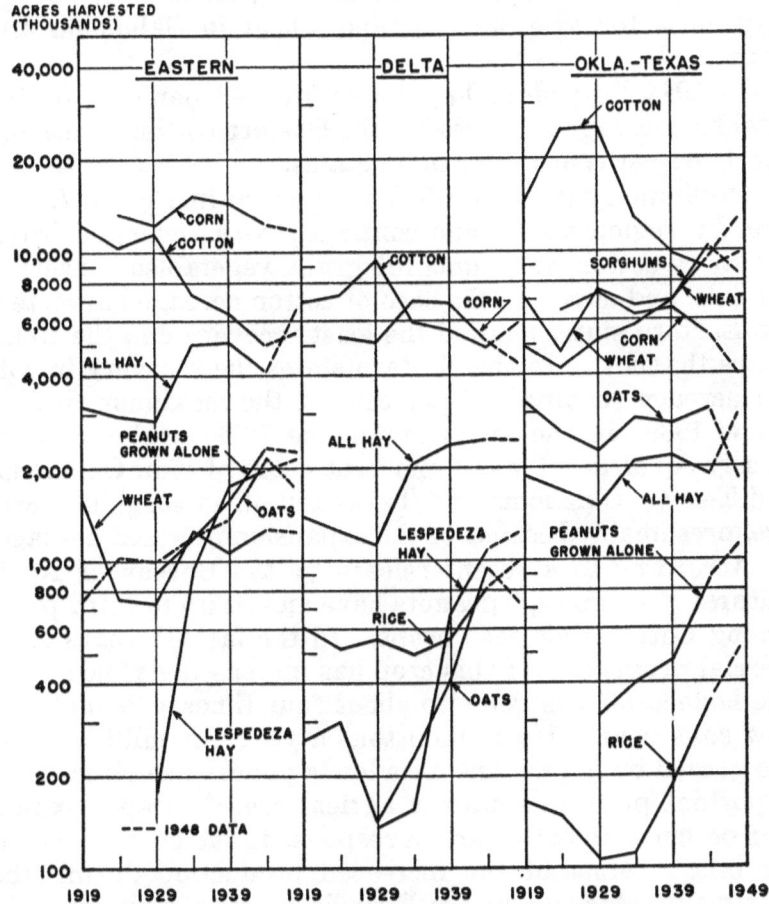

FIGURE 7. TRENDS IN ACREAGE HARVESTED OF IMPORTANT CROPS IN DIFFERENT REGIONS OF THE COTTON BELT, BY CENSUS YEARS

The decrease in cotton acreage after 1929 and of corn more recently gave impetus to large increases in hays and grains; and to increases in the production of peanuts in the Eastern states and Oklahoma and Texas, and sorghums for grain in the latter region also. Rice acreage and production have shown large increases in Arkansas, Louisiana, and Texas.

number of farms growing cotton decreased over one-half (55 per cent) in Oklahoma and Texas, and one-third in both the Delta states and the Eastern cotton states.

From the standpoint of percentage increase in acreage harvested from 1929 to 1944, Lespedeza hay, peanuts grown alone, oats, all hay, and wheat excelled in the Eastern states; Lespedeza hay, oats, rice, and all hay in the Delta states; and peanuts grown alone, sorghums, rice, barley, vegetables for sale, all hay, and wheat in Oklahoma and Texas.

In 1944 Lespedeza hay constituted 49 per cent of the total hay acreage harvested in the Eastern cotton states and nearly 44 per cent in the Delta states.

Preliminary data for 1948 are plotted in Figure 7. Region by region the trends continued with reversals being shown by cotton, sorghums for grain, vegetables harvested for sale, and oats. In the case of cotton acreage harvested, the Eastern states showed the least recovery and the Delta states the most. In the Eastern states the recovery in cotton acreage regained 47 per cent of the maximum decline below 1939; in the Delta states the 1939 level was very closely equaled but was 3 per cent short of it in Oklahoma and Texas. Oklahoma and Texas fell off in sorghum acreage, presumably because of the expansion in wheat acreage.

According to a recent release by the Bureau of Agricultural Economics, "peanuts have moved up to third place among Cotton Belt cash crops. In the last 35 years commercial production of this crop has increased sixfold; acreage hogged-off has gone up about four times. Peanut hay now runs nearly 1½ million tons a year. A million acres are grazed by hogs. The once lowly goober has risen to an important place in southern agriculture."[6] Rapid expansion occurred in both wars in response to the heavy demand for oils. "Most of the increased production during the first war took place in the Georgia-Florida-Alabama area and in Texas." In World War II it again took place in the newer areas, increasing 2.5 times in Oklahoma and Texas, 75 per cent in the Southeast, and only 15 per cent in the Virginia-Carolina areas. As expected after the last war

[6] *The Agricultural Situation*, Vol. 32 (March-April, 1948), pp. 11-13.

there was considerable shrinkage in the acreage and production of the crop, this occurring mainly in Texas and the Upper Piedmont section of Georgia and Alabama which showed heavy shifts to other crops. However, the Southeastern region continued to account for about one-half of the production of peanuts, thus reducing the importance of the Virginia-Carolina area as a major region of peanut production. In contrast, the wartime expansion in peanut acreage and production associated with World War II has been maintained because of favorable prices for peanuts relative to cotton.[7] With regard to prospects and future adjustments, the B.A.E. says that "prospects for consumption of peanuts are reasonably good. During the next few years it will probably not equal wartime figures but the longer-term trends will probably again be resumed at levels much above prewar. Under assumed conditions of full employment the quantity of picked and threshed peanuts that will probably be in demand has been estimated at perhaps four-fifths of the wartime production, or nearly 50 per cent above the prewar level. Consumer incomes will be a major influence in determining the size of the market for edible nuts. A promising opportunity lies in the probable development of new products made from peanuts."[8]

PASTURE

Below is listed the total acreage of pasture land by regions and states in 1944, with the percentage increase from 1929 to 1944:

	Thousand acres in 1944	Percentage increase 1929 to 1944
Eastern Cotton States		
North Carolina	2,718.0	-4
South Carolina	1,851.7	3
Georgia	5,902.9	27
Alabama	6,210.9	51
Tennessee	6,040.0	17
Total	22,723.5	22
Delta States		
Arkansas	6,362.1	68
Louisiana	3,920.6	75
Mississippi	7,804.0	46
Total	18,086.7	59

[7] *Loc. cit.*   [8] *Loc. cit.*

Oklahoma-Texas

Oklahoma	19,229.6	31
Texas	108,524.5	25
Total	127,754.1	26

The data indicate that the Delta states showed the largest percentage increase in pasture area from 1929 to 1944 and the Eastern states the least. The individual states making largest relative gains were Louisiana, Arkansas, Alabama, and Mississippi; while those states having the least percentage gains were South Carolina and Tennessee; North Carolina showing a decline of 4 per cent. However, a large proportion of pasture land in the Eastern and Delta states is in the low quality woodland pasture, 43 and 41 per cent respectively. Although a much lower percentage of Oklahoma and Texas pastures are in woodland (16 per cent), a considerable proportion is arid range-land which often is not worth any more, if as much, for grazing as woodland in the humid regions. However, the distribution of pasture land between types improved from 1929 to 1944 in all regions, since the increases were very largely in all types of pasture other than woodland. These classes, plowable pasture and other types of pasture not woodland, represented 84, 78, and 92 per cent of the total pasture acreage increases in the Eastern states, the Delta states, and in Oklahoma and Texas respectively. The shift in pasture distribution toward the higher quality acreages and the absolute increase in pasture area have an important bearing on the livestock development in the different regions under consideration.

LIVESTOCK

In numbers on farms January 1, Oklahoma and Texas led in all cattle during 1940-46 with 11.2 million head, on the average 2.4 times the number in the Eastern cotton states and 2.7 times the number in the Delta states. The Eastern cotton states led in number of hogs at 6.3 million head during this period, while there were just over half this number in the other two regions. The Eastern states and Oklahoma and Texas averaged close to 48 million head of chickens, or almost twice the number in the Delta states.

Regional Trends

From 1925-29 to 1940-46, the above three enterprises expanded in all three regions, all cattle increasing above the 1915-19 level and hogs falling short of it from 10 to 14 per cent. The Delta states showed the greatest expansion in all cattle and hogs from 1925-29 to 1940-46, 60 and 45 per cent respectively, and was just short of the 22 per cent gain in chickens by Oklahoma and Texas. The Eastern states and Oklahoma and Texas were close together in the increases in all cattle and hogs, the former excelling slightly in the expansion in hogs, 32 per cent, and the latter in all cattle with 38 per cent as compared to 35 per cent. (See Table 7.)

TABLE 7
AVERAGE NUMBER OF ALL CATTLE, HOGS, AND CHICKENS ON FARMS IN REGIONS OF THE COTTON BELT BY PERIODS

	All cattle	Milk cows	Hogs	Chickens
Eastern states				
1910-14	3,729	1,554	6,502	......
1915-19	4,199	1,664	7,276	......
1920-24	4,182	1,731	6,693	......
1925-29	3,447	1,614	4,757	41,975
1930-32	3,656	1,723	4,650	39,387
1933-39	4,173	1,917	5,176	39,724
1940-46	4,669	2,000	6,290	48,634
World War II peak*	5,142	2,122	7,715	57,439
1948	4,841	2,012	5,979	43,187
Delta States				
1910-14	2,586	1,029	3,544	......
1915-19	3,117	1,108	3,626	......
1920-24	3,050	1,100	3,007	......
1925-29	2,566	1,040	2,236	20,468
1930-32	2,835	1,127	2,261	20,795
1933-39	3,511	1,350	2,873	20,123
1940-46	4,117	1,444	3,251	24,593
World War II peak*	4,563	1,535	3,820	29,066
1948	3,942	1,330	2,725	19,634
Oklahoma-Texas				
1910-14	8,341	1,449	3,710	......
1915-19	9,756	1,524	3,941	......
1920-24	9,905	1,533	3,621	......
1925-29	8,103	1,685	2,633	38,508
1930-32	8,710	1,935	2,763	40,472
1933-39	9,834	2,183	2,703	35,673
1940-46	11,170	2,363	3,456	47,047
World War II peak*	12,359	2,490	4,541	55,621
1948	11,057	2,055	2,484	39,611

* World War II peak: Cattle in 1945; hogs and chickens in 1944; milk cows in 1945 in the Eastern and Delta states, and in 1944 in Oklahoma and Texas.
Source: Official estimates of the United States Department of Agriculture, Crop Reporting Board.

Data for these livestock enterprises for 1948 are also shown in Table 7. Even in this year cattle and hogs remained at high levels though reflecting the respective cycles. The peak year during the war was 1945 for cattle and 1944 for hogs and chickens. There was only a small drop by 1948 from the war peak for cattle in the Eastern states but a very large drop in the Delta states. All these regions showed a comparatively large drop by 1948 from the World War II peak for hogs, but the Eastern states declined the least and Oklahoma and Texas the most. In the case of chickens, all regions had declined below the 1940-46 level by 1948, but only the Delta states below the 1933-39 level.

The number of milk cows on farms is also shown in Table 7. The data show that they were more numerous in the Eastern cotton states than in either of the other two cotton regions until the period 1925-29, when Oklahoma and Texas forged ahead. They have since maintained a substantial lead over the Eastern cotton states, currently the second-ranking region of the three regions in milk cows. The Eastern and Delta states indicate some expansion in number of milk cows during World War I, and there were further gains in the Eastern states during 1920-24 but a slight contraction in the Delta states. On the other hand, Oklahoma and Texas showed an expansion by periods from 1910 to 1948 but most rapidly after 1925-29. The other two regions likewise had the most rapid expansion in number of milk cows on farms after this period (1925-29). The percentage increases from 1925-29 to 1940-46 were 24 per cent in the Eastern states, 39 per cent in the Delta states, and 40 per cent in Oklahoma and Texas. The expansion of the enterprise was thus comparatively the greatest in Oklahoma and Texas, with the Delta states a close second, and the least in the Eastern states.

From the peak year during the war (1945 in the Eastern and Delta states and 1944 in Oklahoma and Texas) to 1948 all regions showed declines in the number of milk cows on farms, but Oklahoma and Texas and the Delta states decreased the most, both of these regions dropping below the prewar, 1933-39 average of these regions. The relative importance of milk cows compared to all cattle in the different regions is shown in the following tabulation:

Regional Trends

Percentage of all cattle which were milk cows

Period	Eastern states	Delta states	Oklahoma and Texas
1910-14	42	40	17
1915-19	40	36	16
1920-24	41	36	16
1925-29	47	40	21
1930-32	47	40	22
1933-39	46	38	22
1940-46	43	35	21
1948	42	34	19

Thus milk cows constitute from two-fifths to one-half of all cattle in the Eastern states, one-third to two-fifths in the Delta states, and from one-sixth to one-fifth of all cattle in Oklahoma and Texas. All regions, similar to the Cotton Belt as a whole, show the alternating tendencies of a high ratio of milk cows during periods of low cattle numbers, depression, and low economic activity, and a low ratio for periods of high cattle numbers and high economic activity. It is also apparent that only Oklahoma and Texas have made some gain in milk cows relative to other cattle from 1910 to 1948.

A livestock enterprise of growing importance in a few cotton states is sheep. Of these states Texas is by far the most important and the state showing the most rapid increases in the enterprise. The rapidity of increase in this state is shown by the fact that the number of stock sheep on farms in Texas increased 323 per cent from 1915-19 to 1940-46, and 110 per cent from 1925-29 to 1940-46. This is the largest increase of any livestock enterprise having any significance in numbers. During the period 1940-46, the number reported January 1 averaged 9.8 million head, over four times the average number of hogs in *Texas* and about 18 per cent greater than the average number of all cattle during the period. These data are of even greater significance, since the sheep cycle has been in the declining phase in Texas since 1943. After Texas, Tennessee has the most sheep of the ten states included in this study and numbers have been holding fairly steady since 1914-19. Sheep are growing in importance in Oklahoma and Louisiana and increased rapidly during the period but are still of comparatively minor importance. In the remaining states the enterprise declined sharply throughout the period from 1910 to 1948, being almost at the vanishing point in South Carolina and Georgia at present. In recent years stock sheep have, however, been on the increase in Mississippi.

LIVESTOCK PRODUCTS

According to census data, Oklahoma and Texas led in the production of eggs in 1944, and the Eastern cotton states in the volume of milk produced and sold. From 1919 to 1944, the greatest percentage increase in whole milk sold occurred in the Delta states, 814 per cent, while in production of eggs and milk Texas and Oklahoma led with 168 per cent and 112 per cent, respectively.

From 1929 to 1944 the largest increase in all three products occurred in the Eastern cotton states, where milk sold increased 133 per cent; milk produced, 24 per cent; and eggs produced, 33 per cent.

From 1944 to 1947 the trends in the production of the three livestock products and sale of whole milk continued, except milk produced, which showed a drop of 1 per cent in the Delta states. However, the greatest relative increases in all three occurred in the Eastern states and the least in the Delta states. With regard to 1948, in view of the sharp drop in chickens (see page 33), it is expected that eggs will show a decrease below 1947 in all regions.

The 1944 and 1947 quantities of these products by regions, with percentage increases from 1919 to 1944, from 1929 to 1944, and from 1944 to 1947, are shown on page 37.

FARM POWER

From 1930 to 1945 the most rapid rate of increase of tractors on farms occurred in the Delta states; Texas and Oklahoma were next, and the Eastern cotton states last. From 1940 to 1945, on the other hand, the Eastern cotton states led with 136 per cent increase; the Delta states were second with 100 per cent increase. While the actual number of tractors added was greater in Oklahoma and Texas, the relative increase was more than twice as great in the Eastern cotton states. However, even with these increases,

Regional Trends

	Unit	Quantity (million units)		Percentage increase		
		1944*	1947†	1919 to 1944	1929 to 1944	1944 to 1947
Eastern States						
Chicken eggs produced	doz.	237	301	78	33	27
Milk produced	gal.	730	806	54	24	10
Milk sold	gal.	247	283	626	133	15
Delta States						
Chicken eggs produced	doz.	115	119	77	25	3
Milk produced	gal.	390	388	87	23	−1
Milk sold	gal.	128	133	814	129	4
Oklahoma-Texas						
Chicken eggs produced	doz.	311	344	168	32	11
Milk produced	gal.	718	732	112	8	2
Milk sold	gal.	241	269	793	123	12

* Census Reports of Agriculture.
† B.A.E. estimates for 1947.

all three regions were far below the rest of the United States in the ratio of tractors to cropland harvested, though the improvement in this respect was more than twice as rapid in the Cotton Belt. In 1945 the rest of the United States had 7.6 tractors per 1,000 acres of cropland harvested,[9] whereas the Cotton Belt as a whole had only 4.6, this being a considerable improvement, since 1940 showed only 2.5 per 1,000 acres of cropland harvested. Oklahoma and Texas led the regions with 5.6 as compared to 3.7 in 1940 while the Eastern states were last with 3.6, representing an increase from 1940 of 2.2 tractors per 1,000 acres of cropland harvested. The Delta states, which showed the greatest relative increase in number of tractors from 1930 to 1945, had 4.1 tractors per 1,000 acres of cropland harvested in 1945 as compared to only 1.9 in 1940 and 0.9 in 1930.

The report by the B.A.E. on farm machinery, previously cited,[10] shows that the pace of expansion in number of tractors continues excellent, with the the most rapid strides, relatively, continuing to be made in the Eastern and Delta states. This report shows an increase in tractors from

[9] Computed by dividing the number of tractors reported on farms at the respective census dates by the acres of cropland harvested the preceding year.
[10] See Chap. I, footnote 12.

January 1, 1945 to January 1, 1947 of 16 per cent in Oklahoma and Texas and 22 per cent in the Southeastern states,[11] and 11 per cent and 26 per cent respectively from January 1, 1947 to May 1, 1948.

The effect of these increases in number of tractors on farms on the number of workstock is shown by the census data for the period through 1945. In general, increases in number of tractors during the period were accompanied by large decreases in the number of workstock on farms. Both the largest absolute decrease and the largest relative decrease occurred in Oklahoma and Texas, where the decrease was consistent throughout the entire 25-year period. From 1920 to 1945, this region lost 1,682 thousand head of workstock, a decrease of 58 per cent. The decrease from 1930 to 1945 was 53 per cent. On the other hand, while the decline in workstock has been significant in the Eastern and Delta states, there seems to have been a reversal of the trend from 1935 to 1940, a slight increase occurring during this period in the Eastern and Delta states. This is associated with the depression increase in subsistence farms, and the great emphasis placed by agricultural workers on home production of workstock from 1935 to 1940. It should be noted that the trend began to be retarded in the Delta states between 1925 and 1930, probably because of the increase in number of small farms from clearing and reclamation operations. However, the decrease in number of horses and mules over the 25-year period was 30 per cent in the Eastern states and 22 per cent in the Delta states, and 14 and 12 per cent respectively from 1930 to 1945.

FARM POPULATION

In the Eastern states farm population has been on the decline since 1920 (as far back as data are considered), with the low being reached in the pre-depression period in 1927. After this date there was some increase through 1933, after which the trend was resumed, slowly at first, then very sharply during the war period.

[11] The Southeastern states include the Eastern and Delta cotton states as defined previously in this study but additionally the four states of Virginia, West Virginia, Kentucky, and Florida. The percentage changes for this region are therefore not strictly comparable with those given for the periods up to 1945, but they are a fair indication of what has happened to the tractor population in the Cotton Belt since the war.

In the Delta states and Oklahoma and Texas farm population reached a maximum in 1933, and the pre-depression low in 1927. From 1921 to 1933, however, the farm population in Oklahoma and Texas was fairly stable, varying hardly more than 100,000 persons between the high and the low. From 1933 to 1945 the most rapid declines occurred in Oklahoma and Texas and the Eastern states, the largest relative rate in the former and the largest absolute decline in the latter, although its percentage decline was the lowest of the three regions.

Taking the changes from 1930 in order to have data comparable with other major changes described heretofore, farm population decreases from 1930 to 1945 varied from 23 to 37 per cent, the Eastern states and Oklahoma and Texas, respectively, representing the extremes, with the Delta states showing a decrease of 27 per cent. It should be noted, however, that in all regions the population decrease occurred primarily in the war period, 1940-45.

During 1945 and 1946 there was a reversal in farm migration and a large percentage of the wartime migrants returned to farms. Farm population estimates of the B.A.E. since 1945[12] are shown only by geographic divisions which do not permit a direct comparison with the Cotton Belt regions under discussion, but the regions for which data are available from B.A.E. estimates are roughly comparable—the South Atlantic region with the Eastern cotton states, the East South Central with the Delta states, and the West South Central with Oklahoma and Texas. Accordingly, the increase in farm population during 1945 and 1946 amounted to 65 per cent of the wartime decrease from 1940 to 1945 in the South Atlantic states, 53 per cent in the East South Central region, and 32 per cent in the West South Central region.[13] In 1947 the direction of normal farm migration was resumed and farm population again declined in all regions from January 1, 1947 to January 1, 1948, except in the South Atlantic region where a

[12] *Farm Population Estimates, January, 1948*, U. S. Dept. of Agri., Bur. of Agri. Econ., June, 1948.

[13] Not a direct measure of the return to farms of wartime migrants because of the influence of births on population increase, but these figures do indicate that the movement was reversed.

small increase occurred. Nevertheless, despite the comparatively large return to farms in 1945 and 1946, the net decrease in farm population from 1940 to 1948 must be regarded as significant; and it is the first period since 1920 that more than a nominal decline occurred except in the Eastern cotton states between 1920 and 1927, when the decrease was apparently greater than occurred from 1940 to 1948 (6 per cent as compared to 5 per cent).[14] The net decline in farm population in these regions from 1940 to 1948 was 5 per cent in the South Atlantic region, 10 per cent in the East South Central region, and 19 per cent in the West South Central region.

NUMBER OF FARMS AND FARM SIZE

As with farm population, there was a tendency for the number of farms to fall off in the post World War I period. Farm people were finding city employment and were leaving the farms idle. Then with the coming of the depression and serious city unemployment, they flocked back to the rural areas and reoccupied the idle farms and caused many subdivisions of those already in active operation.

In the Eastern states the number of all farms declined sharply from 1920 to 1925, then remained constant through 1930, followed by a sharp increase until 1935, the number in 1935 being just short of the number in 1920. From 1935 to 1940 an even sharper decrease occurred. However, during World War II (1940-45) there was a net increase of 8 thousand farms—North Carolina, South Carolina, and Georgia showing an increase of 29 thousand farms, and Tennessee and Alabama a decrease of 21 thousand farms. The tendency to increase farms in North Carolina, South Carolina, and Georgia is evidently associated with the increasing popular tendency of city workers to take up a farm residence, either because of a shortage of city houses or the desire to keep anchored to a farm.

In the Delta states the trend was toward an increase in the number of farms until 1935 and an equally positive

[14] On the basis of the net decrease in the South Atlantic region from 1940 to 1948, which may or may not be equivalent to the actual decrease which occurred in the Eastern cotton states. But since these states constitute a fairly high proportion of the South Atlantic region, the decrease is probably a reasonably good approximation.

downward trend thereafter, although the number of farms dropped from 1920 to 1925.

In Oklahoma and Texas the increase was consistent through 1935 after which the decline in number of farms was rapid.

From 1935 to 1945, the percentage decrease in number of farms varied from 11 to 23 per cent, the Eastern states and Oklahoma and Texas being the extremes; also from 1930 to 1945 the number of farms decreased from 6 to 21 per cent, the same regions being the extremes.

These decreases in number of farms, coupled with an increase of 5 to 12 per cent in all land in farms from 1930 to 1945, led to an increase in the size of farms (basis of land area) of 12 to 42 per cent, the Eastern cotton states[15] and Oklahoma and Texas being respectively the extremes in both measures of increase.

The decline from 14 to 10 per cent in cropland harvested during the period 1929 to 1944 was accompanied by a comparatively greater decline in number of farms. Consequently, the acreage of cropland harvested per farm increased in all regions, 2 per cent in the Eastern states, 12 per cent in the Delta states, and 14 per cent in Oklahoma and Texas.

The most significant trends in number of farms have, however, occurred in the number of farms growing cotton. In the Eastern states the trend has been consistently downward since 1919; in the Delta states since 1929; and in Oklahoma and Texas since 1924. From these peaks until 1944, the decrease in number of cotton farms was 40 per cent in the Eastern states, 33 per cent in the Delta states, and 57 per cent in Oklahoma and Texas. The decline of cotton farming in the Cotton Belt since these peaks is shown dramatically by the fact that at the peak number of cotton farms in each region, 84 per cent of all farms (1929) grew cotton in the Delta states, 82 per cent (1924) in Texas and

---

[15] The biggest increases in size of farm in this region during the period occurred in Alabama, Tennessee, and Georgia. North Carolina had a small decrease, while South Carolina remained about constant. Over the longer period from 1920, however, the sharpest increases in size have taken place in Georgia, with more moderate changes occurring in South Carolina and Alabama. See U. S. Census of Agriculture, 1945, Vol. II, Chap. II (Reprint), p. 73, for further details on these and the other states included in this analysis.

Oklahoma, and 70 per cent (1919) in the Eastern states. By 1944 the proportion of all farms growing cotton had declined to 68, 43, and 48 per cent respectively. Thus the Delta states had the highest percentage of farms growing cotton at the peak and in 1944 still had the highest proportion. Oklahoma and Texas were second in percentage at the peak (1924) but in 1944 had the lowest proportion. Therefore, it appears that farms growing cotton have declined relatively the most in Oklahoma and Texas and the least in the Delta states, but there has been a larger increase in size of farms in Oklahoma and Texas and consequently a greater tendency toward large-scale cotton farms.

Since the recent increases, 1947 to 1948, in cotton acreage (those in the latter year moving the acreage to approximately one million acres below the 1939 level in the Eastern cotton states, approximately 300,000 acres in Oklahoma and Texas, and about equal to the 1939 acreage in the Delta states), it is apparent that some, and perhaps considerable, increase in number of farms growing cotton has occurred since 1945; but it is probable that the increase in number of units has been held in check by the rapid increase in tractors and other forms of mechanization since 1945. This means further enlargement of producing units.

DISTRIBUTION OF CASH FARM RECEIPTS

The change in relative contribution to total farm receipts from marketings of crop and livestock enterprises in different regions of the Cotton Belt is shown in Table 8.

These percentages of total receipts from farm marketings show that cotton has declined from 1924-29 to 1941-45 the most relatively in Oklahoma and Texas and the least in the Delta states, dropping in *emphasis* from 56 to 23 per cent in the former and from 67 to 50 per cent in the latter. The Eastern cotton states were intermediate between these extremes but even there cotton lost nearly one-half of its position. The enterprises which have been strongest in replacing cotton in the different regions are as follows:

> *Eastern cotton states:* tobacco, truck crops, dairy products, hogs, peanuts, and cattle and calves.

TABLE 8

Shifts in Relative Importance of Sources of Receipts from Farm Marketings in Different Regions of the Cotton Belt by Selected Periods, 1924 to 1947

Source	Eastern States				Delta States				Oklahoma-Texas			
	1924-29	1935-39	1941-45	1947	1924-29	1935-39	1941-45	1947	1924-29	1935-39	1941-45	1947
Cotton and cotton seed	50.4	33.6	26.1	26.2	67.3	57.4	50.5	51.6	55.5	32.9	23.1	23.9
Tobacco	13.7	24.3	24.5	24.2	....	....	....	....	....	....	....	....
Rice	....	....	....	....	4.6	5.0	6.9	6.4	....	1.2	2.0	2.2
Wheat	0.7	0.9	0.7	1.2	....	....	....	....	0.7	7.7	7.7	15.4
Truck crops	2.5	2.4	8.1	2.2	2.5	2.4	2.3	1.7	6.9	3.4	4.2	2.5
Peaches	1.6	1.3	1.6	1.0	0.4	0.6	0.7	0.4	1.8	0.2	0.2	0.2
Peanuts	2.4	3.7	5.8	5.3	....	....	0.1	....	0.2	0.5	1.6	1.7
Pecans	0.2	0.1	0.6	0.4	0.3	0.2	0.4	0.2	0.2	0.3	0.5	0.5
White potatoes	1.2	1.2	1.2	0.8	0.5	0.7	0.7	0.3	0.3	0.3	0.3	0.3
Sweet potatoes	0.8	1.1	1.0	0.7	0.8	1.1	1.1	0.8	0.3	0.4	0.3	0.3
Total crops	81.3	76.8	71.8	71.5	84.8	77.9	72.5	71.4	71.1	53.4	49.0	56.1
Cattle and calves	3.2	4.9	5.2	6.3	3.3	6.4	7.5	10.7	11.9	19.1	20.7	22.7
Dairy products	5.2	7.0	6.9	6.6	4.8	6.5	6.5	5.8	5.5	10.3	9.0	7.0
Hogs	3.7	5.3	6.9	7.6	2.7	4.3	5.6	6.1	2.9	4.1	6.1	4.3
Eggs (chicken)	3.9	3.3	4.5	3.7	2.8	2.5	3.5	2.5	3.6	4.4	6.4	4.4
Chickens	2.0	1.8	3.7	3.5	1.3	1.9	3.7	3.0	1.8	1.6	2.2	1.5
Total livestock and livestock products	18.7	23.2	28.1	28.5	15.2	22.1	27.4	28.6	28.9	46.6	51.0	43.8
Total receipts from farm marketings	100.0	100.0	100.0	100.0	100.0	100.0	100.0	100.0	100.0	100.0	100.0	100.0
Government payments	....	9.1	4.5	1.3	....	11.6	6.4	1.7	....	12.6	5.2	1.2

Sources: 1. *Cotton:* Hearings before the Subcommittee of the Committee on Agriculture, House of Representatives, Seventy-Eighth Congress, Second Session, Dec. 4 to 9, 1944, pp. 600-7
2. *Cash Receipts from Marketings by States and Commodities, Calendar Years, 1924-44,* U. S. Dept. of Agri., Bur. of Agri. Econ., Washington, D. C., January, 1946, pp. 83-121.
3. *The Farm Income Situation,* U. S. Dept. of Agri., Bur. of Agri. Econ.; current issues.

Delta states: cattle and calves, rice, dairy products, hogs, and chickens and eggs.

Oklahoma-Texas: cattle and calves, dairy products, wheat, chicken eggs, hogs, and truck crops.

The distribution of cash receipts for 1947 is shown for comparison. This is an excellent year to use for this purpose because it is the second full postwar year and cotton production was close to the prewar level. There is, therefore, a better chance to see how the different enterprises held up in the receipts distribution. The conclusion is that in general the pattern of receipts was about the same in 1947 as it was during the war period, 1941-45. The only notable exceptions are decreases in eggs and truck crops, the latter of which showed a very large decline in relative importance in the Eastern states; and increases in wheat and cattle and calves, both gaining most notably in Oklahoma and Texas. In the case of cattle and calves further note should be made of the rapid gain in emphasis which has occurred in the Delta states since the depression, this area showing suprising strides in this respect during the war period, 1941-45, and from then to 1947. But the Delta changes in cattle are in line with the large increases in feed crops and pasture area, the latter being relatively large as compared to the other regions.

Below is listed the important sources of receipts by states for 1947.[16] The contributing enterprises are ranked and the receipts shown in *million dollars rounded.* No enterprise is listed which had receipts of less than 10 million dollars in 1947.

North Carolina

1. Tobacco 404
2. Cotton lint 78
3. Dairy products 34
4. Peanuts 32
5. Hogs 28
6. Chickens 27
7. Eggs 26
8. Corn 17
9. Cattle and calves 17
10. Forest products 16
11. Truck crops 12
12. Wheat 11
13. Cottonseed 11
14. Potatoes 10

South Carolina

1. Cotton lint 120

[16] *The Farm Income Situation,* FIS 99, U. S. Dept. of Agri., Bur. of Agri. Econ., June-July, 1948, pp. 28-32.

Regional Trends

2. Tobacco 65
3. Hogs 22
4. Cottonseed 16
5. Dairy products........... 14
6. Cattle 11
7. Peaches 10

Georgia

1. Cotton lint.............. 122
2. Peanuts 72
3. Hogs 50
4. Tobacco 49
5. Chickens 31
6. Dairy products........... 29
7. Cattle and calves........ 28
8. Forest products 23
9. Truck crops............. 18
10. Cottonseed 17
11. Eggs 17
12. Corn 11

Alabama

1. Cotton lint.............. 169
2. Cattle and calves........ 36
3. Hogs 33
4. Peanuts 24
5. Dairy products........... 24
6. Cottonseed 22
7. Eggs 14
8. Forest products.......... 14
9. Corn 12
10. Chickens 11

Tennessee

1. Tobacco 78
2. Cotton lint.............. 78
3. Cattle and calves 64
4. Dairy products........... 63
5. Hogs 54
6. Eggs 26
7. Corn 20
8. Cottonseed 15
9. Chickens 12
10. Forest products......... 10

Arkansas

1. Cotton lint 220
2. Cattle and calves 53
3. Cottonseed 40
4. Hogs 36

5. Rice 33
6. Dairy products.......... 25
7. Chickens 23
8. Eggs 13
9. Soybeans 11
10. Forest products 10

Mississippi

1. Cotton lint.............. 281
2. Cottonseed 42
3. Cattle and calves........ 42
4. Dairy products........... 30
5. Hogs 20
6. Forest products 14
7. Eggs 13
8. Chickens 10

Louisiana

1. Cotton lint.............. 84
2. Rice 51
3. Cattle and calves........ 46
4. Sugar cane for sugar..... 29
5. Hogs 25
6. Dairy products........... 21
7. Cottonseed 13

Oklahoma

1. Wheat 189
2. Cattle and calves........ 181
3. Dairy products........... 62
4. Cotton lint.............. 46
5. Hogs 39
6. Eggs 34
7. Peanuts 13
8. Chickens 11
9. Cottonseed 10

Texas

1. Cotton lint.............. 465
2. Cattle and calves........ 407
3. Wheat 210
4. Dairy products........... 119
5. Cottonseed 98
6. Sorghums for grain....... 86
7. Eggs 79
8. Hogs 72
9. Truck crops............. 59
10. Rice 56
11. Sheep and lambs......... 34
12. Peanuts 32

13. Chickens	29	17. Turkeys	19	
14. Corn	28	18. Oats	13	
15. Wool	27	19. Mohair	11	
16. Grapefruit	24	20. Oranges	11	

Comparisons of this sort are difficult because of differences in size and resource adaptation in the different states. However, it does serve to demonstrate that many enterprises contribute importantly to the income in most of the states. Most states had from ten to twelve important sources, though Texas had twenty and South Carolina and Louisiana had only seven. It is also to be noted that despite all the trends away from cotton, receipts from cotton lint were sufficient to lead all sources in seven states, in five of these by a wide margin. Tobacco was the leading source of receipts in two states—North Carolina and Tennessee—and wheat the leading source in Oklahoma. It is of great interest that cattle and calves were second as a source in four states, in two of which the receipts from the enterprise were a close second. Cattle and calves, hogs, and dairy products are found as important contributors to receipts in all ten states, and chickens and eggs in all except two states. Few of the other enterprises show any uniformity of occurrence by states. Some are peculiar to certain states which developed them and appear to be making rapid progress in most cases toward further development. The most important of these products by states (in terms of millions of dollars of receipts in 1947) are:

1. *Peanuts*
    Georgia 72
    North Carolina........... 32
    Texas 32
    Alabama 24
    Oklahoma 13
2. *Rice*
    Texas 56
    Louisiana 51
    Arkansas 33
3. *Truck crops*
    Texas 59
    Georgia 18
    North Carolina........... 12
4. *Specialties*
    Louisiana: Sugar cane
        for sugar 29
    South Carolina: Peaches... 10
    Arkansas: Soybeans....... 11
    Texas:
        Sorghum for grain.... 86
        Sheep and lambs...... 34
        Wool 27
        Grapefruit 24
        Turkeys 19
        Mohair 11
        Oranges 11

CHAPTER III

Farm Organizational Changes

SIZE OF FARM

ALTHOUGH DURING the period 1929 to 1944 acreage harvested declined in the regions from 4 to 10 per cent, total land in farms increased from 5 to 12 per cent;[1] the difference between the decline in cropland harvested and the increase in total land in farms going almost entirely to pastures, which increased 59 per cent in the Delta states, 22 per cent in the Eastern states, and 26 per cent in Oklahoma and Texas—80 to 90 per cent of these increases occurring in pasture types other than woodland. Consequently, in view of the comparatively large decrease in number of farms in all three regions, the average land area per farm increased significantly from 1930 to 1945 in all areas. Oklahoma and Texas showed the greatest increase in size and the Eastern states the least, 42 and 12 per cent, respectively, the Delta states being intermediate with an increase of 34 per cent. Furthermore, acreage of cropland per farm increased in all regions also, since the decrease from 1930 to 1945 in number of farms, 6 to 21 per cent, was sufficient to overcome the decrease in total acreage harvested.

As shown in Figure 8, the general increase in size of farms in the different regions has been accompanied by an increase in extensive crops,[2] which have tended to displace intensive crops.[3] These trends had by 1944 caused average acreage of intensive crops per farm to decline below the acreage of extensive crops in the Eastern states and Oklahoma and Texas, being in the latter region just over one-

[1] From 1930 to 1945.
[2] Wheat, oats, barley, hay, cowpeas and soybeans, and sorghums.
[3] Tobacco, cotton, orchards, vegetables for sale, white potatoes, and sweet potatoes.

third of it. As a matter of fact the data indicate that both regions moved to a favorable position with respect to extensive crops about 1934, the Eastern states having slightly more intensive than extensive crops per farm, but the average farm in Oklahoma and Texas in 1934 had an excess of extensive over intensive crops of 32 per cent. In the Delta states the acreage of intensive crops declined but not as much relatively as in the other two regions, while extensive crops per farm showed the highest percentage expansion. But even so the acreage of intensive crops in the Delta states in 1944 still exceeded that of the extensive crops by 22 per cent.

The acreage of medium intensive crops[4] per farm increased from 1929 to 1939 in the Eastern and Delta states, with decreases occurring between 1939 and 1944; Oklahoma and Texas showed an increase from 1934 to 1939 only, with no change between 1939 and 1944. Despite the decrease from 1939 to 1944 in the Eastern and Delta states, this category of crops exceeded in 1944 the acreages of extensive and intensive crops per farm by 58 and 94 per cent, respectively, in the Eastern states and by 7 and 31 per cent in the Delta states. In Oklahoma and Texas, on the other hand, the medium intensive crops occupied in 1944 a considerably smaller acreage per farm than extensive and intensive crops, the former occupying roughly three times the acreage of intensive crops and four times that of the medium intensive crops, or an area per farm in extensive crops 64 per cent greater than the other two types combined.

From either standpoint, cropland harvested or total land per farm, the average farm was closely the same size in the Eastern and Delta states in 1944. In Oklahoma and Texas, however, farms averaged nearly three times the acreage harvested and four times the land area of the average farm in the other two regions.

CROPLAND USE

The resulting cropland use from these trends is shown in Figure 9. In 1944 the Delta states had the highest percentage of cropland harvested in intensive crops and Okla-

[4] Rice, corn, and peanuts.

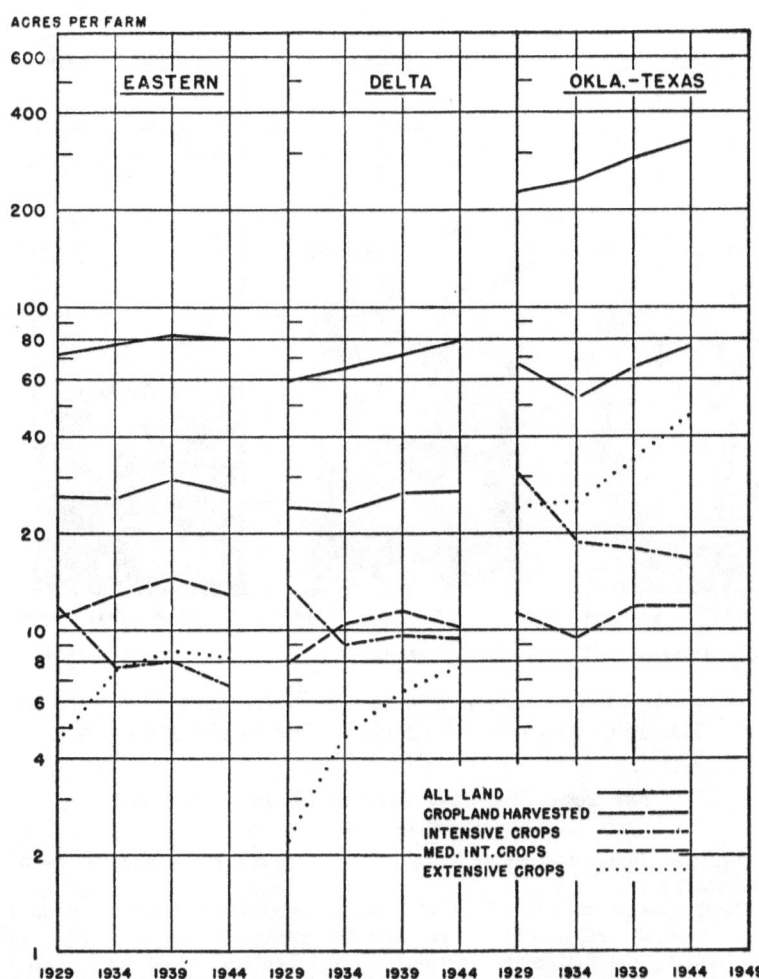

FIGURE 8. TRENDS IN AVERAGE FARM ORGANIZATION IN DIFFERENT REGIONS OF TEN COTTON STATES, BY CENSUS YEARS

Since 1929 farms have been increasing in size and expanding the acreage of extensive crops at the expense of intensive crops in all regions, but more rapidly in Oklahoma and Texas.

homa and Texas the lowest, 35 and 22 per cent, respectively, with the Eastern states having 25 per cent. Because of wheat and grain sorghums, Oklahoma and Texas were highest in the percentage of cropland harvested in extensive crops with 62 per cent, the Delta states being lowest with 28 per cent. In summary, the Eastern states led in the percentage of harvested acreage in medium intensive crops;

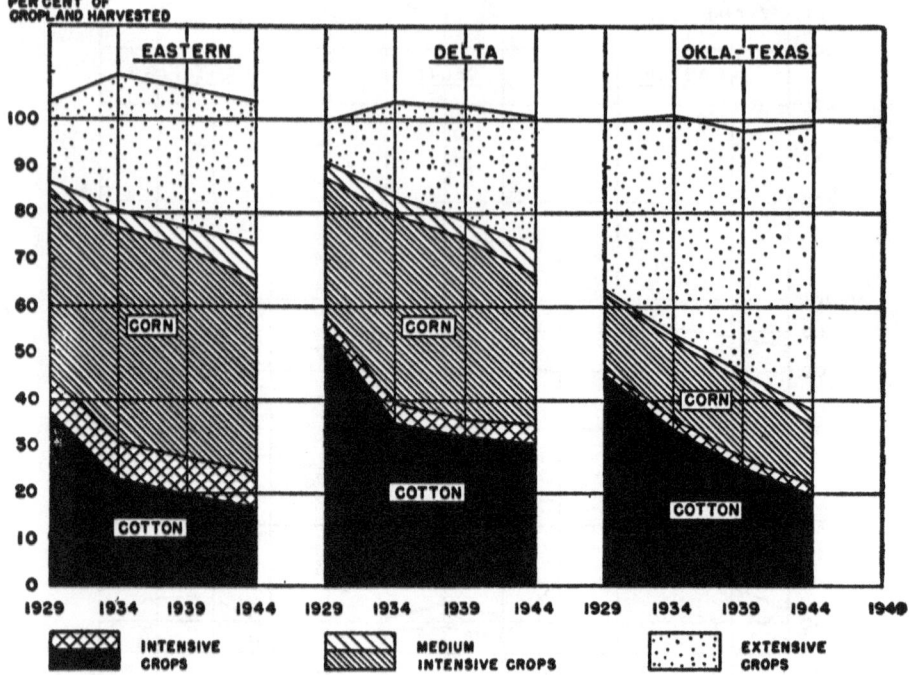

FIGURE 9. PERCENTAGE OF CROPLAND HARVESTED OCCUPIED BY MAJOR CATEGORIES OF CROPS IN DIFFERENT REGIONS, BY CENSUS YEARS

(THE TOTAL PER CENT EXCEEDS 100 IN MOST YEARS BECAUSE OF DOUBLE-CROPPING.)

The most intensive cropland use is found in the Delta and the least in Oklahoma-Texas.

The decline in the percentage of cropland harvested devoted to cotton and the increase in the proportion in extensive crops are the most significant trends during the fifteen-year period. In the Eastern cotton states and the Delta states corn increased in emphasis from 1929 to 1939 but since then has lost position rapidly.

Oklahoma and Texas in extensive crops; and the Delta states in intensive crops.

NUMBER OF LIVESTOCK PER FARM

As shown in Table 9, the number of cattle per farm was the lowest in the Eastern states, from 2.9 to 4.4 head, and the highest per farm in Oklahoma and Texas, varying from 11.6 to 21.5 head during the 25-year period. The comparatively larger number of cattle per farm in Okla-

TABLE 9
TRENDS IN LIVESTOCK PER FARM BY REGIONS

Livestock enterprise and year or period	Number* per farm		
	Eastern	Delta	Oklahoma and Texas
Workstock			
1920.....................	1.8	2.3	4.6
1930.....................	1.6	1.8	3.7
1935.....................	1.4	1.6	3.1
1940.....................	1.6	1.8	2.8
1945.....................	1.4	1.9	2.2
Per cent change:†			
1920 to 1945.............	−22	−17	−52
1930 to 1945.............	−12	6	−41
All cattle			
1917-21..................	3.4	5.1	15.9
1927-31..................	2.9	3.6	11.6
1933-37..................	3.4	4.8	14.1
1942-46..................	4.4	7.3	21.5
Per cent change:			
1917-21 to 1942-46........	29	43	35
1927-31 to 1942-46........	52	103	85
Hogs			
1917-21..................	5.8	5.7	6.2
1927-31..................	4.0	3.1	3.9
1933-37..................	4.0	3.8	3.9
1942-46..................	5.7	5.5	6.5
Per cent change:†			
1917-21 to 1942-46........	−2	−4	5
1927-31 to 1942-46........	42	77	67
Chickens			
1927-31..................	35	30	59
1933-37..................	31	27	50
1942-46..................	46	44	91
Per cent change:			
1927-31 to 1942-46........	32	47	54

* For all cattle, hogs and chickens, the numbers were taken from U. S. D. A. estimates as of January 1. The average for five years centered *approximately* at the census date, was compared to the number of farms.
† Per cent decreases are shown with a minus.

homa and Texas is due to the fact, as shown above, that the average farm has four times the land area and three times the cropland area of the other two regions. However, throughout the cotton states the number of cattle per farm increased rapidly during the 25-year period, the increases being of the following order: 29 to 43 per cent from 1917-21 to 1942-46; and 52 to 103 per cent from 1927-31 to 1942-46. The Delta states showed the greatest relative increase per farm between both periods, although both the Eastern states and Oklahoma and Texas showed a very rapid increase per farm from 1927-31 to 1942-46, 52 per cent and 85 per cent respectively.

The number of hogs per farm is not greatly different among the regions, although Oklahoma and Texas had the largest number during 1942-46, with about one hog more per farm during this period than either of the other two regions. Even though the number of hogs per farm expanded consistently from 1927-31 to 1942-46, the average number per farm had not reached the 1917-21 level in 1942-46 in any of the regions except Oklahoma and Texas. From 1927-31 to 1942-46 the percentage increase in the number per farm was from 42 to 77 per cent, the least percentage increase occurring in the Eastern states and the greatest in the Delta states. The fact that hogs are about equally significant in the average farm set-up in all regions is due to the fact that the larger farms in Oklahoma and Texas are counterbalanced by the relatively greater importance of corn in the farm set-up in the other two regions and especially in the Eastern states.

Oklahoma and Texas have generally had close to double the number of chickens per farm of the other two regions. The greater grain acreage in Oklahoma and Texas is apparently a factor. Although there was a decline in the number of chickens per farm from 1927-31 to 1933-37 in all regions the number per farm in 1942-46 was from 32 to 54 per cent above the 1927-31 level. In view of the decrease in total number of chickens on farms in 1947 and 1948, there has undoubtedly been a decrease in number per farm in the three regions below the high levels reached during the war.

Until 1935 the number of workstock per farm in Oklahoma and Texas was double the number per farm in either of the other two regions. Since then they have been from 57 to 75 per cent higher than the number per farm in the Eastern states and from 16 to 56 per cent greater than in the Delta states. However, despite the trend toward larger farms, the number of workstock per farm tended to decline in Oklahoma and Texas throughout the 25-year period, and more rapidly than in the other two regions because of the relatively more rapid rate of mechanization and the trend toward a more extensive system of agriculture. Although declining earlier, the number of workstock per farm in the Eastern states and the Delta states increased after 1935 and were practically at the 1925 level in 1940. This is due to the increase in size of farms without as much mechanization as in the Western states and to the greater emphasis placed on home production of workstock by agricultural workers during the period. However, the long-time trend toward fewer workstock per farm was again resumed in the Eastern states between 1940 and 1945, but they showed some further increase per farm in the Delta states during this period. The percentage decrease in number of workstock per farm from 1920 to 1945 was 22 per cent in the Eastern cotton states, 17 per cent in the Delta states, and 52 per cent in Oklahoma and Texas; whereas from 1930 to 1945 there was a decrease of 12 per cent in the Eastern states and 41 per cent in Oklahoma and Texas; the Delta states, however, had an increase in workstock per farm during the period of 6 per cent.

NUMBER OF LIVESTOCK PER 100 ACRES OF CROPLAND HARVESTED

Table 10 shows the relative density of livestock per 100 acres of cropland harvested. By periods, it appears that the Delta states had the largest number of cattle[5] per 100 acres of cropland harvested plus pasture land, while the Eastern states had the greatest density of chickens per 100 acres of cropland harvested. The Eastern and Delta states had about equal density in hogs, but both had more than twice as many per 100 acres of cropland harvested as Oklahoma and Texas. The greater density of hogs and chickens in the Eastern states appears to be due, as stated previously, to the higher percentage of cropland in corn and higher yields than in the other regions; and the lower relative number of all cattle in the Eastern states than in the other regions is probably associated with the relatively smaller acreage and poorer quality of pasture, a high per-

[5] Average number for five years centered at the census date.

centage of which is woodland pasture. The increase per 100 acres from 1927-31 to 1942-46 varied from 27 to 38 per cent for all cattle, 42 to 56 per cent for hogs and 30 to 36 per cent for chickens. The Delta states showed the largest increase in all cattle (38 per cent) and in hogs (56 per cent), and Oklahoma and Texas in chickens (36 per cent).

TABLE 10

TRENDS IN NUMBER OF LIVESTOCK PER 100 ACRES OF CROPLAND HARVESTED (PLUS PASTURE ACREAGE IN THE CASE OF ALL CATTLE) BY REGIONS

Livestock enterprise and period	Number* per 100 acres of cropland harvested		
	Eastern	Delta	Oklahoma and Texas
All cattle†			
1927-31	6.8	9.1	5.5
1933-37	7.9	11.2	6.6
1942-46	9.2	12.6	7.0
Per cent increase from 1927-31 to 1942-46	35	38	27
Hogs			
1927-31	15	13	6
1933-37	16	16	7
1942-46	21	20	9
Per cent increase from 1927-31 to 1942-46	42	56	46
Chickens			
1927-31	132	124	89
1933-37	123	115	94
1942-46	172	161	120
Per cent increase from 1927-31 to 1942-46	30	30	36

* For all cattle, hogs and chickens, the numbers were taken from U. S. D. A. estimates as of January 1. The average for five years, centered at the census date for cropland harvested, was compared to the total acreage of cropland harvested (plus land in pasture in the case of all cattle).
† Number per 100 acres of cropland harvested plus pasture acreage.

Table 11 compares the density of workstock with the density of tractors per hundred acres of cropland harvested. For the census years 1930, 1935, 1940, and 1945, the Delta states had the highest number of workstock per 100 acres of cropland harvested, while Oklahoma and Texas had the lowest, with from 15 to 58 per cent fewer relatively than the Delta states, and, except in 1935, from 7 to 44 per cent fewer than the Eastern cotton states. Tractors per 100 acres harvested increased in all areas during the period but only in Oklahoma and Texas did they increase consistently as workstock decreased. In the Eastern and Delta states the number of workstock per 100 acres of cropland harvested dropped from 1930 to 1935 but little change occurred after that date, whereas the relative number of tractors increased from 260 to 356 per cent. From 1930 to 1945 the number of workstock per 100 acres of cropland harvested in Oklahoma and Texas declined 46 per cent, while the relative number of tractors increased 300 per cent. It appears that mechanization was a strong force in the transformation of the agriculture in Oklahoma and Texas, increasing farm size and displacing workstock. Its effects are not as apparent in the other two regions, probably because mechanization has not progressed sufficiently far as yet, apparently being superimposed on the existing agriculture.

TABLE 11

TREND IN NUMBER OF WORKSTOCK AND TRACTORS PER 100 ACRES HARVESTED BY REGIONS

Year	Number per 100 acres of cropland harvested*					
	Eastern		Delta		Oklahoma and Texas	
	Workstock	Tractors	Workstock	Tractors	Workstock	Tractors
1930	6.0	.10	7.5	.09	5.6	.14
1935	5.3	n.a.	6.9	n.a.	5.9	n.a.
1940	5.3	.14	6.8	.19	4.3	.37
1945	5.4	.36	7.1	.41	3.0	.56
Per cent change from 1930 to 1945	−10	260	−5	356	−46	300

* Cropland harvested applies to the year preceding the inventory of tractors.
n.a. means data not available.
Source: Computed from basic data obtained from the Census Reports of Agriculture.

LIVESTOCK INCREASE IN TEN COTTON BELT STATES VERSUS LIVESTOCK INCREASE IN THIRTY-EIGHT OTHER STATES

The percentage increases of important livestock enterprises in ten Cotton Belt states and its regions are compared to the percentage increases in the thirty-eight other states in Table 12. The data show that all cattle made larger percentage increases in the Cotton Belt regions by a large margin between both periods used in the comparison, 1915-19 to 1940-46 and 1925-29 to 1940-46; whereas hogs declined in the period from 1915-19 to 1940-46 in these regions but increased in the thirty-eight other states as a

TABLE 12

COMPARISON OF PERCENTAGE INCREASE OF SPECIFIED CLASSES OF LIVESTOCK IN COTTON REGIONS WITH THAT FOR THIRTY-EIGHT OTHER STATES FROM 1915-19 TO 1940-46 AND 1925-29 TO 1940-46

Livestock enterprise and region	Percentage increase	
	From 1915-19 to 1940-46	From 1925-29 to 1940-46
All cattle		
Eastern states	11	35
Delta states	32	60
Oklahoma and Texas	14	38
10 cotton states	17	41
38 other states	9	26
Hogs		
Eastern states	−14	32
Delta states	−10	45
Oklahoma and Texas	−12	31
10 cotton states	−12	35
38 other states	14	10
Chickens		
Eastern states	n.a.	16
Delta states	n.a.	20
Oklahoma and Texas	n.a.	22
10 cotton states	n.a.	19
38 other states	n.a.	9

n.a. means the data are not available.
Source: Compiled from official estimates of the U. S. D. A.

whole. However, from 1925-29 to 1940-46, the percentage increase of hogs in the cotton regions was much larger than in the thirty-eight other states. This is not significant as it might seem, because the decrease in hogs in the Cotton Belt regions from 1919 to 1926 gave a much lower base from which the percentage increases were calculated. Data for chickens are available only from 1925, but on the basis of increases from 1925-29 to 1940-46 the percentage increases are almost 2 to 1 greater than in the other thirty-eight states.

In the case of sheep, comparisons are made only on the basis of Texas, but the differences in the relative changes are phenomenal. Texas increased stock sheep 323 per cent from 1915-19 to 1940-46 and 110 per cent from 1925-29 to 1940-46, whereas this enterprise remained practically constant in the rest of the United States.

Table 13 shows the number of livestock of different types in the ten cotton states and certain regions of the Cotton Belt as a percentage of the number in the thirty-eight other states. The increase or decrease in the size of this proportion shows the interregional change in the national economy. Thus it is apparent that chickens are definitely developing more rapidly in the cotton regions, while hogs are declining in them, though there has been a reversal in the trend since 1933 but not sufficient to even approach the 1910-14 proportion. All cattle declined to a small extent relative to the thirty-eight other states after 1910-14, but exceeded this level again in 1933-39 and 1940-

TABLE 13

TREND IN SPECIFIED CLASSES OF LIVESTOCK IN TEN COTTON STATES AND CERTAIN COTTON REGIONS AS PERCENTAGE OF THIRTY-EIGHT OTHER STATES BY PERIODS

Livestock and period	Average number in 38 other states (million head)	Number in specified regions expressed as a percentage of number in 38 other states		
		10 cotton states	Oklahoma and Texas	Eastern and Delta states
All cattle				
1910-14....	42.9	34.1	19.4	14.7
1915-19....	52.4	32.6	18.6	14.0
1920-24....	51.2	33.5	19.4	14.1
1925-29....	45.5	31.0	17.8	13.2
1930-32....	48.1	31.6	18.1	13.5
1933-39....	50.9	34.4	19.3	15.1
1940-46....	57.3	37.3	19.5	17.8
Hogs				
1910-14....	39.3	35.0	9.4	25.6
1915-19....	45.6	32.6	8.6	24.0
1920-24....	49.6	26.8	7.3	19.5
1925-29....	47.2	20.4	5.6	14.8
1930-32....	46.9	20.6	5.9	14.7
1933-39....	37.9	28.4	7.1	21.3
1940-46....	51.9	25.0	6.7	18.3
Chickens				
1925-29....	350.6	28.8	11.0	17.8
1930-32....	351.0	28.7	11.5	17.2
1933-39....	319.3	29.9	11.2	18.7
1940-46....	381.0	31.6	12.3	19.3

Source: Compiled from official reports of U. S. D. A.

46 in the Eastern and Delta states, although only in 1940-46 was the 1910-14 relative percentage exceeded slightly in Oklahoma and Texas. It is apparent therefore that for the long period the growth trend of all cattle in the ten cotton states as a whole relative to the rest of the United States is not definitely established, but the trend in the Eastern and Delta states seems sufficiently strong and of such duration as to be regarded as significant and promising. Stock sheep in Texas show the most important livestock trend of all classes of livestock studied. This is shown most emphatically by the following ratios: as an average, Texas had 6 per cent of all U. S. stock sheep in 1914-19, 12 per cent during 1925-29, and 22 per cent on the average from 1940 to 1946. The increase in Texas stock sheep coincides with the general shift of sheep production toward the Western range areas.

Table 14 compares the number per farm and per 100 acres of cropland harvested (plus pasture for all cattle). Although the number of all cattle and chickens per farm in the ten Cotton Belt states as a whole is one-half the number per farm in the rest of the United States, and in the case of hogs per farm from one-third to one-half,[6] the percentage increase in number per farm was greater between both periods in the case of all cattle and almost three times greater in the case of hogs and chickens from 1927-31 to 1942-46. Density, that is, the number of animals per 100 acres of cropland harvested (plus pasture land for all cattle), shows even more striking changes than the number per farm. Although the number of all cattle was 85 per cent and the number of hogs about two-thirds as dense in the ten cotton states during 1927-31 and 1933-37 as in the thirty-eight other states, the margin had closed to about 95 per cent for cattle and three-fourths for hogs by 1942-46; chickens closed from three-fourths to over nine-tenths. These changes represent increases in density in the ten cotton states from 1927-31 to 1942-46 of about three times the increase in density in the rest of the United States. In 1942-46 the Delta states had a 50 per cent greater density of all cattle than the thirty-eight other states, the Eastern

[6] Oklahoma and Texas have averaged higher than the thirty-eight other states in all cattle in most of the periods under examination.

states had about the same density in hogs, and the Delta and Eastern states combined had from 6 to 13 per cent more chickens; however, Oklahoma and Texas had one-fifth less cattle, three-fifths less hogs, and one-fifth less chickens per 100 acres of cropland harvested (plus pasture in the case of cattle). The relatively greater intensity of the agriculture in crop farm operations in the Eastern and Delta states than in the thirty-eight other states undoubtedly accounts, at least in part, for the surprisingly greater relative density of livestock in these Southeastern cotton states.

TABLE 14

COMPARISON OF NUMBER OF SPECIFIED CLASSES OF LIVESTOCK PER FARM AND PER 100 ACRES OF CROPLAND HARVESTED IN TEN COTTON STATES AND IN THIRTY-EIGHT OTHER STATES BY PERIODS

Livestock	Number per farm*		Number per 100 acres of cropland harvested†	
	10 cotton states	38 other states	10 cotton states	38 other states
All cattle				
1917-21..................	6.9	13.7	n.a.	n.a.
1927-31..................	5.4	12.4	6.3	7.6
1933-37..................	6.6	12.6	7.5	9.0
1942-46..................	9.3	17.0	8.2	8.5
Per cent incresae from				
1917-21 to 1942-46..........	35	24	n.a.	n.a.
1927-31 to 1942-46..........	72	37	30	12
Hogs				
1917-21..................	5.9	11.7	n.a.	n.a.
1927-31..................	3.7	13.0	10.2	18.1
1933-37..................	3.9	9.4	12.2	18.5
1942-46..................	5.8	15.2	15.0	20.6
Per cent increase from				
1917-21 to 1942-46..........	−2	30	n.a.	n.a.
1927-31 to 1942-46..........	57	17	47	14
Chickens				
1927-31..................	40	97	109	135
1933-37..................	35	79	109	155
1942-46..................	56	112	145	152
Per cent increase from				
1927-31 to 1942-46..........	40	15	33	13

* Based on number of farms as reported in the closest Census for each period.
† Based on acres of cropland harvested as reported in the closest Census. All cattle are based on cropland harvested plus acreage of pasture land.
n.a. means data are not available.
Source: Compiled from official estimates of U. S. D. A.

CHAPTER IV

Mechanization

IT HAS BEEN estimated that around 1820 one farm worker in the United States supported a total of 4.5 persons at home and abroad with food, fiber, and other farm raw materials; by 1945 he was supporting 14.5 persons.[1] This change represents roughly the increase in farm efficiency from both labor and land. Through the introduction of new and better fertilizers, improved varieties of seeds, better insect control, etc., the land has been made to produce more bountifully. This is represented by the steady increase in yields per acre. Since about 1920 crop production per acre in the United States has increased 25 per cent.[2]

The productivity of farm labor has likewise become more efficient. This is shown by the increase of 50 per cent in output per worker in agriculture in the United States since 1920,[3] which has been due to the higher land productivity mentioned above and to an increase in mechanical aids, although the upward trend in the level of education of farm workers should not be ignored as a factor.

Efforts of man to ease the drudgery of labor and to find better methods of doing things have over the centuries been a major force in the advance of civilization and a chief means by which the rise in the standard of living of the masses of humanity has been achieved. When each family was dependent on what the woman could cultivate with a crooked stick and what the head of the household could slay as a hunter, there was no need for exchange (for there was no surplus to exchange) and no possibility of a city culture. When man domesticated the horse and trained it

[1] Martin R. Cooper, et al., *Progress of Farm Mechanization*, U. S. Dept. of Agri., Misc. Pub. No. 630, 1947, p. 5.
[2] S. E. Johnson, *Changes in Farming*, p. 72.
[3] *Ibid.*, p. 71.

Mechanization

as a beast of burden, he made a considerable advance. At this point in the evolution of civilization exchange became necessary because the men of the soil supplied the necessary food and fiber for a city population, which in turn provided other types of goods necessary for the comfort and ornament of the home.

In the last forty years or thereabouts the farmer has been harnessing another form of power, the gas engine. Of course prior to 1910 there were many inventions which made important contributions, through mechanical aids, to his labor productivity. Notable among these were the reaper, binder, mower, and various types of multiple horse-drawn equipment.

Cooper, Barton, and Brodell in their *Progress of Farm Mechanization,* previously cited, give changes in labor requirements for three important staple crops since 1800. These crops are wheat, corn, and cotton. The results which are most striking are given in Table 15.

Because some of the great labor-saving devices have been developed in connection with grain farming, the greatest reduction in labor requirements per acre and per bushel

TABLE 15
TREND IN LABOR REQUIREMENTS OF THREE MAJOR STAPLE CROPS
IN THE UNITED STATES, 1800 TO 1940

Item	About 1800	About 1840	About 1880	About 1900	About 1920	About 1940
Wheat						
Man-hours per acre	56	35	20	15	12	7.5
Yield per acre, bushels	15	15	13.2	13.9	13.8	15.9
Man hours per 100 bushels	373	233	152	108	87	47
Corn						
Man-hours per acre	86	69	46	38	32	25
Yield per acre, bushels	25	25	25.6	25.9	28.4	30.3
Man hours per 100 bushels	344	276	180	147	113	83
Cotton						
Man-hours per acre before harvest	135	90	67	62	55	46
Harvest	50	45	52	50	35	52
Total	185	135	119	112	90	98
Yield per acre of lint, pounds	154	154	196	198	160	257
Man-hours per bale	601	439	304	283	281	191

Source: U. S. D. A., Misc. Pub. 630, p.3.

occurred in wheat. From 373 hours per 100 bushels about 1800 to 47 hours per 100 bushels in 1940 is the startling increase in labor efficiency which developed in the production of this great food crop. Thus the labor requirement in 1940 is just one-eighth what it was in 1800. In the case of corn the 1940 requirements are 24 per cent of those about 1800, and those of cotton, 32 per cent. Both of the latter have been affected by multiple-row equipment and in recent years by sharp upward trends in yields. However, corn farmers took advantage of a ratio of man to animals much earlier and more completely than did cotton farmers. The latter because of the necessity of having a large supply of hoe and harvest labor developed the farm organization and equipment set-up around the family. However, prior to the tractor, multiple-row equipment appears to have been used in Texas in cotton production. But even there, and particularly in West Texas, the most rapid strides were made in using this form of labor-saving equipment in the twenties.

If we look back at the tabular data again, it is apparent that the chief decrease in labor to produce cotton came from reductions in pre-harvest labor (89 hours between 1800 and 1940), which caused a decline of 48 per cent in total labor requirements per acre. The changes in pre-harvest labor reflect the shift in the Cotton Belt to the more arid areas, to larger fields and farms, to the change from a slavery economy, and to the use of multiple-row equipment.

USE OF TRACTOR POWER IN FARMING OPERATIONS

In view of their adaptability, generality of use, and comparatively reasonable investment, tractors and the equipment which may and should be used with them, occupy a unique and highly significant place in Southern agriculture.

The small general-purpose tractor, which came on the market in the last fifteen years, has undoubtedly extended tractor use on cotton farms in areas which otherwise would not have been subject to mechanical power. Where found on farms it is used mainly in land preparation of cotton and corn and for practically all operations in grain production.

Mechanization

The Bureau of Agricultural Economics, U. S. D. A., recently published a study on tractor use by crops and operations in 1939 and 1946. A summary of these results is shown in Table 16.

TABLE 16
IMPORTANCE OF TRACTOR POWER IN PERFORMING MAJOR OPERATIONS OF SPECIFIED ENTERPRISES BY REGIONS, 1939 AND 1946

Enterprise and operation	Percentage of total of specified operations performed by tractor machines									
	South-east*		Delta†		Okla.-Texas		Corn Belt‡		U. S.	
	1939	1946	1939	1946	1939	1946	1939	1946	1939	1946
All crops										
Breaking land...	12	38	11	35	49	82	69	92	55	82
Disking........	23	53	19	48	50	86	69	92	57	85
Harrowing......	9	31	9	29	41	79	52	86	43	77
Small grains										
Breaking land...	13	41	26	42	71	89	71	91	71	90
Disking........	24	56	36	55	71	91	70	92	70	91
Harrowing......	10	32	23	38	65	87	54	85	58	85
Drilling seed....	7	36	23	38	71	89	30	70	49	79
Harvesting.....	32	62	35	54	80	90	71	91	69	90
Corn										
Breaking land...	11	36	13	32	34	68	73	92	51	78
Disking........	21	51	21	45	35	75	72	93	53	81
Harrowing......	9	30	11	25	26	63	56	87	39	72
Planting........	2	13	4	12	23	60	9	44	13	41
Cultivating.....	3	10	5	16	22	65	47	82	30	64
			Mid-South§				Mountain Pacific‡			
Cotton										
Breaking land...	10	38	16	42	48	84	81	94	30	60
Harrowing......	8	29	13	37	40	81	67	89	25	54
Planting........	2	13	4	16	42	78	64	81	21	43
Cultivating.....	2	11	6	18	40	82	69	87	21	45

* Virginia, North Carolina, South Carolina, Georgia, Florida, and Alabama.
† Mississippi, Arkansas, and Louisiana.
‡ Ohio, Indiana, Illinois, Iowa, and Missouri.
§ The Delta states plus Tennessee and Missouri.
‡ New Mexico, Arizona, and California.
Source: A. P. Brodell and J. A. Ewing, *Use of Tractor Power, Animal Power, and Hand Methods in Crop Production*, U. S. Dept. of Agri., Bur. of Agri. Econ., F. M. 69, July, 1948, pp. 9-28.

The data are of interest to this discussion from two major standpoints. They show the trend in mechanization of operations between 1939 and 1946 and the degree of mechanization in 1946. The table shows comparisons between the different subregions of the Cotton Belt, the Corn Belt, and the United States as a whole for all crops, small grains, corn, and cotton.

It is apparent from the data that the pace of mechanization has been very rapid in all regions shown, and in the United States, but more rapid in relative increase in the Southeastern and Delta states than in any of the other regions; although these regions are still less than half as mechanized as the other regions given in the table, and as the United States, in most of the operations except disking. By 1946 Oklahoma and Texas were about eight-tenths mechanized in land preparation of all crops as compared to nine-tenths in the Corn Belt; in contrast, the Delta states were from 29 to 48 per cent, and the Southeastern states from 31 to 53 per cent, mechanized. Of the three crops reported in Table 16, small grains were the most mechanized and cotton the least. Grains were from 79 to 90 per cent mechanized in the United States, with Oklahoma and Texas and the Corn Belt being both equal to these extremes; however, the Southeastern and Delta states were in two operations (harrowing and drilling seed) less than half as mechanized, varying from 32 to 38 per cent of total work performed in the different operations. In all the regions mentioned above, disking was the operation most highly mechanized, while drilling seed was the least mechanized operation in the United States and the Corn Belt and harrowing land the least mechanized in the three cotton regions.

In corn culture only five operations were reported on in 1946—breaking land, disking, harrowing, planting, and cultivating. In all regions shown, disking was the highest percentage mechanized and planting the lowest, except in the Southeastern states where the percentage of land cultivated by mechanized means was even lower. The Corn Belt, except in planting, was from 82 to 93 per cent mechanized as compared to 63 to 75 per cent for Oklahoma and Texas. In the Delta and Southeastern states, on the other hand, the percentages were some fraction of those given above, planting and cultivating varying between 10 and 16 per cent, harrowing and breaking land between 25 and 36 per cent, and disking between 45 and 51 per cent.

Only four production operations, breaking land, harrowing, planting, and cultivating, are given for cotton. It is seen that these operations were only 43 to 60 per cent mechanized in the United States as a whole in 1946, falling to the lowest percentage of the three crops considered. However, two regions, Oklahoma and Texas and the Mountain and Pacific cotton states, show materially higher ratios, from 78 to 84 per cent in the former and 81 to 94 per cent in the latter. Thus the Western states of the Cotton Belt are better than eight-tenths mechanized in all operations exclusive of chopping, hoeing, and harvesting, which are not shown. In comparison, the Southeastern and Mid-South states were from 11 to 18 per cent mechanized in the planting and cultivating jobs, 29 to 37 per cent in harrowing, and from 38 to 42 per cent in breaking land. In all regions the land-breaking operation is the most mechanized and planting the least, except in the Southeastern states where cultivation is the least mechanized.

It should be noted that in two crops, grains and corn, disking was the most mechanized in all regions, and the planting operation the least; in the case of cotton, breaking land was the highest and planting seed the lowest. One important exception to the above generalization may be made regarding the Southeastern states. While all regions were least mechanized in the planting operations in corn and cotton, this region is lowest in cultivation of both crops. This is true despite the more rapid relative rate of mechanization that has occurred in the Southeast since 1939, which should have given the region a higher proportion of the smaller and more adaptable tractors of recent models.[4] It is not believed that the Southeastern cotton growers are less ingenious in the use of farm machinery. But they are probably prevented from as full exploitation of it for cultivation purposes as in other regions because of the prevalence of and need for terraces and contour farming, which causes a comparatively large number of short rows and hence seriously hinders tractors and tractor equipment in

[4] During the war years when tractors were purchased at a very high rate in the Southeast, it appears that rationing of scarce metals for complementary machines may have been a more important factor in limiting expansion in them than in the tractor population. Since 1945 it appears that farmers have made very rapid increases in the items for which data are available. See Table 17, below.

cultivation. Further development and extension of the practices of strip farming would tend to eliminate short rows and therefore increase the use of tractors in this operation.

From 1939 to 1946 the relative mechanization of the operations in land preparation for all crops increased from one-half to three-fourths in the United States, and from 70 to 90 per cent in Oklahoma and Texas. In the other two cotton regions the increases by operations were between 130 and 245 per cent. In grain farming, the degree of mechanization of the operations from land preparation through harvesting increased from 12 to 34 per cent in Oklahoma and Texas, over 50 per cent in the Delta states, and over 100 per cent in the Southeast. In the case of cotton and corn, the percentage of the operations from land preparation through cultivation handled by mechanized equipment more than doubled from 1939 to 1946 in the three regions, although a few operations in some of these regions had a many-fold increase.

The smallest percentage increase (16 to 33 per cent) in relative mechanization of the four cotton production operations occurred in the irrigated cotton states from 1939 to 1946; however, even in 1939, these states were comparatively highly mechanized, from 64 to 81 per cent of these operations being performed by tractor machines. They were in the lead among the Cotton Belt regions in this respect that year, and despite the relatively small increase in the seven-year period, remained in the lead in 1946 with 81 to 94 per cent of the land-breaking, harrowing, planting, and cultivating operations mechanically performed. At these ratios the region was, in 1946, 57 to 93 per cent more highly mechanized than the Cotton Belt as a whole. On the other hand, the Southeastern and Mid-South states, in spite of very high percentage increases from 1939 to 1946, still had in 1946 a comparatively low degree of mechanization of cotton production, and only in the breaking of land (38 to 42 per cent mechanized) and harrowing of land (29 to 37 per cent mechanized) could it be said that tractor power and tractor machines were used extensively.

Mechanization

TRACTOR-DRAWN MACHINERY

Tractors furnish a high and flexible power capacity but, unless they are harnessed effectively, the labor saving may not be great. Because of the nature of the region's agriculture maximum use of equipment with tractors has not been made. This is particularly true of the specialized cultivation equipment. But as the adoptions of the small, general-purpose types of tractors become more widespread, and as there is a movement away from cotton and similar intensive types of farming, it is expected that increasing attention will be given to buying, along with the tractor, its full complement of equipment. More reasonably priced equipment and increased knowledge on the part of farmers as to how to use it most effectively should further the tendency.

Only limited statistics are available since 1942 on the employment of tractor-drawn machines in the Cotton Belt, and then not according to the regions which have been customarily used in the analysis thus far. Available data on machinery of interest in this discussion are given in Table 17. As in the case of the tractor, the two regions shown— the Southeast (corresponds closely to the Eastern and Delta cotton states) and Oklahoma and Texas— have had very large increases in tractor-drawn equipment. The largest relative increases have occurred in the Southeast, and while only two items are shown for the period January 1, 1945 to May 1, 1948, both (tractor-drawn moldboard plows and mowers) had more rapid increases than in the period from January 1, 1942 to January 1, 1945. War rationing of scarce metals was an important factor in retarding the rate in the earlier period.

Particular note should be made of the changes in binders which are in part tractor drawn. The decline is of interest because it is due to displacement by combines. Both are very important labor-saving devices in the harvest operations, but combines make a far greater saving in labor because the harvest operation occurs simultaneously with the cutting job; furthermore, combines are more versatile, being, after proper attachments are connected and necessary adjustments made, suitable to harvesting many other

TABLE 17

TRENDS IN NUMBER OF SPECIFIED KINDS OF FARM MACHINERY
IN THE SOUTH, 1942 TO 1948

Region and type of equipment	Number on farms in thousands			Per cent increase		
	Jan. 1, 1942	Jan. 1, 1945	May 1, 1948	Jan. 1, 1942 to Jan. 1, 1945	Jan. 1, 1945 to May 1, 1948	Jan. 1, 1942 to May 1, 1948
*Southeast**						
1. Tractor-drawn:						
a. Moldboard plows	63.7	77.4	288.0	21.5	272.1	352.1
b. Disk harrows	114.6	128.4	‡	12.0	‡	‡
c. Disk plows	48.0	54.6	‡	13.8	‡	‡
d. Disk plows— one way	18.0	22.6	‡	25.6	‡	‡
e. Row-crop planters	12.6	20.7	‡	64.3	‡	‡
f. Grain drills	13.6	13.7	‡	0.7	‡	‡
g. Row-crop cultivators	46.3	76.7	‡	65.7	‡	‡
h. Mowers	24.2	29.8	105.0	23.1	252.3	333.9
i. Windrow pick-up balers	3.5	5.7	‡	62.9	‡	‡
j. Combines	18.4	31.8	‡	72.8	‡	‡
2. Binders†	99.2	90.6	‡	−8.7	‡	‡
3. Milking machines	4.7	8.4	‡	78.7	‡	‡
Oklahoma-Texas						
1. Tractor-drawn:						
a. Moldboard plows	65.0	75.0	155	15.4	106.7	138.5
b. Disk harrows	57.0	62.0	‡	8.8	‡	‡
c. Disk plows	45.0	48.0	‡	6.7	‡	‡
d. Disk plows— one way	70.0	72.6	‡	3.7	‡	‡
e. Row-crop planters	105.0	117.7	‡	12.1	‡	‡
f. Grain drills	70.0	68.6	‡	−2.0	‡	‡
g. Row-crop cultivators	110.0	141.0	‡	28.2	‡	‡
h. Mowers	20.0	25.4	‡	27.0	‡	‡
i. Windrow pick-up balers	4.0	5.6	‡	40.0	‡	‡
j. Combines	39.0	40.8	‡	4.6	‡	‡
2. Binders†	72.0	65.0	‡	−9.7	‡	‡
3. Milking machines	3.0	5.4	‡	80.0	‡	‡

* Includes Va., W. Va., N. C., S. C., Ga., Fla., Ky., Tenn., Ala., Miss., Ark., and La.
† Of which 19 and 48 percentages in the Southeast, and Oklahoma and Texas respectively were drawn by tractor power.
‡ Means the data are not available.

Source: 1942 and 1945, A. P. Brodell and M. R. Cooper, *Number and Duty of Principal Farm Machines*, U. S. D. A., Bur. of Agri. Econ., F. M. 46, Mimeo., Nov., 1944, pp. 26-39; 1948, D. O. Mesick, *Farm Machinery*, ibid., Mimeo., Mar. 15, 1949, pp. 4-5.

types of seed. Of the two regions the Southeast shows the most rapid increase in combines. From January 1, 1942 to January 1, 1945 combines increased 73 per cent in the Southeast but only 5 per cent in Oklahoma and Texas, the differences in the rates of change of the two regions being partly due to the differences in the number of combines on farms January 1, 1942 (18.4 thousand as compared to 39.0 thousand). However, according to B. A. E. estimates the two regions together increased an additional 54 per cent from January 1, 1945 to May 1, 1948, which rate of increase is double that of the three-year period ending January 1, 1945. The rapid increases which have occurred in the number of combines are a strong reflection of some of the important shifts in agriculture referred to heretofore; namely, the trend toward more grains and hays, larger farms, and a shift in farm organization from the specialized to the more generalized types with greater emphasis on extensive crops.

EFFECT OF TRACTORS ON SOUTHERN AGRICULTURE

Although tractors are being introduced in all regions of the Cotton Belt at quite a rapid pace,[5] particularly in the Eastern cotton states and the Delta states, they pose new problems of farm organization and management which many operators, because of inexperience, will find serious difficulty solving. One problem has been the displacement of workstock. Farmers in the Eastern cotton states have neither promptly nor as a rule displaced as many work animals as necessary. As a consequence, where tractors are found on farms in combination with workstock, a surplus of power exists for the size of farm unit, which seriously limits the available work for both. In one study the cost of mule power was found to be about 50 per cent higher per hour and that of tractors about 22 per cent higher per hour where both types of power were combined on the same farm.[6]

Another problem is the inadequacy of the size of unit

[5] From 1940 to 1945 tractors on farms increased 136 per cent in the Eastern cotton states, 100 per cent in the Delta states, and 61 per cent in Oklahoma and Texas. From 1945 to 1947 the increases were 22 per cent in the Southeast and 16 per cent in Oklahoma and Texas. From January 1, 1947 to May 1, 1948 further increases of 26 per cent and 11 per cent respectively occurred in the two latter regions. (From U. S. D. A. official reports.)

[6] Ben T. Lanham, Jr., *Farm Power and Equipment Costs in Northern Alabama*, Agri. Expt. Sta. of the Ala. Polytechnic Institute, Bul. 260, March, 1947, pp. 12 and 29.

for tractor power, which results in a seriously limited volume of work for it. Greene and others found that the average farm with tractor power in the middle Piedmont of North Carolina had only 72 acres of cropland, or about double the acreage of non-tractor farms.[7] They found also that, despite the comparatively large proportion of the tractor hours being spent on custom work, about 32 per cent, they were "not used to capacity or anything near capacity." However, in spite of the inefficiency caused by this failure to achieve the rated capacity of the tractor and equipment they found that the saving during 1945 in cost of tractor power over horse power was 8 per cent for cotton, 19 per cent for corn, and 20 per cent for wheat.[8] Tractors give an elasticity and flexibility in farm operations which have advantages not readily evaluated in costing. For instance, in the study by Greene cited above, yields of crops on tractor farms were above those on horse farms, which may be partly attributed to advantages in operation with tractor power, although it is suspected that the farmers able to buy tractors had more fertile farms and used more progressive methods.

The Committee on Industrialization in the South have used number of tractors as an over-all index of mechanization and have projected the growth rate to obtain a forecast of mechanization in this region during the next twenty years, 1946 to 1965.[9] The method is described as follows: "The Tractor population in the 13 States of the Cotton South[10] was taken as 465,000 in 1945 (estimate of the U. S. Dept. of Agri.) on the basis of the 1930-40 annual rate of growth, 6⅔ per cent, the tractor population was projected to 1,691,000 in 1965. The figure of 465,000 in 1945 allows for an increase of 210,200 between 1940 and 1945. The projected increase is 1,226,000 between 1945 and 1965. Probably by 1965 there would be no more than 2 million bona

---

[7] R. E. L. Greene, *et al.*, *Farm Mechanization in the Piedmont*, N. C. Agr. Expt. Sta. Tech. Bul. 84, August, 1947, pp. 3, 6, and 12.

[8] *Ibid.*, p. 27.

[9] *A Study of the Agricultural and Economic Problems of the Cotton Belt*, Hearings before Special Subcommittee on Cotton of the Committee on Agriculture, House of Representatives, Eightieth Congress, First Session, July 7 and 8, 1947, p. 554.

[10] Alabama, Arkansas, Florida, Georgia, Kentucky, Louisiana, Mississippi, North Carolina, Oklahoma, South Carolina, Tennessee, Texas, and Virginia.

Mechanization 71

fide commercial farms, averaging 50 acres each, in the South and about 75 per cent or 1.5 million of them would be using tractors and other mechanizations. On the basis of our tractor projection to 1.7 million in 1965, this would mean that there would be a trifle more than one tractor per farm by 1965."[11] On the basis of a net farm labor displacement of 1.303 men per tractor, the committee estimated the net cumulative displacement in the South because of the prospective tractor increase at 1,598,266 farm laborers by 1965. It estimated the net displacement from the cotton-picker and flame cultivator at 518,210 workers by 1965. Thus the expected labor displacement by the tractor and associated machinery is three times as great as the cotton-picker and flame cultivator. The total displacement in the twenty-year period, given in round numbers, is 2,116,500 workers, but because of expected population growth in the South, the actual number of farm workers would decline only from 4,897,000 in 1945 to 3,714,000 by 1965, a total reduction of 1,183,000 below the 1945 number.[12] Even this latter figure looms large, when the number of persons in the workers' families is considered. Although we may hesitate to accept these estimates because they are too high,[13] it is obvious that the South is in for considerable mechanization, which is overdue, and that this cannot occur without drastic readjustments in the region's agriculture and considerable displacement of its labor. Both are necessary in the interest of efficiency and higher farm incomes.

Ownership of a farm tractor offers many inducements to farmers, and especially to the more progressive and the younger farmers. With a tractor much of the drudgery of farm work can be eliminated. In a rush, work can be done more quickly without serious strain on labor or work animals. Timeliness of operations is especially important where the soil is of the stiff, clay type; for the soil can be kept in better tilth, more work can be accomplished on it, and undoubtedly higher crop yields will be obtained. There is a degree of flexibility possible with tractor power which cannot be obtained with animals, since speed, power, and endurance are present all out of proportion to the man-

[11] *Ibid.*, pp. 619-20. [12] *Ibid.*, pp. 620-21.
[13] For further analysis of trends in farm population, see Chapter VI.

team used with it. Consequently there is keen interest on the part of practically all farmers in obtaining this useful type of power. Each improvement in tractors which makes them adaptable to a wider range of farms and conditions, each comparative reduction in cost, and each improvement in farm income strengthens these incentives, and increased farm income gives farmers the purchasing power to make their wants an actuality.

But tractors have a certain type of inflexibility. They are not widely adaptable to cotton farms in the Eastern states and not fully to those in the Delta states, to tobacco farms, and to certain other types of intensive farms. But operators of all such farms have an equal desire to escape farm drudgery. They persuade themselves that such equipment will help out in land preparation, grain cutting, etc., and if there is purchasing power available, which has been increasingly so in recent years, a tractor is frequently introduced on cotton farms and similar types under conditions which are not suitable for its efficient operation. Even though tractors do help out on such farms, the farmer finds all sorts of complications which he did not anticipate—idle horsepower, disadvantages from following the old sharecropper system, etc. Consequently, when tractors are introduced on cotton farms, the operator is either planning a shift in the type of the farm, or will eventually be forced to such a shift, wholly or in part, after an initial period of experimentation. He will find that with a tractor his cotton farming operations as a whole are less efficient and when the opportunity arises, difficulty with labor usually, may shift over to a more extensive type of farm altogether. This would eliminate most or all of the sharecropper units; and often cotton as the leading cash crop would be eliminated, while on other units it would be greatly reduced in importance as a cash crop.

Figure 10 shows that there is a strong association between the increase in number of tractors on farms and the increase in number of non-cotton farms in the different regions, although the ratio of the change varies in the different regions.[14] The line of relationship shows that,

[14] It is to be noted that while the increase in number of tractors on farms in the Cotton Belt undoubtedly caused an increase in number of farms of

Mechanization

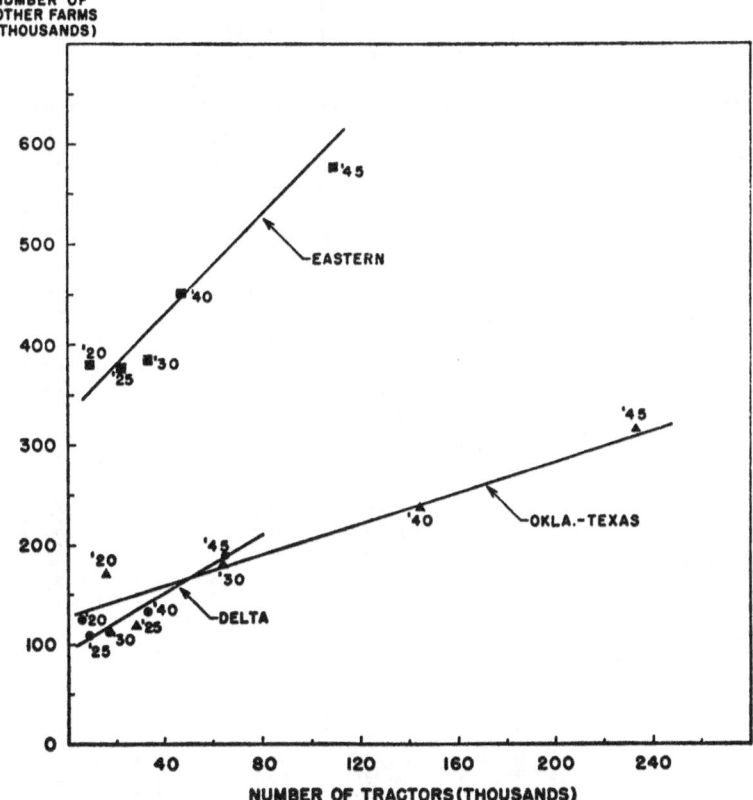

FIGURE 10. RELATION OF TRACTORS ON FARMS TO NUMBER OF OTHER (NON-COTTON) FARMS, BY CENSUS YEARS

The number of types of farms other than cotton farms are *associated* with increases in the number of tractors on farms—one tractor to 2.5 other farms in the Eastern cotton states, to 1.3 other farms in the Delta states, and to ¾ of a farm of another type in Oklahoma and Texas.

during the census years in the 25-year period, an increase of one tractor in the Eastern cotton states was associated with an increase of 2.5 non-cotton farms; in the Delta states, one tractor with 1.3 non-cotton farms; and in Oklahoma and Texas, an increase of one tractor with ¾ of a non-cotton farm. These differences reflect the extent to which tractors are used not only in the operation of other

---

certain types, the entire increase in all farms of types other than cotton was not caused by the introduction of tractors. The ratios, therefore, show association and not necessarily causation in full.

TABLE 18
TREND IN NUMBER AND IN RATIO TO ALL FARMS OF SHARECROPPERS ACCORDING TO COLOR IN DIFFERENT REGIONS OF THE COTTON BELT BY CENSUS YEARS, 1920 TO 1945

Region and census year	Number of sharecroppers		Percentage of all farms which were sharecroppers		
	White	Colored	White	Colored	Total per cent
Eastern					
1920............	107,923	159,277	8.4	12.4	20.8
1925............	127,927	150,604	10.7	12.6	23.3
1930............	174,890	159,432	14.6	13.3	27.9
1935............	164,163	148,344	13.0	11.7	24.7
1940............	126,197	111,371	11.4	10.0	21.4
1945............	101,349	124,104	9.1	11.1	20.2
Per cent decrease 1930 to 1945....	42	22	....	....	....
Delta					
1920............	34,926	130,907	5.5	20.5	26.0
1925............	46,917	144,475	7.7	23.6	31.3
1930............	79,084	180,671	11.0	25.2	36.2
1935............	72,088	180,647	9.8	24.6	34.4
1940............	49,999	162,781	7.6	24.7	32.3
1945............	33,041	126,631	5.6	21.4	27.0
Per cent decrease 1930 to 1945....	58	30	....	....	....
Oklahoma-Texas					
1920............	47,369	29,938	7.5	4.8	12.3
1925............	68,361	36,085	10.3	5.4	15.7
1930............	85,369	40,808	12.2	5.8	18.0
1935............	61,752	28,356	8.6	4.0	12.6
1940............	28,893	15,880	4.8	2.7	7.5
1945............	16,746	10,205	3.0	1.9	4.9
Per cent decrease 1930 to 1945....	80	75	....	....	....
10 Cotton Belt States					
1920............	190,218	320,122	7.5	12.6	20.1
1925............	243,205	331,164	9.8	13.4	23.2
1930............	339,343	380,911	13.0	14.6	27.6
1935............	298,003	357,347	11.0	13.2	24.2
1940............	205,089	290,032	8.7	12.3	21.0
1945............	151,136	260,940	6.7	11.5	18.2
Per cent decrease 1930 to 1945....	56	32	....	....	....

Source: Census Reports of Agriculture, 1920, 1925, 1940 and 1945.

farms but also cotton farms. As previously shown,[15] tractors are used in Oklahoma and Texas more extensively not only on other farms but also on cotton farms than in the

[15] Cf. above, pp. 62-66.

Mechanization

Eastern cotton states, with the Delta states falling between these extremes.

EFFECT OF MECHANIZATION AND OTHER TECHNOLOGICAL CHANGES ON TENANCY

The changes in number of farms in the different regions of the Cotton Belt, discussed in the earlier chapters, have been accompanied by very important changes in the number of tenants, and particularly in the number of sharecroppers. The turning point in the number of tenant farmers in the South was reached in 1935, although the relative number of tenants began declining with the 1930 Census.[16] However, in the case of sharecroppers the decline both in numbers and in percentage began in 1930. This important trend is true of all three regions of the Cotton Belt and applies to both white and colored sharecroppers. In all three regions, however, white sharecroppers have shown a sharper retrenchment in numbers and in ratio to all farms than have the colored sharecroppers. Among the three regions, Oklahoma and Texas have led in both respects in the downward trend of white and colored sharecropers, the Delta states next, and the Eastern cotton states last. For the Cotton Belt as a whole the decline in white sharecroppers was 56 per cent from 1930 to 1945 and in colored sharecroppers 32 per cent. (See Table 18.) Relative to the period since 1945, a recent study released by the Bureau of Agricultural Economics establishes that the trends continued through 1947.[17]

These trends mean much to the future of Southern agriculture, for as the sharecropper becomes a declining force in it many of the evils associated with a shiftless, unstable tenure system (such as over-emphasis on inter-tilled cash crops and other careless practices leading to heavy soil erosion) will become progressively less.

The reasons why these important changes have happened in Southern agriculture since 1930 will now be in-

[16] Max M. Tharp, *The Farm Tenure Situation in the Southeast*, S. C. Agri. Expt. Station in cooperation with the U. S. Dept. of Agri., Bul. 370, January, 1948, p. 3.

[17] Carl C. Taylor, et al., *Trends in the Tenure Status of Farm Workers in the United States Since 1880*, U. S. Dept. of Agri., Bur. of Agri. Econ., July, 1948, pp. 21-24.

vestigated. For one thing, conditions—an efficient and fair source of farm credit, farm programs which tended to insure a certain minimum income to farmers, and improvement in business conditions after 1933—were more favorable to ownership and there was not only an increase in the relative number of owner-operators during the period but also in actual numbers.[18] During World War II this tendency further accelerated because farm incomes were favorable to tenants becoming owners, and many did, apparently. However, and much more important to our analysis, many tenants, and especially sharecroppers, were displaced by tractors. The effect of an increase in number of tractors on the number of other types of farms is given in Figure 10, above, while the effect of a change in number of other types of farms on the number of cotton farms is shown in Figure 20, below.[19]

But there is another important force at work tending to displace sharecroppers. This is represented by the technological changes in agriculture which have raised crop yields. Under conventional sharing agreements in effect with the sharecropper system that is, the half-and-half arrangement, any improvement in yields above a certain relationship relative to the normal labor requirements tends to cause a shift to hired labor, or other kinds of labor. Likewise any improvement in mechanization which tends to lower labor requirements has the same effect even where yields have not increased. Actually, both of these forces have been operating in the Cotton Belt since 1930. They have been very powerful in reducing the number of tenants, and particularly sharecroppers.

It is well known that the wage rate in the South tends to fluctuate with the price of cotton, lagging changes in cotton price by about one year and showing somewhat less flexibility.[20] As shown in Figure 11, farm wage rates in South Carolina varied directly with the price of cotton received by farmers in the United States. During the period 1923 to 1941, the wage rate per hour without board averaged 60 to 75 per cent of the price of cotton per pound. This

[18] *Census of Agriculture, 1945*, Vol. II, Chap. III (Reprint), p. 145.
[19] See Chap. VII, pp. 136-37.
[20] M. R. Cooper, *Production Costs and Returns*, U. S. Dept. of Agri., Bur. of Agri. Econ., June, 1939, p. 26.

Mechanization

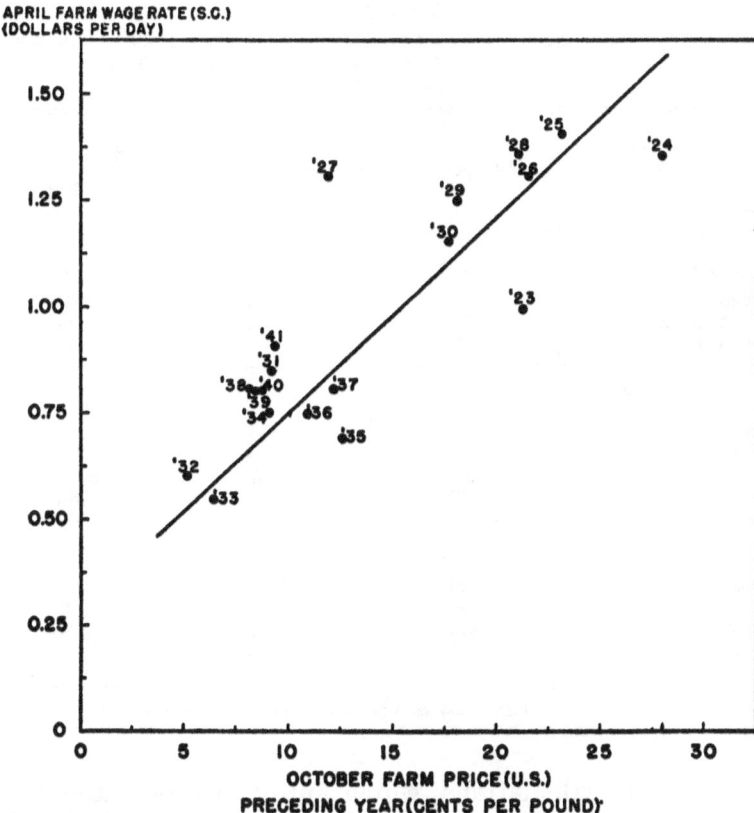

FIGURE 11. RELATIONSHIP OF PRICE OF COTTON RECEIVED BY FARMERS IN U. S. PRECEDING OCTOBER TO APRIL WAGE RATE PER DAY WITHOUT BOARD FOR FARM LABOR IN SOUTH CAROLINA, 1923 TO 1941

During the period an increase in October farm price of cotton of one cent per pound caused farm wage rates the following year to increase from 6 to 7.5 cents per day.

relationship would vary somewhat from state to state depending on customary yields, costs of other factors, relative supply of farm labor as influenced by off-farm employment, etc. Holcomb and Aull, in a prewar study of sharecropper labor in South Carolina, have calculated net returns from cropper and wage labor under several cotton price and yield assumptions.[21] Their results are shown in Table 19.

[21] E. J. Holcomb, and G. H. Aull, *Sharecroppers and Wage Laborers on Selected Farms in Two Counties in South Carolina*, S. C. Agri. Expt. Sta., Bul. 328, 1940, p. 67.

TABLE 19

NET RETURNS PER ACRE TO FARM OPERATOR IN COTTON PRODUCTION WITH CROPPER AND WAGE-LABOR UNDER DIFFERENT YIELD AND PRICE SITUATIONS

Prices and wage rates	Yield per acre	Type of labor	
		Sharecropper	Wage hand
Lint 7¢ lb.		(Net return per acre)*	
Seed $16.67 ton	150	$ 2.34	$— 0.57
Wage rate $0.50	250	6.13	5.70
per day without	350	9.90	11.95
board	450	13.69	18.23
Lint 9¢ lb.			
Seed $20.00 ton	150	$ 4.04	$ 0.21
Wage rate $0.75	250	8.96	8.09
per day without	350	13.87	15.97
board	450	18.79	23.85
Lint 11¢ lb.			
Seed $23.33 ton	150	$ 5.73	$ 0.96
Wage rate $1.00	250	11.78	10.46
per day without	350	17.82	19.94
board	450	23.86	29.43

* Prices of fertilizer and ginning; bagging and ties held constant; other factors were omitted.
Source: S. C. Agri. Expt. Sta. Bul. 328, p. 67.

Taking their calculations, which apply to wage rates 60 to 75 per cent of the price of cotton, it is apparent that yields of 250 pounds and under clearly show a greater net return from using sharecropper labor, whereas the yields of 350 and 450 pounds show greater net returns from wage labor. From the calculations it is not possible to establish accurately the margin between using the two types of labor. In order to do this accurately, detailed cost accounts over a period of years would be necessary. But the margin is obviously between 250 and 350 pounds.[22] The conclusion is that low yields favor the use of sharecropper labor and high yields that of hired hands; the higher the price of cotton the more favorable relatively becomes the net returns from using hired labor on farms with comparatively high

[22] This assumes that the supply of farm labor, on which the farm wage rate (price of cotton ratio, 1923-41) rests, does not become less plentiful. If the supply should become scarcer the ratio would rise, thus raising the point of indifference between the use of sharecropper and hired labor.

Mechanization

yields of lint cotton per acre. Therefore, it is inescapable that both the rapid increase in cotton yields since 1933 and the trend toward mechanical aids, which began much earlier but which has not shown very rapid progress until recently, have contributed importantly to the reduction in the relative number of sharecropper farms since 1930. This has apparently occurred as a result of the more favorable returns in general from using hired labor instead of sharecropper labor,[23] and from displacement of sharecroppers altogether by the tendency toward larger farms caused by mechanization and other factors.

SUMMARY

1. Agricultural technological improvements, both those affecting mechanical aids to labor and those influencing rates of production, have made phenomenal strides since about 1820. This is shown by the fact that about 1820 one farm worker could supply only 4.5 nonfarm persons; by 1945 this ratio had increased to one to 14.5, an increase of 222 per cent.

2. During the last century or so technological improvements in cotton farming have been comparatively slow as compared to the improvements in some of the other staple crops. In wheat the labor required to produce an acre declined from 56 hours about 1800 to 7.5 about 1940, a decrease of 87 per cent; in corn production the decrease was 71 per cent; but in cotton production it was only 47 per cent. During the 140-year period little change occurred, on the average, in the absolute amount of labor required to harvest an acre of cotton, although there was a relative decline per bale because of the upward trend in yields per acre caused by improvements in production techniques. On the other hand, labor requirements per acre prior to harvest showed comparatively large decreases during the period, amounting to 66 per cent. These decreases were due to shifts in the production area to more arid climates, to the change from the slave economy, to multiple hitches in land preparation and cultivation, and, in recent years, to the increase in use of tractor power in land preparation and more limitedly for cultivation.

[23] Taylor, *op. cit.*, p. 31.

3. Of great consequence for the displacement of labor and rearrangement of the Cotton Belt's agriculture is the farm tractor and accompanying equipment. Tractors on farms increased 82 per cent from 1940 to 1945, and according to the Committee on Industrialization of the Cotton Research Committee, there will be 1,691,000 tractors in the thirteen Southern states by 1965, or more than a threefold increase from 1945 to 1965, which, considering the readjustments in farms expected, will give an average of one tractor per farm by 1965. The committee further estimated that the total displacement from tractors and all mechanical aids would be 2,116,500 by 1965, of which 1,598,266 would be from tractors and associated equipment and 518,210 from the cotton-picker and flame cultivator. However, taking into account the expected population increase from 1945 to 1965, the total displacement below the 1945 number would amount to 1,183,000 workers.

4. Farmers are attracted to the purchase of a tractor by the possibilities for removing drudgery from farm work, by timeliness and flexibility in farm operations, etc. But in the case of a cotton farm, inefficiency appears in the use of work animals, and difficulties with the customary (sharecropper) labor arrangements arise. Consequently, work animals will be eliminated over time but sharecroppers even more quickly. When this latter occurs, in addition to eliminating one or more sharecropper units, the operator is likely to eliminate all or practically all cotton acreage. Therefore, it appears that the tractor is a great force in eliminating cotton acreage and cotton farms, especially in the Eastern cotton states. During the period 1920 to 1945 an increase of one tractor was associated with an increase of 2.5 non-cotton farms in the Eastern cotton states, 1.3 non-cotton farms in the Delta states, and 0.75 non-cotton farm in Oklahoma and Texas.

5. Another great force in the elimination of sharecropper units is the upward trend in cotton yields in recent years which has been due to a more complete and effective application of known technology and to improvement in land quality by more careful selection of the acreage allotment under the A.A.A. Since the sharecropper is paid a

Mechanization

fixed share of the crop as a wage, any improvement in yields above that yield level which is just sufficient to return the cropper the current wage rate tends to cause the operator to shift to hired labor in order that he, the operator, may reap the benefit of the higher land productivity. The farm wage rate in the Cotton Belt tends to fluctuate with the price of cotton, although lagging and tending to be somewhat less flexible than it, and bears a fixed ratio to the price of cotton. In South Carolina the wage rate per hour without board varied from 60 to 75 per cent of the price of cotton per pound between 1923 and 1941. Consequently, according to calculations by Holcomb and Aull for South Carolina, with a labor requirement of roughly 130 hours per acre of cotton, yields of lint cotton in excess of 250 pounds per acre show a more favorable return from the use of hired hands than cropper labor. Therefore, upward trends in yields constitute, along with tractors, the great forces in Southern agriculture tending to reduce sharecropper units and hence the total number of farm units.

CHAPTER V

The Mechanical Harvesting of Cotton

COTTON PICKING is one of the most disliked of farm jobs. It is tiresome and backbreaking, and with hoeing and chopping included, the enterprise is first-class drudgery. But being an important fiber-source for clothing, cotton has always found a ready market, although seldom at a price which would return a living wage to the producers. In fact, cotton lint is one of the most salable commodities. In small Southern towns it can be disposed of at all seasons of the year with about as much ease as a twenty-dollar bill. This characteristic gives the producer an independence in disposing of his crop which he well likes, and it is a strong force in keeping him from changing to other types of farm enterprises.

WEST TEXAS STRIPPER

Many attempts have been made to remove the drudgery from the cotton harvest by machinery, efforts in this regard going back to 1850.[1] A Texas bulletin published in 1932 on the subject lists something like 750 patents issued for different types of mechanical cotton pickers between 1870 and 1931;[2] and there has been no lack of them since. About ten years ago it seemed that the Rust brothers had the answer, but despite high labor cost and other favorable conditions for the introduction of their device during the war years, it has not received widespread adoption. The large number of patents indicates several things: first, that there is wide interest in the problem of harvesting cotton mechanically; second, that this interest has extended over a long period; and third, that despite all these well-meaning efforts no solution has been reached as yet. This

[1] Texas Agri. Expt. Sta., Bul. 452, August, 1932, p. 5.
[2] *Ibid.*, pp. 60-72.

problem has resisted solution for so long that new efforts which claim a quick, complete solution should be greeted with extreme skepticism, although the problem should not be regarded as insoluble in this modern age. However, there is no easy answer, for the cotton boll is very difficult to handle mechanically, and the wide range of climatic conditions under which the crop is grown complicates the mechanical adaptations.

To date the best answer to mechanical harvesting of cotton has been obtained in West Texas.[3] Here the labor required to grow the crop is comparatively small for two reasons: multiple-row equipment and a subhumid climate which eliminates hoeing except in some years. Consequently, the agriculture is not as intricately tied in with a family labor supply, although migratory labor, largely Mexican, is employed in the harvesting season. This type of labor is unreliable, perhaps even more so than the Negro sharecropper of the East. When wages are good elsewhere, or if the crop is large, farmers in West Texas have often had serious difficulty getting the crop snapped.[4] It was during two of these bumper-crop years that farmers discovered a practical answer, the sled-stripper, to harvest the crop. Strippers were first put into operation in 1914 but were not used extensively until 1926.[5] In 1926 West Texas farmers had more than a normal crop of cotton and less migratory labor than usual for harvesting it, so in the emergency the sled-stripper first adapted to the cotton harvest forty to fifty years before, was widely used to strip the ripened bolls, leaves and all, from the stalk. The sleds in 1926 were made on the farm or by local blacksmiths at an average cost of $18.61.[6] One man and a team harvested from 4 to 5 acres of cotton a day, but improvements in gin equipment to remove burrs and other trash from the cotton had to be installed. West Texas gins have kept up with these developments, made necessary in part by the practice of snapping the cotton.

[3] Texas Agri. Expt. Sta., Buls. 362, 452, 580 and 686; and Progress Report No. 952.

[4] The entire boll is removed in a fast snapping action of the hand. Twice as much cotton can be snapped as picked per day.

[5] Texas Agri. Expt. Sta., Bul. 362, p. 21.

[6] *Loc. cit.*

The sledding of cotton comes at the end of the harvest season, after frost. Some cotton may have already been snapped. But in any event a considerable proportion of the crop is left in the field; and the delay in harvesting until after frost when all bolls are ripe lowers the grade, so that there is a price discount. A recent report on progress in mechanical harvesting of cotton, gives an estimate of the waste which varies from 2 to 7 per cent more than from hand-snapping, and a reduction in the Grade Index of 5 to 11 percentage points below the hand-snapped.[7] These losses are based on a 1944 study after commercial companies and the Texas Agricultural Experiment Station had experimented with different types of strippers and methods of harvesting, and had developed varieties more specific for stripping. The earlier strippers, while cheaply constructed, left much more cotton in the field and caused a greater grade discount. Not only do the current models of strippers show improvements in waste and grade discount over the earlier models, but they have increased the operating capacity. In the 1944 study, Progress Report No. 952, three types were studied: the double-roller, the single-roller, and the finger-type. "Three workers, including one to haul cotton to the gin, usually harvest from 10 to 14 acres per 7-hour operating period in cotton being harvested exclusively by machines, and from 14 to 16 acres[8] in cotton that has been hand-snapped. To accomplish equal units of hand-snapping would require from 18 to 20 adult workers."

During the season the average acres harvested by each type of machine were as follows:

Double-roller stripper	178 acres
Single-roller stripper	247 acres
Finger-type stripper	257 acres

However, farmers using the machines in 1944 estimated that each type could probably average 400 acres in a normal season.[9]

[7] Texas Agri. Expt. Sta., Progress Report No. 952, August, 1945, pp. 23 and 26.
[8] The rate with the home-made sled was 4 to 5 acres per man and two horses, but the ratio cited here includes ginning, which apparently was not included in the rates given for the earlier machines.
[9] Texas Agri. Expt. Sta., Progress Report No. 952, p. 1.

Despite the mechanical progress which has been made, Mullins concludes in the Progress Report cited that "the combined effects of these factors (harvesting costs, including overhead, waste, and grade loss) under the 1944 wage-price relationships, indicate that to the extent workers were available during the early part of the season it was profitable to hand-snap instead of waiting until machine strippers could be used. After frost had occurred and significant weathering had taken place, the advantages were definitely in favor of machine harvesting."[10]

Although the general idea is that West Texas is to a considerable extent mechanized, and the evidence as regards the production is that some type of multiple-row equipment, either tractor- or horse-drawn is almost universally used, the progress in mechanical harvesting has not been as great as is generally believed. Mullins, in giving a brief review of the development of mechanical harvesting in West Texas, shows the following ratios for the different methods of harvesting:[11]

	Proportion of crop harvested by:		
	Hand picking	Hand snapping	Sleds and/or strippers
1925	50	45	5
1926	32	34	34
1931	3	95	2
1931–35	4	94	2
1944	not given	not given	18–20

Ginners estimated that in 1944 about 100,000 bales were harvested by sleds or tractor-mounted strippers.[12] The quantity harvested in 1926 was probably considerably greater because of the size of the crop. Even so, the volume of cotton harvested mechanically over the years has been comparatively small. It is worthy of note also that it was only during large crop-years, as in 1926, or when labor was unduly scarce or high, as in 1944, that growers turned to mechanical devices to any significant extent. This does not mean that they will not do so in the future; but it does mean that there are serious reasons why farmers,

[10] Loc. cit.
[11] Ibid., pp. 5 and 7.
[12] Loc. cit.

in an area where the maturity characteristics of the crop give it an advantage over other areas for mechanical harvesting, have not adopted more widely a device which is reasonably cheap and simple to operate. The explanation probably lies in the waste and grade loss of a comparatively valuable crop, and the generally plentiful supply of cheap, migratory labor which, except in an emergency, makes hand-snapping more profitable. The importance of these factors is pointedly stated in one of the earlier Texas reports on mechanical harvesting of cotton as follows: "The development of a successful mechanical cotton harvester has been slow, due not only to the mechanical problems encountered in handling the fiber, but also to the belief of cotton growers that any machine could not gather practically all of the cotton. However, with the spread of cotton culture into West Texas, where few laborers are required to produce large crops, and help for the harvest is sometimes hard to secure, many farmers rather than lose most of the crop produced, began using mechanical devices, such as sleds of their own make to harvest as much of it as they could. . . ."[13] In the fall of 1926, the farmers of Northwest Texas were confronted with a scarcity of labor, high charges for picking and hand-snapping, low prices for cotton, weather conditions adverse to harvesting by hand, and an unusually large crop. These conditions forced the farmers to adopt more rapid and mechanical methods of harvesting in order to save the crop and show a profit. Cotton sleds, or strippers . . . were used extensively; and several thousand bales of cotton were harvested by this method almost entirely, with machines built by the farmers themselves and by local blacksmiths."[14] Another author describes these devices as innovations for use in emergency situations, and for harvesting "bollies," or the late part of the crop.[15] He is of the opinion that "the use of mechanical devices for harvesting depends a good deal upon weather conditions during the harvesting season. During years when sled-strippers have been used extensively, unfavor-

---

[13] Texas Agri. Expt. Sta., Bul. 452, p. 5.
[14] *Ibid.*, p. 14.
[15] Troy Mullins, Texas Agri. Expt. Sta., Progress Report No. 952, p. 5.

able weather as a rule has been responsible for preventing normal harvesting by hand-snapping. During the 1944 season, weather conditions contributed to the unusual interest in mechanical harvesters. However, the relatively scarcer labor supply, coupled with the high wage rates and the improved bargaining position of the migratory laborers, also stimulated interest in mechanical harvesters. Approximately 30,000 to 35,000 workers migrated into the High Plains area during the 1944 harvesting season. This compares with about 50,000 such workers employed in the area in 1942.''[16]

THE MISSISSIPPI DELTA COTTON PICKER

The other cotton region in which interest in mechanical harvesting has been centered is the Mississippi Delta. Here the technical problems which must be overcome are entirely different from those in West Texas. The chief difference is that the climate is quite humid, which causes luxuriant growth and slow maturity of the crop, extending over several weeks. This means, if the quality of the crop is to be protected, that harvesting must be done in stages, that is, as repeat operations. Consequently, the stripper type, which cleans the crop at one operation, is not suitable. Therefore, the inventors and farm machinery people have had to concentrate on an entirely different type of machine. This has been some form of the picker type—a mechanical imitation or substitute for human hands. The most recent machine, introduced in the Delta in 1943, is of this type. Developed by the International Harvester Company, the description of the machine, as quoted from company literature in a recent Mississippi Agricultural Experiment Station Bulletin, is as follows: " 'The pickers are provided with two vertical and parallel revolving drums between which the cotton plants pass as the machine moves forward along the rows. Each drum is equipped with cam-actuating picker bars on which are mounted spindles having numerous tiny needles or barbs which catch the lint. The rotative speed of the picker drums is synchronized with the traveling

[16] *Ibid.*, p. 6.

speed of the tractor so that the projecting rotating picker spindles enter and withdraw from the plants without any raking action and without disturbing the unopened bolls or otherwise injuring the plants. As the rotating spindles penetrate the plants and contact the lint in the open bolls, the barbs catch the cotton and extract it. As the cam-actuated picker bars carry these cotton-laden spindles around, they are withdrawn from the plants and the cotton is removed by rubber doffers which rotate in close proximity to the spindles and thus remove the cotton. Before the spindles contact the open bolls, they pass moistened rubber pads which moisten the spindles to assist in doffing the cotton. There is a water tank and metering system which supplies water to the rubber pads in uniform amounts controlled by the operator to give best results.

" 'After removal from the spindles the cotton is conveyed by vacuum to a separate chamber where considerable trash is removed. It is then blown up into the storage basket by air pressure produced by fan equipment. As the cotton enters the basket it passes along a grating which further assists in removing trash. The basket holds approximately one-half bale of seed cotton. When the basket is filled, the cotton is dumped into a wagon or truck by a mechanism powered by the Farmall hydraulic lift.

" 'The driver is the only attendant required to operate the machine. He sits comfortably above the drum box where he has a full view of the row of cotton plants being picked, which flow continuously through the drum box.' "[17]

It is apparently an ingenious and complicated machine, and *appears* to answer all the mechanical difficulties encountered in picking the crop in a humid region. Obviously, the operator must be more than just a driver; he must have real ability and intelligence.

Welch and Miley studied twelve machines under actual farm operating conditions in 1944.[18] They averaged 43 ten-hour days of picking, and harvested 186 bales of cotton. Detailed figures from one plantation show an average

[17] Frank D. Welch, and D. Gray Miley, *Mechanization of the Cotton Harvest*, Miss. Agri. Expt. Sta., Bul. 420, June, 1945, pp. 12-14.
[18] *Ibid.*, p. 14.

The Mechanical Harvesting of Cotton

coverage of 4.7 acres per day, which is about the acreage rate for the early types of sled-strippers in West Texas. The seed cotton wasted was 7 per cent greater than by hand, and the grade lower by 1.4 commercial grades. Both are very important cost items, but the authors are of the opinion that ginning equipment will be developed which will remove most or all of the grade loss. Breeding of new varieties will also help solve the problem of grade loss. The itemized and comparative costs are summarized below:

	Cost per bale	
	By machine	By hand
Cost of picking:		
Direct costs	$ 3.84	....
Interest & depreciation[19]	3.54	....
Total	7.38	$37.76[20]
Loss in grade	18.40	....
Loss of cotton as waste	7.62	....
Total all costs	33.40	37.76
Difference in favor of machine-picked cotton	4.36	....

The major items of cost in 1944 in order of importance were grade loss, waste, and picker costs, the latter of which included direct operating costs and interest and depreciation on the picker and associated equipment; and the percentages of total costs represented by the above items were 55, 23, and 22 per cent respectively. Thus, as in the case of the Texas strippers, grade loss and waste account for the bulk of the cost, with the picker costs being comparatively minor. But despite the very high grade loss the total machine cost per bale was $4.36, or 12 per cent less than hand picking under 1944 conditions—scarce and comparatively high-priced labor, cotton prices at nearly 22 cents per pound, and yield at close to a bale to the acre. All were exceptional

---

[19] The cost of the pickers averaged $3,924, including $1,250 for the tractor, leaving a net of $2,674 per machine. Depreciation was calculated at 20 per cent per year, though only one-fourth of the charge on the tractor was included since the tractor may be used for other farm work.

[20] Calculated on the basis of 1,600 lbs. of seed cotton. Even at a lint return of 33.3 per cent, only 1,440 lbs. would be required for a 500-lb. bale. Perhaps the bales averaged greatly in excess of 500 pounds throughout the study. But it would have been less confusing to have converted everything to a 500-lb. bale equivalent.

conditions, and it is hoped that prices will not return to that level or below. However, the advocates of uncontrolled production and unlimited competition in cotton production envision a world price much lower than 20 cents.

Data on the picker and its equipment under Delta conditions,[21] assembled by the Bureau of Agricultural Economics for 1947, show important changes in some of the overhead charges. The depreciation rate on both the picker and the tractor is materially less, being 14.3 per cent and 10 per cent respectively, as compared to a rate of 20 per cent on each in the calculations of Welch and Miley. The grade loss is 1.0 commercial grades as compared to 1.4 in the 1944 experiments. Offsetting these improvements in the techniques of operating the picker from 1944 have been big increases in the prices of fuel and oil and in the picker and complementary equipment. Large increases in the wages of labor and in the piece rate for picking cotton by hand have also occurred. However, the increase in the cost of picking by hand has not been nearly so much as occurred in the prices of the picker and the tractor, as is shown below:

	Percentage increase, 1944 to 1948
Labor cost for picking cotton by hand in Mississippi, per 100 pounds of seed cotton	55
Gasoline, per gallon	27
Lubricating oil, per gallon	20
Purchase price of:	
1. Tractor[22]	97
2. Picker	130

In a progress report on mechanical harvesting of cotton in the Mississippi Delta, released May, 1949, by the Mississippi Agricultural Experiment Station in cooperation with the Bureau of Agricultural Economics, are given results from cost studies of the operation of the picker for 1945, 1946, and 1947, with the 1947 data adjusted to the 1948

[21] Supplied by Mr. Grady B. Crowe, Agricultural Economist, Bureau of Agricultural Economics, Delta Experiment Station, Stoneville, Miss., in a letter dated March 10, 1949.

[22] Used primarily for general farm work. The time employed in picking was additional so that about one-fourth of the tractor overhead is chargeable to the picking operation.

selling prices for the picker and tractor.²³ Below are given the data for 1947 and then also adjusted to 1948 equipment prices:

	1947	1948ᵃ
Machine costs:		
Direct costs	$ 8.81	$ 8.81
Interest and depreciation	5.96	9.42
Total	14.77	18.23
Loss in grade	7.90	7.90
Loss of cotton as waste	13.00	13.00
Total all costs	35.67	39.13
Cost of hand picking	37.44ᵇ	48.80ᵇ
Difference in favor of machine picking	1.77	9.67

ᵃ The interest and depreciation charges for operating the picker and tractor were adjusted to 1948 prices; all other charges for 1948 were taken equivalent to 1947.
ᵇ Based on Mississippi average picking rates, as reported in *Farm Labor*, Bur. of Agri. Econ., Nov. 12, 1948, p. 7.

In the averages for 1947 are represented 26 machines and 2,827 bales of cotton, or an average of 109 bales per machine, about 40 per cent less volume than was harvested by the 12 machines studied by Welch and Miley. Data were obtained from records kept by farmers, by interviews, and from observation of machines operating under plantation conditions. Harvest conditions were favorable through October but the weather was wet thereafter.²⁴

The results above show some important differences with the 1944 findings of Welch and Miley, not so much in total costs as in their distribution. In the 1944 study the cost of operating the picker and tractor constituted 22 per cent of total cost, while in 1947 it was 41 per cent and in 1948, 47 per cent, indicating a reversal in the relative importance of picker operating costs, from the lowest to the highest proportion of *total* costs per bale, and therefore from the least important element of cost to the most important. This reversal is due to the decline in grade loss from $18.40 in 1944 to $7.90 in 1947.

The 1948 cost figures enable two important conclusions. In the first place, the mechanical picker is still showing a margin of profit over hand picking, $9.67 or 20 per cent,

[23] Grady B. Crowe, *Mechanical Cotton Picker Operation in the Yazoo-Mississippi Delta: A Progress Report*, Mississippi Agricultural Experiment Station in Cooperation with United States Department of Agriculture, Bureau of Agricultural Economics, issued May, 1949.
[24] *Ibid.*, p. 5.

even though the volume of cotton picked in 1947 (and assumed to be the same in 1948) was only 109 bales, or 40 per cent less than in 1944. And secondly, despite the very great increase in the price of picking equipment from 1944 to 1948, the total cost of picking a bale is only $5.73 higher, the large increase in picker costs being to a considerable extent offset by the reduction in grade loss.[25]

Should cotton prices decline to 20 cents or below, it is obvious that picker equipment priced as in 1948 would perhaps be too expensive to show an advantage over hand picking. It is expected, however, that if cotton prices decline to that level some adjustments in farm machinery sale prices will occur. But the history of prices indicates that adjustments in general farm machinery prices[26] occur only after a time lag, and then not proportionately.

In addition to the market price for cotton, yield per acre has a vital bearing on the economy of using the machine. If the average performance is 4.7 acres per day,[27] and 43 days the working period during the cotton harvest season, then the acreage capacity would be 202 acres. Since the acreage which may be harvested mechanically is limited by the picker's capacity, the cost per bale will be greatly influenced by the yield per acre because with high yields there will be more units to which to distribute the overhead. The price of cotton has a bearing on the cost of waste and

[25] In the report cited, Crowe points out that mechanical harvesters are generally located on large farms, which usually have one or two machines per farm. They are used to supplement hand pickers as needed, or are used solely for scrapping, that is, clean-up picking of cotton late in the season. In this latter capacity the grade loss from machine picking may differ little from hand picking, and often may show a grade premium. Although the favorable season for harvesting cotton through October in 1947 could be a factor in the relatively lower grade loss than in 1944, it appears that this new technique in the employment of the picker may be the outstanding reason for the improvement in this respect. However, introductions of improved ginning equipment especially adapted to the cleaning of mechanically harvested cotton during the period should not be overlooked as a factor in the decline in grade loss.

[26] There is no historical price series on cotton picker equipment because of its recent development, but it is obvious that the price behavior of such equipment would be similar to that of general farm machinery since the conditions under which both are produced are roughly the same.

[27] Welch and Miley, *op. cit.*, p. 14, as reported for one machine. However, Crowe in the report cited above states that "the average seasonal capacity of the machine is estimated to be between 150 and 200 acres."

loss of grade but a more important effect on the cost of hand picking, since, with a reasonably adequate supply of picking labor, the rate for picking varies directly with the price of cotton.

In order to show the economic effects of yield per acre and price of lint cotton on potential use of the mechanical cotton picker, Welch's and Miley's data, modified by the data supplied by Crowe, have been re-examined under several yield and price possibilities. The following assumptions were made in applying these data:

1. Cotton lint wasted was taken as 7 per cent. The corresponding loss of cotton seed was not included in the cost of waste, since it was considered that the value of the cotton seed would be recovered as fertilizer in the fields where wasted. However, the normal profit on bagging and ties was included as a cost.

2. A grade loss of one commercial grade was allowed. Crowe, upon whose studies this estimate is based, is of the opinion, however, that under normal conditions the grade loss will be higher. The grade discount at different cotton prices was determined from the regression line of the relationship of strict low middling to middling (both 15/16 inch cotton) on the ten designated markets, 1937 to 1947.

3. Direct costs (variable costs) assume a decline proportionately with the price of cotton. Labor, which is the major variable cost, declined almost to the same extent[28] as the index of farm prices in both of the major recession periods after World War I, 1920 to 1921 and 1929 to 1932, although with approximately a one-year lag.

4. Interest and depreciation on the picker and tractor were computed according to the following rates.[29] For depreciation, the rate was 10 per cent on tractors[30] with one-fourth being chargeable to the cotton harvest, while on the mechanical picker it was 14.3 per cent.[31] The interest charge was determined by applying 5 per cent to the aver-

[28] *Agricultural Statistics, 1940*, pp. 572-73.

[29] Rates are as supplied by Crowe and pertain to the crop-year 1947.

[30] Cost when new, less 10 per cent as the trade-in value, and "straight-line" depreciation applied at the rate of 10 per cent.

[31] "Straight-line" depreciation without allowance for trade-in or scrap value.

age investment of each piece of equipment,[32] only one-fourth of the interest cost thus derived being charged to the cotton picker.

5. The purchase price, original cost, on both the picker and its accompanying tractor assumes a decline one-half as great as the assumed decline in the price of cotton. However, the calculations for a price of 30 cents per pound of lint cotton assume 1948 sales prices for tractors and pickers without adjustment since such a price for cotton is sufficiently near that for which the 1948 crop sold to make an adjustment unnecessary. The assumption that the purchase price of these two pieces of equipment would show some, though less than proportionate,[33] response to certain possible adjustments downward in cotton prices permits a realistic analysis; and the net effect is a limited flexibility over time in the fixed costs of mechanical harvesting of cotton.

6. Calculations were made on the basis of 500-pound bales, with bagging and ties being included to derive total production figures.

7. The picking rate at the three different cotton prices was determined from the regression line of the relationship of the hand-picking rate to the market price of cotton between 1939 and 1947.

[32] One-half the purchase price for the picker; one-half the purchase price for the tractor plus the 10 per cent allowed as trade-in value.

[33] During the two major price recessions which have occurred in our economy since World War I, general farm machinery showed some response to the decline in farm prices but less than a proportionate decline after a time-lag of about one year. From 1920 to 1921 the index of farm prices declined 41 per cent, while the index of the farm price of farm machinery declined 15 per cent from 1920 to 1922, or about 40 per cent as much as the former. However, in the 1929 to 1932 recession the ratio of the decline in the index of farm machinery prices to that of the index of farm prices was considerably less, being only 18 per cent. On the other hand, the type of price reaction expected in the next few years will occur as a postwar adjustment and should resemble more nearly the 1920 to 1921 adjustment, although it is not expected, because of reasonably good farm price controls, that the adjustment will occur either so rapidly or to the same extent. Hence in the above analysis the change in the prices of the picker and the tractor has been taken in ratio with the change in cotton prices as in the 1920 to 1922 relationship; a decline in picker equipment equal to one-half that in cotton prices was adopted, however, in the interest of simplicity in calculations. See *Agricultural Statistics, 1940*, pp. 572-73.

Calculations were made under these assumptions at 25-acre intervals up to 200 acres[34] with three yield levels—250, 350, and 450 pounds—and selling prices of 20, 25, and 30 cents for each yield level. The results show that the picker would be profitable at all three price levels under certain yield conditions. A selling price of 20 cents per pound and a yield of 450 pounds of lint cotton per acre is at the point of indifference in the use of the picker over hand picking with 150 acres of cotton harvested. At a selling price of 25 cents the 350- and 450-pound yields reach this point at 165 and 100 acres respectively, and also at a selling price of 30 cents when 145 and 90 acres are harvested, assuming normal hand-picking rates. However, if the 1948 picking rates prevail, the point of indifference is indicated for all three yields (with a cotton price of 30 cents) at comparatively low acreages harvested. (See Figure 12.)

The significance of this analysis is not that an advantage of the picker over hand picking is established under certain conditions as regards yield at all three prices, but that, at a price of 20 cents for cotton, only the high-yielding farms (450 pounds) which operate the picker at near its acreage capacity show an advantage for the machine over hand picking. This indicates that the high-yielding farms with sufficient acreage to use the picker to near capacity should have a reasonably safe bet in the deflationary period ahead, provided the reaction does not get out of hand. On the other hand, the low-yielding farms (250 pounds) may expect their profit margin to disappear and the intermediate yielding farms will be similarly affected if the price deflation goes very far. Since the price declines assume a less than proportionate decline in the prices of picker equipment (only 50 per cent as great), it appears that if cotton prices decline as much as one-third, the great majority of farmers with necessary capacity will not be able to own pickers; and some of those who now have them or buy them in the meantime will be unable to buy replacements. But the farm machinery companies may help greatly in such a

---

[34] To 150 acres for yields of 350 and 450 at a selling price of 30 cents, however.

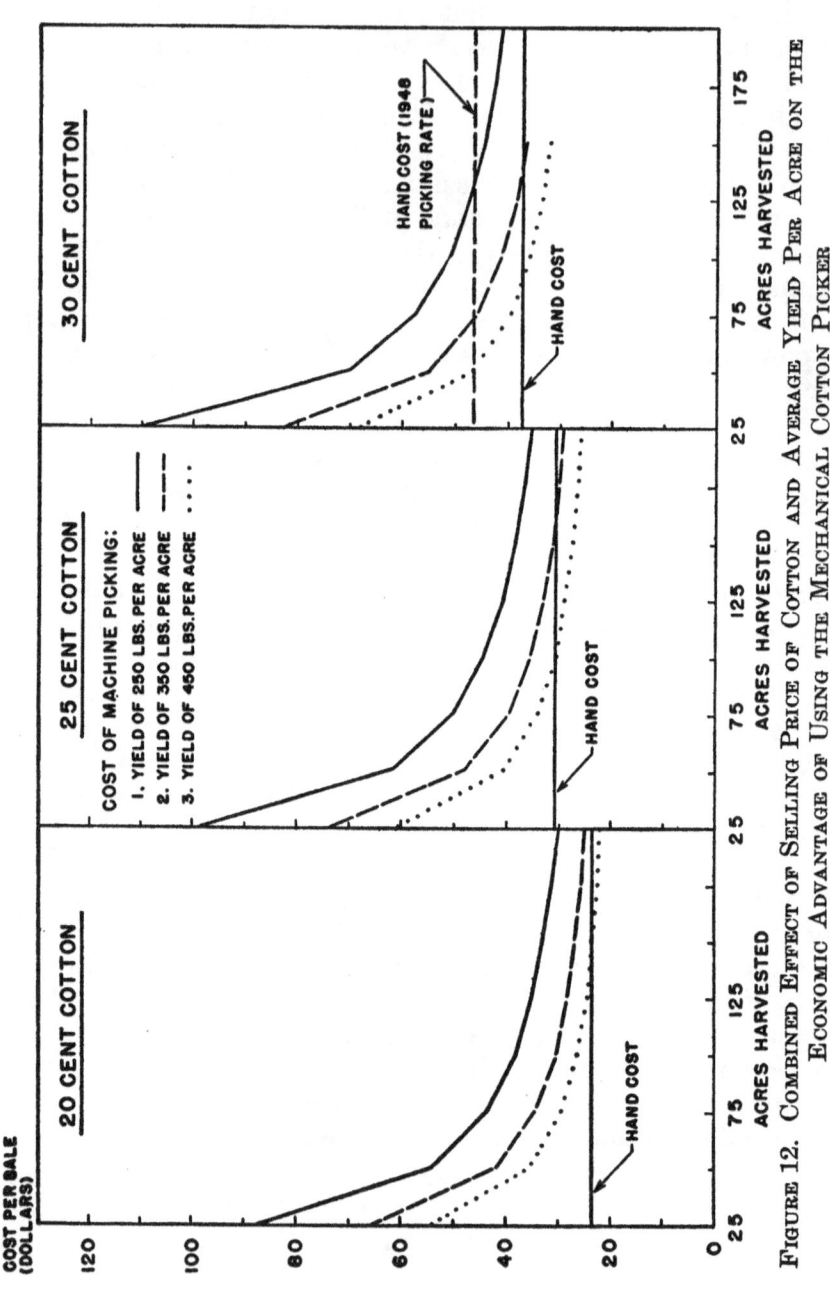

FIGURE 12. COMBINED EFFECT OF SELLING PRICE OF COTTON AND AVERAGE YIELD PER ACRE ON THE ECONOMIC ADVANTAGE OF USING THE MECHANICAL COTTON PICKER

At a selling price for lint cotton of 20 cents per pound an advantage over hand picking would appear only with a yield of 450 pounds, the point of indifference being 150 acres. At 25 cents, two yields—350 and 450 pounds—reach the margin when 165 and 100 acres respectively are harvested; while if the selling price is 30 cents, all three yields show a favorable return from the picker over hand picking at comparatively low acreages of cotton harvested with 1948 hand picking rates; however, with normal hand picking rates, only the 350 and 450 yields show a favorable return at 145 and 90 acres respectively.

period by following a more flexible pricing policy in permitting all picking equipment to decline more nearly proportionately with cotton prices. This would help keep overhead costs down. Equally important effects on profitableness in the use of pickers, and perhaps more probable of achievement than such a price policy from farm machinery companies, are reductions in the quantity of cotton left in the field and in the grade loss from the mechanical picking.[35] More times over with the harvester and appropriate developments in ginning equipment should go a long way toward keeping the latter within reasonable cost limits.[36]

EFFECT OF MECHANICAL PICKER ON THE COTTON BELT'S AGRICULTURE

In Texas, two operators, with any one of the 1944 models of the stripper did the work of 18 to 20 cotton snappers,[37] while in the Mississippi Delta the mechanical picker with one operator accomplished the work of about 40 hand pickers.[38] Although a hand snapper will harvest twice as much

[35] According to Crowe, more and better ginning equipment is being installed each year for the cleaning of machine-harvested cotton.

[36] Ginning experiments in the Mississippi Delta on machine-harvested cotton, as cited by Crowe, have been largely unsuccessful in removing particles of grass from the lint. Under present conditions the most feasible solution to grade loss from this kind of trash is the practice of clean cultivation and late control of grasses from flaming. Both methods and particularly the first would add considerably to the cost of producing cotton and would therefore become an added cost to mechanical harvesting. However, he reports a recent development in ginning equipment to clean lint after it is ginned, which appears to offer good possibilities for the removal of more foreign matter from machine-harvested cotton.

[37] Cf. p. 84.

[38] A. Raper, *Role of Agricultural Technology in Southern Social Change*, U. S. Dept. of Agri., Bur. of Agri. Econ., May, 1946, p. 9. There is, however, considerable difference of opinion concerning the number of hand pickers displaced. In *Fortune* (May, 1949, p. 85) it is stated that after desirable conditions as regards varieties and skill of operator are more fully met, the displacement in California should be 22 hand pickers. In an article in *Life* (Oct. 31, 1949, p. 83), entitled "The New South," it is given as 25 hands for large cotton farms near Greenville, Mississippi. The varying estimates are probably due to the differences in assumptions as regards utilization of machine capacity and the maturity of the hand pickers. Failure to utilize the mechanical picker to capacity results in diseconomies and, as shown above, its advantage over hand picking becomes questionable. Many women and children help to pick cotton and they constitute a very important element in its harvest in most sections of the Cotton Belt. But such labor lowers the average picking rate and raises the potential displacement of hand labor

cotton as a hand picker, the mechanical picker has the edge in labor saving over the stripper by a considerable margin, apparently about 2 to 1. However, a large part of the difference between the two machines is due to the higher yields in the Mississippi Delta, which are more than double those in Texas. Although the acreage per day for the 1944 stripper in Texas is more than triple the acreage per day for the mechanical picker of Mississippi, this advantage does not cancel the favorable ratio of yield in Mississippi, for a crew of two men is required to handle the latest type of stripper in Texas.

E. L. Langsford, Bureau of Agricultural Economics, in a report entitled *Cotton Production in War and Peace* (F. M. 45, 1944, p. 25), spelled out the effect of the types of mechanical harvesters discussed here on labor requirements per acre in cotton production. These estimates are shown in Table 20 under different assumptions, or possibilities, as to further progress in mechanizing the other jobs in producing cotton. In the High Plains area the two-row mechanical stripper complemented by four-row tractor equipment is estimated to reduce total man labor requirements by 72 per cent, or from 22.6 hours to 6.4 hours per acre. In the Delta the one-row mechanical picker and the same complement of cultivating equipment shows an estimated reduction of 67 per cent, or from 141 to 46 hours. Mechanizing the troublesome hoeing and chopping operations by a flame cultivator[39] would, according to Langsford, cause a further reduction of 21 hours per acre, giving an over-all possible reduction of 82 per cent and a total saving of 116 man hours per acre. Assuming maximum mechanization, he estimates the man hours per bale at 15 in the High Plains area and 28 in the Delta,—only 28 per cent of the labor required in the High Plains area when two-row tractor equipment is used and the crop harvested by hand

by the mechanical picker. Consequently, if capacity use of the picker and average quality hand pickers are assumed, it appears likely that the displacement may be nearer the highest estimate (Raper's).

[39] Danielson and Crowe, reporting in *The Agricultural Situation*, March, 1949, pp. 12-13, on the results of a study of flame cultivation in the Mississippi Delta in 1947, reach the conclusion "that although the flamer has been greatly improved, it is not yet the full solution to the problem of weed control."

TABLE 20

ESTIMATED MAN LABOR NEEDED PER ACRE TO PRODUCE COTTON WITH DIFFERENT TYPES OF POWER AND EQUIPMENT AND VARIOUS METHODS OF HARVESTING, IN SPECIFIED PRODUCTION AREAS

Production area	Type of equipment	Method of harvesting	Prepare seed bed and plant	Cultivate	Chop and hoe	Total pre-harvest	Pick or snap	Total man hours for all operations*	
								Per acre	Per bale
			Hours	Hours	Hours	Hours	Hours	Hours	Hours
High Plains	2-row tractor	Snapped by hand	1.2	1.4	3.0	5.6	17.0	22.6	54
High Plains	4-row tractor	Snapped by hand	.7	.7	3.0	4.4	17.0	21.4	51
High Plains†	4-row tractor	2-row mechanical stripper	.7	.7	3.0	4.4	2.0	6.4	15
Blackland	2-row tractor	Picked by hand	2.4	2.6	10.0	15.0	30.0	45.0	143
Sandy Lands	1-row mule	Picked by hand	14.0	10.0	20.0	44.0	30.0	74.0	235
Delta	1-row mule	Picked by hand	10.0	13.0	33.0	56.0	85.0	141.0	160
Delta	4-row tractor	Picked by hand	5.0	4.0	33.0	42.0	85.0	127.0	143
Delta†	4-row tractor	1-row mechanical picker	5.0	4.0	33.0	42.0	4.0	46.0	52
Delta‡	4-row tractor and flame cultivator	1-row mechanical picker	5.0	3.0	13.0	21.0	4.0	25.0	28
Coastal Plains	½-row mule	Picked by hand	15.0	21.0	35.0	71.0	50.0	121.0	230
Coastal Plains	1-row mule	Picked by hand	12.0	12.0	35.0	59.0	50.0	109.0	208

* Does not include hauling to gin.
† It should not be inferred that tractors, mechanical harvesters and flame cultivators can or will be used only in the first areas in which these machines are adopted.
‡ Four times over with a 2-row flame cultivator, 3 hours per acre, plus 10 hours hand chopping. Labor needed has been based on yield per acre as follows: High Plains, 200 pounds; Blackland, 150 pounds; Sandy Lands, 150 pounds; Delta, 425 pounds; Coastal Plains, 250 pounds. These yields very closely approximate averages obtained during recent years.

Source: E. L. Langsford, *Changes in Cotton Production in War and Peace*, U. S. Dept. of Agri., Bur. of Agri. Econ., F. M. 45, December, 1944, pp. 24–25. Notes *, †, and ‡ are quoted directly from Langsford.

snapping and 12 per cent of that required in the Delta when cultivated by one-row mule equipment and the crop picked by hand. (See Table 20.)

On the basis of the saving in labor shown above, lower cost of production may be expected on some farms even at the present price of cotton and purchase price of the mechanical picker and equipment, if the machines are operated to capacity. But if the picker is to be of permanent benefit to the Delta, but more particularly to the Eastern Cotton Belt, the picker and equipment must be sold at a more reasonable price. Should the equipment be sold at a level low relative to the price of cotton, costs of producing the crop would drop and the price of lint correspondingly, therefore putting it on a more competitive basis in world markets. Also the tendency of production to shift to the Delta, West Texas, and the irrigated areas would be further accelerated. The small cotton farms in the Eastern cotton states and elsewhere would be subject to very heavy economic pressure, and family incomes on such farms would shrink. Cotton production may or may not be discontinued on such farms, depending upon whether alternative employment can be found elsewhere. On the other hand, an exceptionally low price for cotton does not favor the mechanical picker. This is true because very expensive labor is employed to manufacture mechanical cotton pickers, flame cultivators, and even tractors, but comparatively low wages are the lot of all farm labor, including the tractor driver and the operator of the mechanical picker; even the return to the farm operator for his labor is comparatively low. The terms of exchange are therefore against farm labor equipped with such expensive machinery, which becomes more unprofitable with each drop in the price of cotton; for, since the wages of factory labor are inflexible, the price of such machines tends to be inflexible also. When the price structure declines into an imbalance from a given adjustment, the price of the farm products tending to move against the farmer and his labor, the *users* of such machinery may, and often too frequently do, encounter difficulty in finding the exchange to make necessary repairs and to pay for replacement.

Any tendency toward mechanization of the harvest will have the generally expected effect on farm organization. Farms must become large; first, by displacement of share-croppers and other labor, and secondly, by consolidation. A limited amount of consolidation will be possible by farmers' purchasing nearby and adjoining units and by renting. However, a strong tendency toward enlargement of farms, which any large-scale movement toward mechanization of the harvest requires, would necessitate considerable consolidation if not complete rearrangement of farms in the areas concerned. Unless economic conditions are favorable to a movement of displaced persons into remunerative industry, such consolidation would not occur except in the natural course of events, by death of owners, expiration of leases, etc., which may require a generation or so. Otherwise, rapid, quick, and complete mechanization of the order anticipated here would occur only on the farms of the requisite capacity already in existence under current legal arrangements, or which might be achieved by minor legal negotiations, such as displacement of share-croppers or the renting of nearby farms.

As to the effect of adoption of the picker upon labor displacement, Welch and Miley estimate that 209,591 persons will be displaced in the ten all-Delta counties.[40] This estimate is arrived at by assuming that a conservative number of farmers with sufficient acreage of cotton to utilize the mechanical picker to capacity would adopt it, on whose farms 73 per cent of the labor might be displaced.[41] This forecast is made for only a part of the Cotton Belt adaptable to mechanical harvesting, although because of high-yielding land and large acreages in the operating unit it does include the area where the picker is most adaptable and where it probably will be purchased in largest numbers.

[40] Welch and Miley, *op. cit.*, p. 22.
[41] *Ibid.* On farms with pickers they assume that the labor force would be adjusted to 100 acres of cropland per family. Crowe reports, however, that up to now (1949) in the Delta, mechanical pickers have been used primarily to supplement the hand labor force; and generally on the plantations which have pickers, only a small part of the total production of cotton is harvested mechanically.

West Texas[42] and the irrigated areas are suitable to mechanical harvesting to a considerable extent. Moreover, in other areas of the Belt there are many farms of sufficient acreage for capacity-use of the picker, but a real difficulty to the picker's introduction in these areas is the comparatively low yields which, as shown above, are a handicap to obtaining efficiency in its use.

The Committee on Industrialization in the South, Project VII, of *A Study of the Agricultural and Economic Problems of the Cotton Belt*,[43] places the net displacement from the flame cultivator and cotton picker at 518,210 workers by 1965, which estimate was admittedly determined by rough methods.[44] Since it exceeds the Welch and Miley figure for ten Delta counties by approximately 309,000 workers, the effects of mechanization on the cotton enterprise in other regions of the Cotton Belt are apparently given considerable weight. It is expected, however, that the estimate of the Committee may be too high for the next generation, for farmers are conservative, and there are many difficulties to adopting the picker.[45] Furthermore, there have been many so-called answers to the mechanical harvesting of cotton in the past. Only ten years ago, some writers became alarmed at the possibility that the Rust brothers' machine would cause widespread displacement of labor in the Cotton Belt, but nothing, or almost nothing, ever came of this attempt at mechanization of the cotton harvest. The recent IHC machine in the Mississippi Delta has received just as many alarming journalistic

[42] Where mechanical harvesting is practiced in the High Plains, some form of stripper-harvester is used on both dry and irrigated lands. (See Texas Agri. Expt. Sta., Progress Report 1134, Oct., 1948.)

[43] Hearings before Special Subcommittee on Cotton of the Committee on Agriculture, House of Representatives, Eightieth Congress, First Session, July 7 and 8, 1947, p. 621.

[44] Estimate based on an assumed reduction in labor requirements of 75 per cent for the proportion (60 per cent) of production expected to be affected by 1965. The total hours of labor saved was converted to man years by dividing by 2,000—the man hours assumed per year.

[45] It should be pointed out that despite the optimism relative to the possibilities of the machine in 1944, a maximum of only 570 pickers, according to Crowe, were in operation at any time in the Mississippi Delta in 1948. Furthermore, only 2.0 per cent of the crop in Oklahoma and Texas and 0.5 per cent in the irrigated states were harvested by machine methods in 1946. (U. S. Dept. of Agri., F.M. 69, July, 1948, p. 28.)

spreads. However, Welch and Miley have wisely concluded that: "Even though there is evidence that the key to complete mechanization of the cotton industry is closer to reality today than ever before, any assumption that there will be a rapid and extensive shift to complete mechanization should be examined carefully. Had the mechanical picker been at the technological stage of development at the outbreak of the war that it is now, and had these machines been available during the war period, there can be little doubt that extensive utilization of mechanical harvesters would have resulted.

"... one of the most significant impacts of technological advancement in agriculture, however, is that farmers do not and cannot apply at equal rates the results of science and invention. New and old techniques continue side by side—the one-horse plow and the tractor operate in adjacent fields; one-horse wagons and modern trucks transport cotton to the same market; and very likely, the power harvester and the laborer armed only with his bare hands and a sack across his back will both continue to harvest the American cotton crop for some time to come."[46]

SUMMARY

1. Although there has been no lack of interest in removing the drudgery from the cotton harvest, as shown by the hundreds of patents for mechanical devices to harvest cotton in the last fifty years or so, no significant progress was made until recent years, and even now the so-called answers hold only a partial solution under limited conditions. The problems which have retarded and seriously limited developments in mechanical harvesting are the complicated arrangement and inflexible qualities of the cotton boll and the comparatively long interval for maturity of the crop.

2. The best solutions to mechanical harvesting of cotton have been reached in West Texas and the Mississippi Delta. In West Texas cotton is produced under subhumid conditions with low labor inputs and the crop matures in a comparatively short period. In the Mississipi Delta cot-

[46] Welch and Miley, *op. cit.*, pp. 19-20.

ton production occurs under typical humid conditions but production is dominated to a considerable extent by a plantation economy. In West Texas, farmers, agricultural scientists, and farm machinery companies have during the last twenty-five years succeeded in producing a practical cotton stripper. It removes leaves, bolls, and other material and is dependent for success on the subhumid climate which produces a comparatively quick maturity of the crop and on adaptations of gins to remove the trash. In the Delta, because of duration of maturity, a picker type of machine has been developed. It simulates hand action and may repeat the harvest operation. The stripper in West Texas requires only a moderate investment;[47] while the Delta picker makes necessary a comparatively large one.[48] The greatest costs in operating both machines, however, are grade loss and cotton left in the field as waste. The more recent models of the West Texas strippers are estimated to displace eighteen to twenty mature cotton pickers; the latest Delta picker, at least 22 hand pickers and perhaps as many as 40. The most extensive adoptions of the machines have occurred in West Texas but even in 1944, a good year for the strippers, only 100,000 bales are estimated to have been harvested by them, although a higher proportion of the crop and perhaps a larger baleage was harvested in 1926 with the crude, farmer-devised sled-strippers. The U. S. D. A. (F. M. 69, July, 1948, p. 28) estimates that 2 per cent of the cotton crop in Oklahoma and Texas and 0.5 per cent in the irrigated states were machine-harvested in 1946, which on the basis of total production in 1946 would be about 60,000[49] and 4,000 bales respectively. The use of sleds, or other types of strippers in West Texas, seems to depend more on unfavorable harvest conditions—scarcity of immigrant labor for snapping, high-priced labor, a comparatively large crop, and adverse harvest weather—than upon other factors.

[47] A new two-row single-roller stripper cost about $900 in 1947. The average investment in 90 machines on 85 farms that year was $870. (See Texas Agri. Expt. Sta., Progress Report 1134, p. 3.)

[48] Reported by Mr. Grady B. Crowe (letter dated January 31, 1949) as $5,672 and $2,466 in the picker and the tractor respectively.

[49] In the progress report cited in footnote 47, it is estimated that 150,000 bales, or 15 per cent of the crop, in the High Plains area of Texas was harvested by tractor-mounted strippers in 1947.

3. Since the investment in the mechanical picker (Delta machine) is comparatively great, the economics of its use are complex. The important factors are amount of waste, grade loss, acreage harvested, yield per acre, and price of cotton. The machine should be used to its acreage capacity, 150 to 200 acres, in order that overhead may be absorbed cheaply. A high yield is necessary in order that the maximum machine acreage will produce enough bales to spread all costs, including waste and grade loss, sufficiently to be competitive with hand picking. The higher the price of cotton the more important waste and grade loss become as cost determinants. Analyses of data published for 1944 by Welch and Miley and of data supplied by Crowe for 1947 and also adjusted to 1948 show that in all three years the picker showed a clear advantage over hand picking. However, in 1944 the machine was used to near capacity, 186 bales being harvested, but the baleage in 1947 was only 109, being similarly assumed for the 1948 adjusted costs.

4. If price deflation occurs during the next few years, and the probabilities for it are strong, the price of cotton is expected, on the basis of past price behavior, to decline more than the selling price of picker equipment. In looking ahead the question which must be answered is: What effect will such an imbalance in this price relationship have on the economic advantage of using mechanical harvesters? In order to answer this question a capacity analysis against cost was performed under three price and yield assumptions. Three cotton prices—20, 25, and 30 cents—and three yields—250, 350, and 450 pounds—were selected for analysis; and, except for the 30-cent price, these prices assume a greater than proportionate (ratio of 2 to 1) decline in cotton price from present levels than the decline assumed for the price of picker equipment. The main conclusion is that profitableness in the use of the picker over hand picking would disappear if the price of cotton should drop to 20 cents for all yield levels, except 450 pounds under the condition of near capacity acreage operation of the picker. It appears, however, that if manufacturers would adopt a more flexible pricing policy for picker equipment, the picker could be kept competitive with hand picking on farms with

moderate yields and with sufficient acreage to insure near capacity-use of the machine. Efforts towards further reducing the loss from waste and grade discount would also aid in accomplishing the same end.

5. The mechanical picker probably will not have the serious repercussions on the Cotton Belt's agriculture generally believed, certainly not in the near future. A fairly limited number of farmers will have the acreage coupled with high yields to afford capacity-use of the machine, required in order to insure an economic advantage over hand picking for some period in the future, considering the contingency of an imbalance in the price structure from deflation. It does not appear that custom work holds an important part of the answer to capacity-use because labor on small farms is already seriously under-employed. However, some farmers may prefer to absorb a small cost disadvantage in exchange for the greater certainty, timeliness, and flexibility of the machine over the managerial difficulties and irritations involved in producing cotton with a large number of sharecroppers. The top estimate on future labor displacement by the picker is about 518,000 workers, which appears to the writer to be the upper limit in view of the rather rough computing methods used and considering the natural inertia and conservatism of farmers. In fact, a reliable source reports that a maximum of only 570 pickers[50] were used at any one time in the Mississippi Delta in 1948. In view of the optimism which greeted the machine upon its appearance, and in some of the journals almost every year since, this is a snail's pace compared to what would seem to be necessary if the machine is to revolutionize cotton production in one generation as thoroughly as the estimates of labor displacement and other repercussions claimed for the picker seem to predict.

[50] The number of stripper type machines (excluding sleds) in operation in the High Plains in 1947 is estimated at 3,000. (*Loc. cit.*) The author of the article in *Fortune* (May, 1949) on California cotton puts the number of mechanical harvesters in operation in that state at one-third of the total production of 1,400 by the International Harvester Company.

CHAPTER VI

Urbanization and Agriculture

URBANIZATION is of interest in a study of this sort because it shows economic progress. As a country matures, if it has a high type of civilization, cities also grow and more rapidly than the over-all population. While a proportionately large urban population is indicative of a general high standard of living of the people, it is also indicative of progress in economic organization, for there are many things which a concentrated population center can do more efficiently than a dispersed one. These are assembling and distributing articles of commerce, providing sanitation, and rendering many other social and economic services. Although large cities are not necessary for industrial development, they both accompany and contribute to it. Through the greater volume of produce arising from industry, cities expand in response to the growing burden of commercial functions. But cities contribute to industrial growth directly by supplying labor, water and sanitary facilities, transportation facilities, locations for markets, and commercial outlets; and by other policies which favor industrial progress in general.

The growth of urban centers and the over-all urban growth are of interest to agriculture from many standpoints, but only two major ones will be considered here—demand for agricultural products and an outlet for excess rural population. The industrial growth which occurs with city growth gives rise to an expanding demand for industrial raw materials. In the Cotton Belt these are mainly cotton and lumber—true products of the soil—and petroleum, iron ore and other minerals mined locally. Growth as such provides an expanding demand for raw materials for industry and perishable products for human consumption, such as milk, eggs, vegetables, and fruits. Hence the nature and character of city growth will determine to a very large extent the pattern of agriculture in the city environs and to some extent in the entire region, depending upon the proportion of the total population in urban centers. But from the standpoint of agricultural balance, the cities with their low birth rates afford an outlet and opportunities for excess farm population. Also, relative industrial growth will afford such opportunities over and beyond the mere maintenance of the city population. The relation of city and industrial growth to rural population demand, or outlet, is perhaps of greatest interest of all to the economic development of not only the region's agriculture but also of its general economy. This determines the extent to which excess population will exist in farm areas and the amount of migration from the region, which depletes the local areas of wealth and human resources. If city demand for labor is sufficiently strong, excess rural population, and often surplus labor from other regions, will be absorbed, thereby affecting the economic status of those who remain on farms—increasing their employment, per capita output, efficiency of output, and finally, per capita income. Consequently the nature, extent, and rapidity of urban growth holds the key to much progress in agriculture and the solution to many of its problems.

URBAN GROWTH

From 1790 to 1860 total population in the United States doubled about every generation; urban population[1] about every 15 years. Since 1860, however, the rate of growth in total population has declined sharply. Total population increased 100 per cent from 1860 to 1890, although the War Between the States was a very important factor in slowing down the rate of increase. Total population doubled again from 1890 to about 1933, a period of 43 years. On the other hand, urban population doubled from 1860 to 1875, in fifteen years; again about 1893, in 18 years; and again about 1916, in 23 years; while from 1916 until 1940 it increased another

[1] Urban population includes all persons in cities, places, or thickly populated areas of 2,500 inhabitants or over. See Sixteenth Census of the United States, 1940, *Population*, Vol. I: *Number of Inhabitants*, p. 18.

Urbanization and Agriculture

50 per cent, in 24 years. Therefore, the rate of growth of urban population has slowed down recently, but relatively less than the rate of growth of total population.[2]

In the ten cotton states, urban growth is of a comparatively recent origin, dating from 1900 both in relative importance and degree of increase. Even in 1910 the ten cotton states had only 4.1 million people living in urban centers and a ratio of just less than 1 city person to 4 rural inhabitants. Although urban population growth was rapid after 1910, the ten Cotton Belt states had in 1940 only 1 urban person to 2 rural persons, the rest of the United States

TABLE 21
PROGRESS OF URBANIZATION IN TEN COTTON STATES AND REST OF UNITED STATES BY CENSUS YEARS, 1890 TO 1940

Region and year	Census date	Total population (000,000)	Urban population (000,000)	Per cent urban population is of total population
10 cotton states				
1890	June 1	13.9	1.7	12.2
1900	June 1	17.4	2.4	13.8
1910	Apr. 15	21.2	4.1	19.3
1920	Jan. 1	23.6	5.8	24.6
1930	Apr. 1	27.3	8.5	31.1
1940	Apr. 1	29.6	10.0	33.8
Per cent increase:				
1910 to 1920		11	41	*
1920 to 1930		16	47	*
1930 to 1940		8	18	*
Rest of United States				
1890	June 1	49.0	20.4	41.6
1900	June 1	58.6	27.8	47.4
1910	Apr. 15	70.8	37.9	53.5
1920	Jan. 1	82.1	48.4	59.0
1930	Apr. 1	95.5	60.5	63.4
1940	Apr. 1	102.1	64.4	63.1
Per cent increase:				
1910 to 1920		16	28	*
1920 to 1930		16	25	*
1930 to 1940		7	6	*

* Not applicable.
Source: Sixteenth Census of the United States, 1940, *Population*, Vol. I: *Number of Inhabitants*, U. S. Dept. of Commerce, Bureau of the Census, 1942, pp. 14, 22, and 23.

[2] Sixteenth Census of the United States, 1940, *Population*, Vol. II: *Characteristics of the Population*, Part 1, p. 18.

having just less than 2 urban inhabitants to 1 other inhabitant. (See Table 21.) Furthermore, despite the Cotton Belt's progress in urbanization, it stood in 1940 about where the entire United States was in 1890.[3]

In Table 21 total and urban population by decades for the ten Cotton Belt states and rest of the United States are shown together with urban ratios and percentage changes in recent decades. It is seen, in line with the discussion above, that total population in the ten cotton states and the rest of the country doubled in 42 and 44 years, or from 1890 to 1932 and 1934 respectively. In the case of urban population the ratio of the 1890 population to that of 1930 was one to five for the cotton states, and one to three for the rest of the nation. During the decade 1930 to 1940, the ten cotton states increased in urban population 18 per cent, all other states only 6 per cent, giving a ratio of 3 to 1.

The important urban centers in the ten Cotton Belt states are shown in Figure 13. The most highly urbanized regions which are also generally important industrial centers are in the Piedmont of the Carolinas and Georgia; the Middle Coastal Plain of the Carolinas; the Birmingham area of Alabama; the Knoxville-Chattanooga region, and Nashville and Memphis vicinities in Tennessee; Shreveport, New Orleans, and Baton Rouge areas, and the gulf counties in Louisiana; Little Rock, Arkansas; East Texas, including Dallas, Fort Worth, Austin and San Antonio; Texas Gulf ports, including Corpus Christi, Galveston and Houston; and Tulsa-Oklahoma City in Oklahoma. These population centers are for the most part rapidly growing. (See Figure 14.) They are the generators of economic activity in their sustenance areas; and will affect vitally the agricultural economy of the environs. As these centers grow through industrialization and other causes, the level of income of the South will rise, a change so necessary for social and economic development.

The important cities[4] in the ten Cotton Belt states in 1940 are listed in Table 22. The region had thirty-six cities of 50,000 population or over that year, Texas leading with

[3] *Loc. cit.*
[4] With 50,000 inhabitants or over.

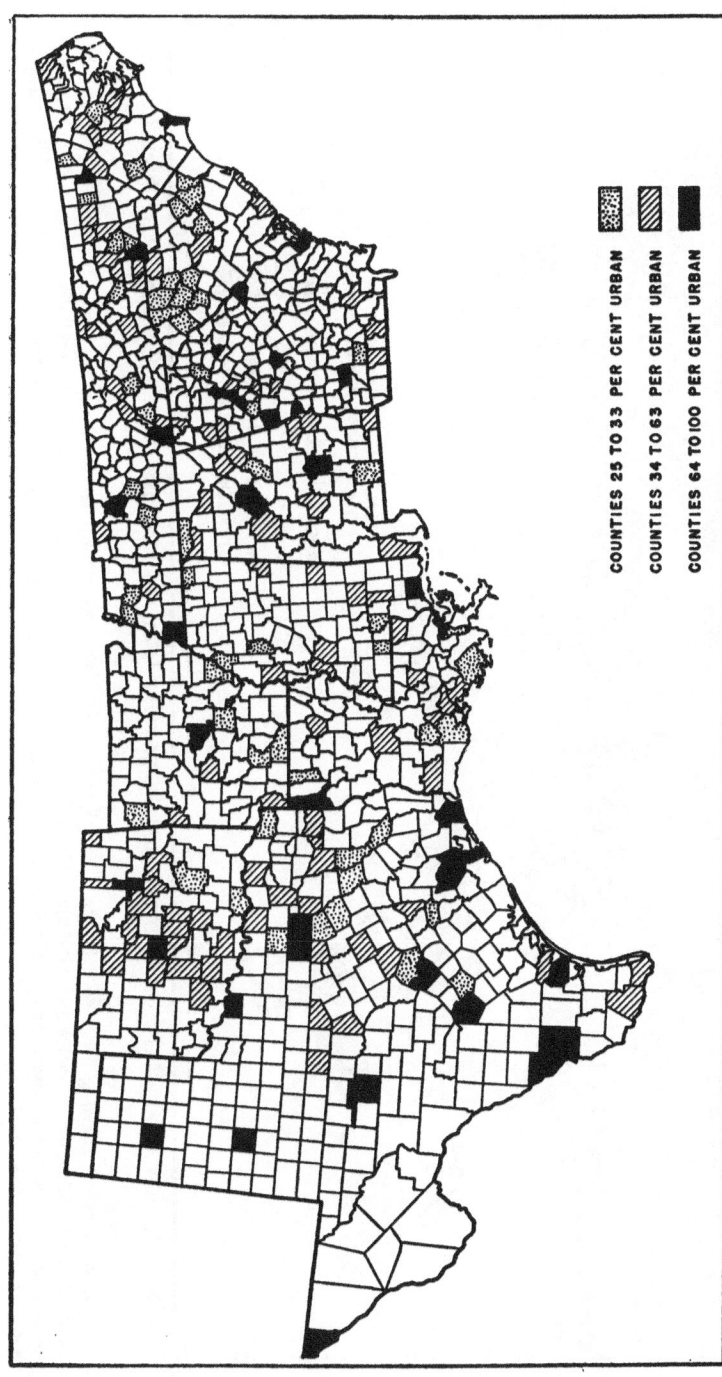

FIGURE 13. IMPORTANT URBAN COUNTIES IN THE COTTON BELT, 1940

(Counties selected on the basis of at least 25,000 total population and 25 per cent or over urban.)

The most highly urbanized regions are the Piedmont of the Carolinas and Georgia; the Middle Coastal Plain of the Carolinas; Central Alabama; Knoxville-Chattanooga, Nashville and Memphis areas of Tennessee; Shreveport, New Orleans, and Baton Rouge areas and coast counties in Louisiana; Little Rock, Arkansas; Tulsa-Oklahoma City; East Central Texas; and the Texas Gulf Coast.

112   *Agricultural Progress in the Cotton Belt*

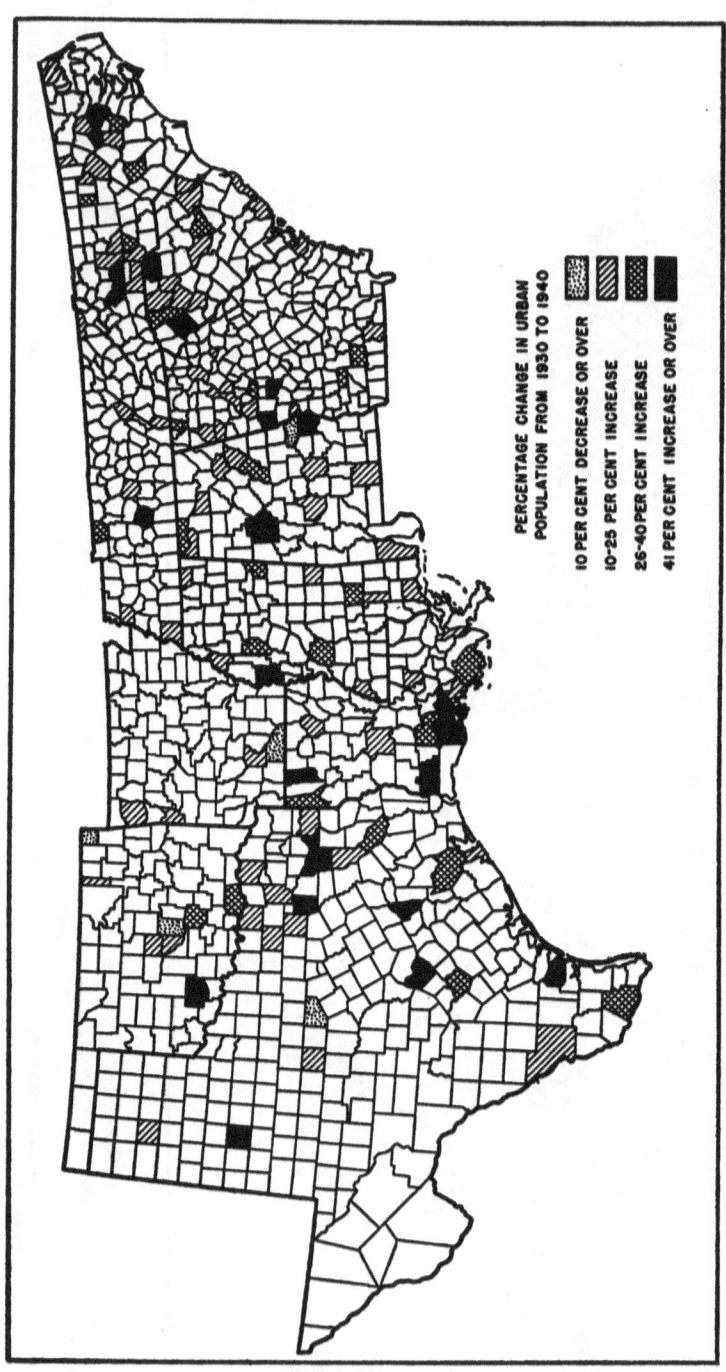

FIGURE 14. RELATIVE RATE OF GROWTH OF IMPORTANT URBAN COUNTIES IN THE COTTON BELT BETWEEN 1930 AND 1940

The centers of urban growth coincide to a large extent with the important areas of urban concentration (cf. Figure 13). Rapidly growing urban counties indicate not only a healthy economic situation but also opportunities for the agricultural interests in the environs to capitalize on the demand for fruits and vegetables, dairy and poultry products, and otherwise to profit from catering to a local city market.

eleven and Arkansas and Mississippi last with only one each. The percentage increase by ten-year periods is shown in the second line. Although the rate of city growth by decades since 1890 has been very rapid, the decade ending in 1890 showed the greatest relative increase and that ending in 1940 the least. Other large relative increases were registered at the decades ending in 1910 and 1920, with 1930 and 1900 not far behind.[5] Some of these large relative increases are misleading because of the small base from which the change was calculated. This is especially true of the early decades given, 1890 and 1900. City growth in the decade through 1910 was influenced strongly by the rapid expansion in railroad tracks and facilities[6] and by the general growth in the textile and other industries which was likewise occurring. The rapid growth from 1910 to 1920 was associated with the expansion of war industries and industries stimulated by the prosperity of World War I, and that from 1920 to 1930 with the postwar high level industrial and economic activity. The poor showing of city growth from 1930 to 1940 was due to the depression conditions of the 1930's which held industrial expansion to a very low level. The effect of a war, and its accompanying high level of economic activity, on city growth was repeated in World War II.[7] As happened after World War I, it is expected that the postwar decade ending about 1955 will record rapid city growth in the South, although probably the percentage increases will fall below that from 1920 to 1930 because of the comparatively larger base from which the change will be computed.

FACTORS IN URBAN GROWTH

Many factors contribute to urban growth, such as commercial expansion, industrialization, etc. Often a single factor will be responsible for the development of an urban center, such as steel production at Birmingham, Alabama;

[5] Arrived at by frequency counts according to percentage increases of the cities in Table 22. For a further check see the 1940 Census of Population, Vol. I, p. 20.

[6] *Statistical Abstract of the United States, 1940,* U. S. Dept. of Commerce, 1941, p. 425.

[7] *Current Population Reports: Population Characteristics,* Bureau of the Census, Series P-20, No. 9, p. 5.

TABLE 22
URBAN PLACES IN THE COTTON BELT OF OVER 50,000 PERSONS IN 1940 WITH POPULATION BY CENSUS DECADES FROM 1890 TO 1940, AND PERCENTAGE INCREASE IN POPULATION IN EACH DECADE

State and city	1890	1900	1910	1920	1930	1940
North Carolina						
1. Charlotte (000)	11.6	18.1	34.0	46.3	82.7	100.9
Per cent increase	63	56	88	36	78	22
2. Winston-Salem (000)	10.7	13.6	22.7	48.4	75.3	79.8
Per cent increase	156	27	66	113	56	6
3. Durham (000)	5.5	6.7	18.2	21.7	52.0	60.2
Per cent increase	169	22	173	19	140	16
4. Greensboro (000)	3.3	10.0	15.9	19.9	53.6	59.3
Per cent increase	58	202	58	25	170	11
5. Asheville (000)	10.2	14.7	18.8	28.5	50.2	51.3
Per cent increase	291	44	28	52	76	2
South Carolina						
1. Charleston (000)	55.0	55.8	58.8	68.0	62.3	71.3
Per cent increase	10	2	5	16	− 8	14
2. Columbia (000)	15.4	21.1	26.3	37.5	51.6	62.4
Per cent increase	53	38	25	43	38	21
Georgia						
1. Atlanta (000)	65.5	89.9	154.8	200.6	270.4	302.3
Per cent increase	75	37	72	30	35	12
2. Savannah (000)	43.2	54.2	65.1	83.3	85.0	96.0
Per cent increase	41	26	20	28	2	13
3. Augusta (000)	33.3	39.4	41.0	52.5	60.3	65.9
Per cent increase	52	18	4	28	15	9
4. Macon (000)	22.7	23.3	40.7	53.0	53.8	57.9
Per cent increase	78	2	75	30	2	8
5. Columbus (000)	17.3	17.6	20.6	31.1	43.1	53.3
Per cent increase	71	2	17	51	39	24
Alabama						
1. Birmingham (000)	26.2	38.4	132.7	178.8	259.7	267.6
Per cent increase	748	47	245	35	45	3
2. Mobile (000)	31.1	38.5	51.5	60.8	68.2	78.7
Per cent increase	7	24	34	18	12	15
3. Montgomery (000)	21.9	30.3	38.1	43.5	66.1	78.1
Per cent increase	31	39	26	14	52	18
Tennessee						
1. Memphis (000)	64.5	102.3	131.1	162.4	253.1	292.9
Per cent increase	92	59	28	24	56	16
2. Chattanooga (000)	29.1	30.2	44.6	57.9	119.8	128.2
Per cent increase	126	4	48	30	107	7
3. Knoxville (000)	22.5	32.6	36.3	77.8	105.8	111.6
Per cent increase	132	45	11	114	36	6
4. Nashville (000)	76.2	80.9	110.4	118.3	153.9	167.4
Per cent increase	76	6	36	7	30	9

Urbanization and Agriculture 115

TABLE 22 (continued)

State and city	1890	1900	1910	1920	1930	1940
Mississippi						
1. Jackson (000)	5.9	7.8	21.3	22.8	48.3	62.1
Per cent increase	14	32	172	7	112	29
Arkansas						
1. Little Rock (000)	25.9	38.3	45.9	65.1	81.7	88.0
Per cent increase	97	48	20	42	25	8
Louisiana						
1. New Orleans (000)	242.0	287.1	339.1	387.2	458.8	494.5
Per cent increase	12	19	18	14	18	8
2. Shreveport (000)	12.0	16.0	28.0	43.9	76.7	98.2
Per cent increase	50	34	75	57	75	28
Oklahoma						
1. Oklahoma City (000)	4.2	10.0	64.2	91.3	185.4	204.4
Per cent increase	....	142	540	42	103	10
2. Tulsa (000)	....	1.4	18.2	72.1	141.3	142.2
Per cent increase	....	....	1208	296	96	1
Texas						
1. Houston (000)	27.6	44.6	78.8	138.3	292.4	384.5
Per cent increase	67	62	77	76	111	32
2. Dallas (000)	38.1	42.6	92.1	159.0	260.5	294.7
Per cent increase	268	12	116	73	64	13
3. San Antonio (000)	37.7	53.3	96.6	161.4	231.5	253.9
Per cent increase	83	42	81	67	44	10
4. Fort Worth (000)	23.1	26.7	73.3	106.5	163.4	177.7
Per cent increase	246	16	175	45	54	9
5. El Paso (000)	10.3	15.9	39.3	77.6	102.4	96.8
Per cent increase	1305	54	147	98	32	− 6
6. Austin (000)	14.6	22.3	29.9	34.9	53.1	87.9
Per cent increase	32	53	34	17	52	66
7. Galveston (000)	29.1	37.8	37.0	44.3	52.9	60.9
Per cent increase	31	30	− 2	20	20	15
8. Beaumont (000)	3.3	9.4	20.6	40.4	57.7	59.1
Per cent increase	....	186	119	96	43	2
9. Corpus Christi (000)	4.4	4.7	8.2	10.5	27.7	57.3
Per cent increase	35	7	75	28	164	107
10. Waco (000)	14.4	20.7	26.4	38.5	52.8	56.0
Per cent increase	98	43	28	46	37	6
11. Amarillo (000)	.5	1.4	10.0	15.5	43.1	51.7
Per cent increase	....	199	590	56	178	20

Source: Sixteenth Census of the United States, 1940, *Population*; Vol. I: *Number of Inhabitants*.

but usually several factors will be responsible, as in the case of Atlanta, which, in addition to being a great commercial center, is a communication center, has important industries, is the capital of a state, and is an important educational center.

In Table 23 are listed the important metropolitan centers in the ten cotton states with their 1940 population and the

TABLE 23
METROPOLITAN POPULATION OF CITIES OF 100,000 OR OVER IN COTTON BELT WITH INDUSTRIAL DISTRIBUTION OF EMPLOYED LABOR FORCE COMPARED TO SPECIFIED LARGE CITIES IN NORTH AND MIDDLE WEST, 1940

City	Population of metropolitan district (000)	Percentage of employed labor force engaged in:					Important industrial lines with approximate percentage of labor force employed
		Agriculture, forestry and fishery	Coal mining, crude petroleum, etc.	Transportation, communication, public utilities, etc.	Wholesale and retail trade	Manufacturing	Construction	
New Orleans, La.	540.0	1.3	0.2	13.7	23.5	17.9	6.2	Food 5; apparel 2.
Houston, Texas	510.4	2.3	2.5	11.0	22.5	20.6	7.4	Petroleum 6; machinery 4; food 3.
Atlanta, Ga.	442.3	1.2	...	9.9	22.4	19.1	6.3	Food 3; textile mfg. 3; apparel 2; printing 2.
Birmingham, Ala.	407.9	0.9	9.7	8.2	17.8	27.2	4.2	Iron, steel, etc. 17; food 2.
Dallas, Texas	376.5	2.7	0.6	8.6	26.4	16.6	6.6	Apparel 3; food 3; printing 2.
Memphis, Tenn.	332.5	4.3	0.1	10.2	23.7	18.8	6.4	Food 3; autos and equipment 2; chemicals 2.
San Antonio, Texas	319.0	3.1	0.8	6.5	24.5	10.7	6.3	Food 4.
Nashville, Tenn.	241.8	2.6	0.1	9.0	19.7	23.7	6.2	Chemicals 4; food 3; printing, etc. 3; apparel 2; iron 2; textiles 2.
Oklahoma City, Okla.	221.2	1.5	4.2	7.9	27.0	12.5	5.3	Food 5; printing 2; machinery 1.
Fort Worth, Texas	207.7	2.4	1.1	10.0	26.4	17.8	5.9	Food 7; petroleum 2; printing 2.
Chattanooga, Tenn.	193.2	2.8	0.6	6.9	16.7	35.7	6.3	Textiles 14; iron and steel, etc. 8; furniture 2; food 3; machinery 1.
Tulsa, Okla.	188.6	2.5	8.5	7.7	23.5	16.8	5.7	Petroleum, etc. 4; iron 2; machinery 2; food 2.
Knoxville, Tenn.	151.8	3.1	1.7	8.4	21.2	27.8	5.6	Textiles 11; food 3; apparel 3.
Charlotte, N. C.	113.0	0.8	0.1	8.4	22.6	25.4	6.4	Textiles 12; food 4; machinery 2; chemicals 2.
New York—Northeastern New Jersey Metropolitan District.	11690.5	0.6	0.1	8.7	20.3	28.4	4.9	Apparel 7; printing 3; textiles 2; food 2; machinery 2.
Chicago, Ill.	4499.1	0.5	0.1	9.9	21.6	35.0	3.8	Iron and steel, etc. 8; machinery 6; food 5; printing 3.
Pittsburgh, Pa.	1994.1	1.3	7.4	8.2	17.7	35.6	4.0	Iron and steel, etc. 19; machinery 4; food 3.

Source: Sixteenth Census of the United States, 1940, *Population*, Vol. II: *Characteristics of the Population*.

distribution of the employed labor force according to major sources of employment and details on relative employment in leading industries. Comparative data are also given for the very large metropolitan centers of New York, Chicago, and Pittsburgh.

The data show that most of the metropolitan centers in the ten cotton states are primarily commercial and secondarily industrial; Knoxville, Chattanooga, Birmingham, and Charlotte being exceptions in showing a high relative employment in some form of manufacturing. It appears that Birmingham and Chattanooga compare favorably in this respect with Chicago and Pittsburgh. In fact, they have a better balance than the two northern cities from some standpoints, in that a proportionately larger labor force is employed in mining, particularly in Birmingham, which places certain basic raw materials at the point of manufacture. It is interesting that in 1940 Birmingham was not far behind Pittsburgh in the percentage (17 to 19) of the population engaged in iron and steel manufacture. But Pittsburgh was ahead of the two southern cities in machinery manufacture, as was Chicago. Metropolitan New York is both an important manufacturing and commercial center. Although it led in the relatively high-valued apparel manufacture, the percentage employed in textiles was low. Several Cotton Belt cities led in textile manufactures but were low in apparel manufacture. Greater emphasis in the region on the manufacture of apparel, machinery, and chemicals seems highly desirable in the interest of better industrial balance and higher incomes.

Further growth of these cities is inevitable, but the rapidity of such growth is an unknown factor, for it depends upon many circumstances. The urban centers dependent on commercial pursuits will grow with the general population and with the expansion in demand for commercial services. So far as industry is concerned, it depends first on the general trend of economic growth in the nation, and then on the factors in regional development, such as the supply of local resources, location of the market for the product, attitude of the city in supplying industrial requirements of water, sanitation, etc., and the quantity and character of the local labor supply.

Although the stimulants to city growth may be present, or potentially so, the stream in growth comes in part from the city inhabitants and from those of the hinterland. Since the reproduction rate in cities is insufficient to maintain their population, the additional persons to supply the deficiency in births and to provide for urban growth come from the rural population, both rural-nonfarm and rural-farm because both categories reproduce in excess of normal replacements and needed expansion. The net reproduction rates for the South[8] are as follows:

	1905-10	1935-40	Per cent decrease from 1905-10 to 1935-40
Urban	764	712	7
Rural-nonfarm	1591	1211	24
Rural-farm	2199	1812	18

Since a rate of 1,000 is required for a stationary population,[9] it is apparent that the urban centers have not been reproducing themselves wheras the rural areas are producing an excess population, the deficiency in the case of the urban centers being about 30 per cent while the excess in the rural-nonfarm is 20 per cent and that in the rural-farm, 80 per cent. It should be noted, however, that from the period 1905-10 to 1935-40 the reproduction rates declined proportionately more in the rural areas than in the urban—24 per cent in rural-nonfarm and 18 per cent in rural-farm, compared to about 7 per cent in the urban centers.

The crude birth rate rose rapidly during World War II and during 1946 and 1947 to rates much above the 1930's and in some years near the 1921 level, raising the question as to whether there has been a reversal in the trend. Thompson, however, largely explains away the bulge in the crude birth rate by the special conditions which influenced the marriage rate and the birth of the first child or first two children. These conditions were: first, the war prosperity which permitted catching up on marriages postponed from

[8] *A Study of Agricultural and Economic Problems of the Cotton Belt*, p. 624.

[9] *Loc. cit.* The reproduction rates are given in percentage with 1,000 as unity. A net reproduction rate of 1,000 means that each generation would just replace itself if death and birth rates of the period continue.

the depression of the 1930's and favored early marriage of the youths of the period; second, the relatively large number of World War I babies reaching maturity; and third, the effect of the war psychology on early marriage and the rearing of a family. Thompson is of the opinion that the temporary inflation in the birth rate will end shortly and the prewar long-run downward trend will be resumed.[10]

Under the assumption that birth rates in the South will return in a few years to the prewar level and resume the 1905-10 to 1935-40 trend, the rural-nonfarm segment of the population should just reproduce itself in about thirty years beyond 1940, which would be around 1970. By that date the rural-farm birth rate should be about 50 per cent in excess and the urban rate 29 per cent deficit, under the assumption that the latter will not change from the 1935-40 rate.[11] Consequently an urban population about 1.7 times the rural-farm should be sufficient to absorb all excess farm population within the region, should all the people composing this farm population excess choose to migrate to cities in the region.

The date when city population may be expected to exceed rural farm population by this ratio is difficult to foretell, since such a forecast depends upon many imponderables, such as progress of industrialization of the region, level of employment, trends in migration, and many other factors which also will tend to affect the validity of the above assumption relative to a declining birth rate. But Figure 15 attempts to determine this date very roughly. The lines forecasting urban and rural-nonfarm populations are simple historical projections based on census data by decades since 1890. Somewhat more elaborate methods were employed to obtain the projection for the rural-farm population. The tentative estimates for the entire United States prepared by the U. S. Department of Agriculture for

[10] Thompson, Warren S., "The Demographic Revolution in the United States," *The Annals of the American Academy of Political and Social Science*, Vol. 262 (March, 1949), pp. 65-66. Thompson is a leading expert on population analysis and his opinions in a matter of this sort deserve great consideration, and they are accepted as my position in the analysis which follows immediately.

[11] See T. Lynn Smith, *Population Analysis* (New York: McGraw-Hill, 1948), p. 227.

the House Committee on Agriculture in 1948 have been used as the basis.[12] These data were adjusted to obtain a forecast for the region by a trend extension of the ratios of the farm population of ten Cotton Belt states to the farm population of the United States for the period 1933 to 1945.

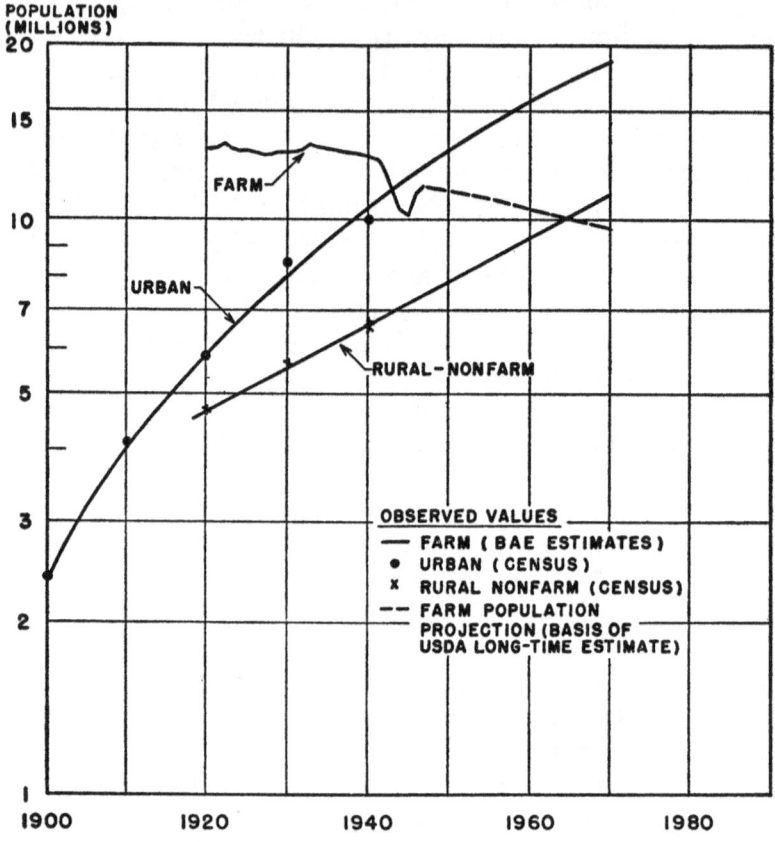

FIGURE 15. PROJECTION OF POPULATION TRENDS BY MAJOR CATEGORIES FOR TEN COTTON STATES

The estimated ratios (by trend line extension) for 1955, 1965, and 1975 were applied directly to the United States farm population estimates to obtain farm population forecasts for the ten Cotton Belt states for these years. The

[12] *Long-range Agricultural Policy*: A Study of Selected Trends and Factors Relating to the Long-range Prospect for American Agriculture for the Committee on Agriculture of the House of Representatives, Eightieth Congress, Second Session, March 10, 1948, p. 27.

results were plotted in Figure 15 and the annual data extended through these points. The method is obviously crude[13] but rests on fairly sound estimates for the United States which were prepared after careful study by the population experts of the Bureau of Agricultural Economics.

Forecasts for the three categories of population, read from the projections in Figure 15, are given in Table 24.

TABLE 24
TRENDS IN GROWTH OF POPULATION CATEGORIES IN TEN COTTON STATES
WITH PROJECTION FORECASTS FOR 1960 AND 1970
(000 omitted)

Year	Rural farm	Rural nonfarm	Urban	Total population
1920............	13,336	4,677	5,842	23,855
1930............	13,143	5,640	8,484	27,267
1940............	12,982	6,576	10,033	29,591
1945-46.........	10,600*	7,100†	11,600†	29,300†
1948............	11,300*	7,700†	11,800†	30,800†
Projected estimates:				
1960............	10,500‡	9,300†	16,000†	35,800†
1970............	9,650‡	11,000†	18,700†	39,350†
Per cent total:				
1960............	29.3	26.0	44.7	100
1970............	24.5	28.0	47.5	100

* Adjusted to farm population estimates by *geographic* regions.
† Based on historical projections. See Figure 15.
‡ Read from Figure 15. See discussion above for method, and footnote 12 for source of original data.

Accordingly it appears that the urban population of these states will perhaps be, even in 1960, below the ratio required to absorb the farm population excess but somewhat above it in 1970, which if taken as the approximate date of the rural-urban population balance would provide a margin for errors in the assumptions. At that date farm population would constitute 24 per cent of the total population as compared to 44 per cent in 1940 and 48 per cent in 1930; and would be in a ratio to city population of 1 to 2 but still far short of the 1940 ratio for the United States.

[13] Incidentally, substantially the same results are obtained under the assumption that net migration from Southern farms would continue at the 1947 rate.

Of the three regions of the Cotton Belt, Oklahoma and Texas are the most highly urbanized, with 43 per cent of the total population in urban centers in 1940 and 35 per cent rural-farm. However, by 1945-46 the percentage of rural-farm was 25 per cent and the percentage of urban a great deal above the 1940 proportion. Oklahoma and Texas are thus presently near the population ratios which we give for the entire ten states for 1970, and would be near a population balance within the region if the reproduction rates were in line. Reproduction rates for Oklahoma and Texas are not currently available but presumably they are not greatly different from rates of the South as a whole, which if true means that the region does not yet have population balance but should achieve it in a few years—certainly long in advance of the Delta states which, with the exception of Louisiana, are the least urbanized of the lot. (See Figure 16.)

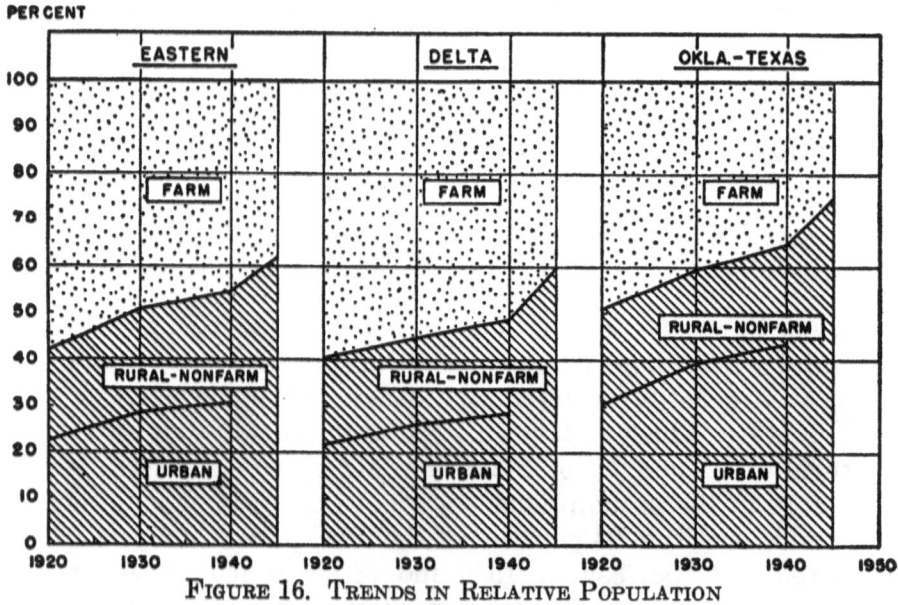

FIGURE 16. TRENDS IN RELATIVE POPULATION DISTRIBUTION BY AREAS

Oklahoma and Texas have the highest percentage of the urban and rural-nonfarm population; the Delta states the lowest. However, the trends in relative distribution are about the same in all areas.

According to a study by the United States Department of Labor, the net migration from the South in 1940-45 was five times greater than in the period 1935-40. However, "only 3 of the Southern States—Alabama, Tennessee, and Texas—[14]moved up the list in the direction of relatively less out-migration. The 13-state area—and every state in it, except only Florida and Virginia, continued to lose population to other areas."[15] This reflects the relatively greater industrial growth of the three cotton states and Virginia; in Florida the shift is toward urbanization but probably because of greater tourist interest and expansion of commercial activity. Where economic opportunity is present, or if it develops, migration from farms will be largely to the local urban centers, and to that extent progress toward a population balance will be accelerated.

EFFECT OF URBANIZATION ON AGRICULTURE

In addition to providing an outlet for excess farm population, cities afford opportunities for part-time employment, and a market for perishable agricultural commodities. According to the data in Table 25, 27 per cent of all farmers reported off-farm work in 1944, averaging 184 days annually. This off-farm work in industry and urban centers thus concerns about 1.6 million farmers and the amount of time involved on the average is considerable. Even at ordinary pay rates the supplementary income is significant. Not a great deal is known about off-farm work of farmers but interest in it on the part of rural scientists is increasing. In a study published by the North Carolina Experiment Station in 1947, McVay, the author, reports that "total family incomes were raised substantially" by earnings from such employment.[16] Off-farm work enabled the

---

[14] A recent Census Bureau release (Series P-25, No. 4) dated October 12, 1947, gives estimates of population by states and changes in population by states from 1940 to 1947. Texas showed the largest increase (10.3 per cent) of any of the ten cotton states. There have also been other recent indications that Southern and other regional migrations have shifted toward the West and Northwest, and Texas seems to be in the axis of migration. This suggests that Texas has opportunities for surplus population already in excess of the ability of local population to supply.

[15] U. S. Department of Labor, *Labor in the South*, Bulletin No. 898, p. 17.

[16] Francis E. McVay, *Factory Meets Farm in North Carolina*, N. C. Agri. Expt. Sta., Tech. Bul. No. 83, p. 22.

TABLE 25
WORK OFF FARM BY FARM OPERATORS IN DIFFERENT REGIONS AND STATES BY CENSUS YEARS

Region and state	Per cent operators reporting				Average days off-farm work			
	1929	1934	1939	1944	1929	1934	1939	1944
United States	30	30	29	27	100	97	137	184
South	31	28	28	26	92	95	135	176
North Carolina	28	25	25	19	93	118	146	173
Texas	27	27	26	27	86	94	143	191
Mississippi	30	22	22	19	72	71	99	111
New York	31	28	31	31	128	137	161	228
Massachusetts	38	34	40	45	170	171	212	268

Source: *Census of Agriculture, 1945*, Vol. II, Chap. IV (Reprint), p. 272.

farm family to more fully utilize its labor, which could not have found full employment on the local farms even with larger acreages because of the short season labor requirements of the main cash crop, cotton. As a rule those who worked off-farm, according to the study, had moderately smaller farms in terms of cropland cultivated and a larger acreage of idle cropland. The adjusted cotton acreage[17] decreased with the percentage of the labor force employed off the farm and with the size of the farm. So that the effect of off-farm work was to increase family income but by a relatively smaller amount because of the reduced cotton acreage and increased idle cropland associated with off-farm work.[18] In other words, while off-farm work arose as a result of unused labor resources seeking utilization, when pursued to a considerable extent, it affected the acreage of the intensive cash crops, cotton and tobacco, which are not subject to mechanization to any significant extent in the counties studied.

Referring again to Table 25, it is apparent that off-farm work is heaviest in the more urban states. It also varies with the business cycle. The average number of days worked in 1944 was much higher than in 1939, although the percentage of farm operators reporting was less in 1944 and the total number of farmers less by about 177,000,[19]

[17] Means that cotton acreage was increased by the addition of tobacco acreage multiplied by 5.
[18] McVay, *op. cit.*, pp. 8-15.
[19] *Census of Agriculture, 1945*, Vol. II, Chap. IV (Reprint), p. 272.

which reduction is a reflection of the absolute decrease in total farms in the United States of about 238,000 from 1939 to 1944.[20] Presumably, many farmers who engaged in off-farm work found employment on a full-time basis during the war prosperity and made the transition to non-farm work completely.

The agricultural products which find a ready market in the cities are milk, eggs, and fresh fruits and vegetables. Since all three classes are bulky, perishable, and of low specific market value, they are not able as a rule to absorb the heavy transportation costs associated with production at great distance from the market. Consequently, such products tend to be produced near the urban center, usually within a certain radius of the city if soil and other natural conditions are reasonably suitable. Hence, as the urban population increases, particularly that in cities of some size, the demand for and subsequent production of these products expand.

As shown by Figures 17 and 18, the sale of milk and vegetables produced for market expanded not in the same ratio as the urban plus rural-nonfarm population but in a geometric ratio. During the period 1920 to 1945, when the non-farm population expanded by 100 per cent, milk sold increased from 500 to 600 per cent, depending upon the region; and from 1930 to 1945 vegetables harvested for sale expanded 400 per cent in the Eastern cotton states and more than that percentage in Oklahoma and Texas. The very large expansion of milk sold is due to a rising level of income associated with urbanization, and to the increasing emphasis on milk by nutritionists as a health-giving and health-protective food. In the case of vegetables harvested for sale, the income and nutrition factors were operative; but in addition, the discovery of new areas suitable for well-established products brought the entire national market to bear. Also, new methods in transportation, mainly in refrigeration, brought the distant fruit and vegetable-producing areas of the Cotton Belt within reach of the great urban centers of the Northeast and Middle West.

[20] *Ibid.*, p. 230.

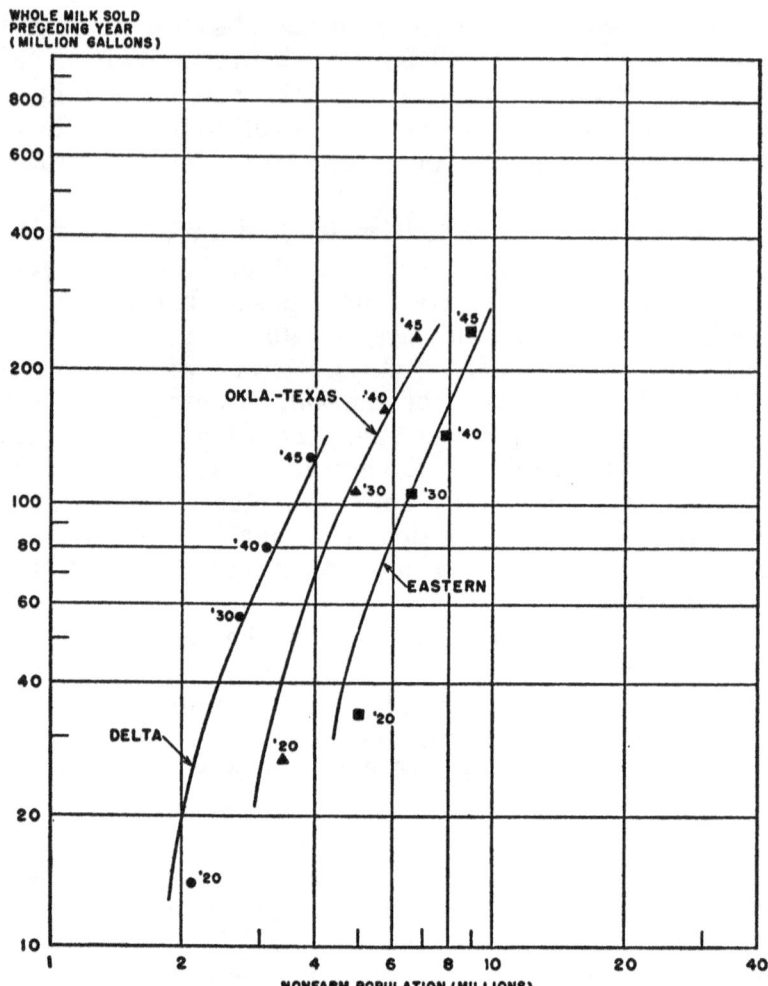

FIGURE 17. RELATION OF NONFARM POPULATION TO MILK SOLD, BY CENSUS DATES

When nonfarm population doubled during the period, whole milk sold increased about 500 to 600 per cent. The regression lines indicate that if the total of rural-nonfarm and urban population increases by this percentage again, milk sold would be expected to expand by 200 to 300 per cent, other things being equal.

In the case of eggs, no data are available in the census on sales by states. But production figures are available; however, these are not directly comparable to urban growth. Since a relatively large quantity of eggs is consumed on

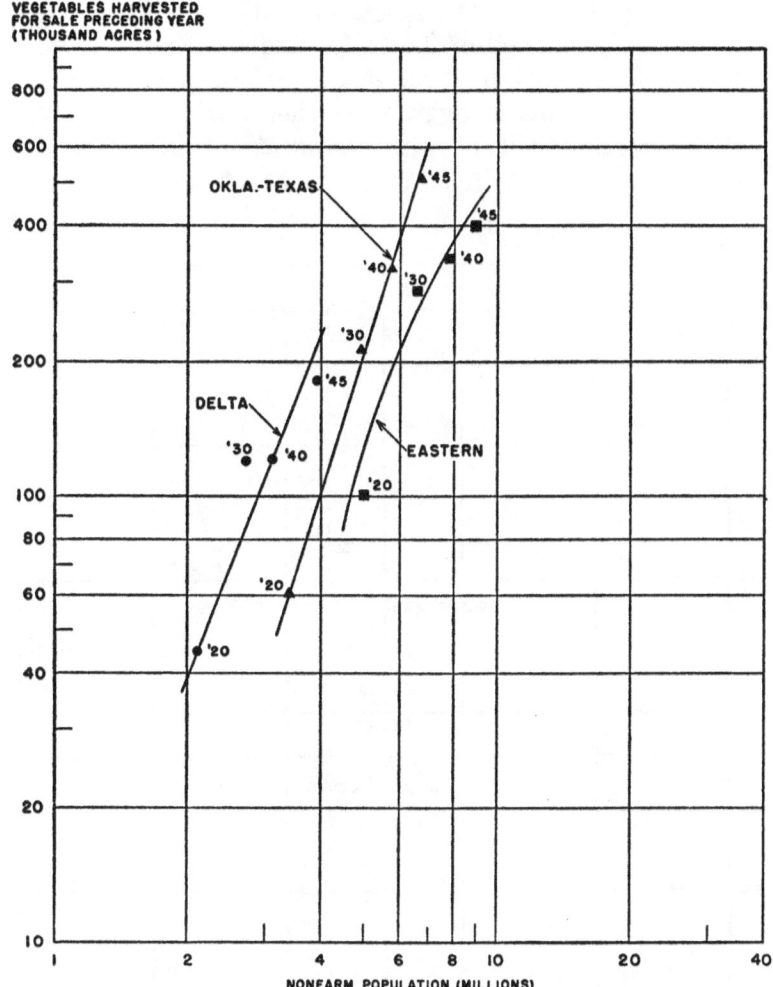

FIGURE 18. RELATION OF NONFARM POPULATION TO VEGETABLES HARVESTED FOR SALE, BY CENSUS DATES

During the period a doubling of the nonfarm population was *associated* with an increase in the acreage of vegetables harvested for sale of 400 per cent in the Eastern cotton states, 800 per cent in Oklahoma and Texas, and 500 per cent in the Delta states.

the farms where produced, a more correct comparison is with total population. Such a comparison is shown in Figure 19. According to the scatter diagrams there given for the different regions of the Cotton Belt, a doubling of the total population was associated with a ratio of change in total eggs produced of 3.5 to 5.5 times. Rising levels of income and transition from small urban places to some extent self-sufficient in eggs and other perishable foods to urban places larger in absolute population but almost completely insufficient in these respects are factors helping to

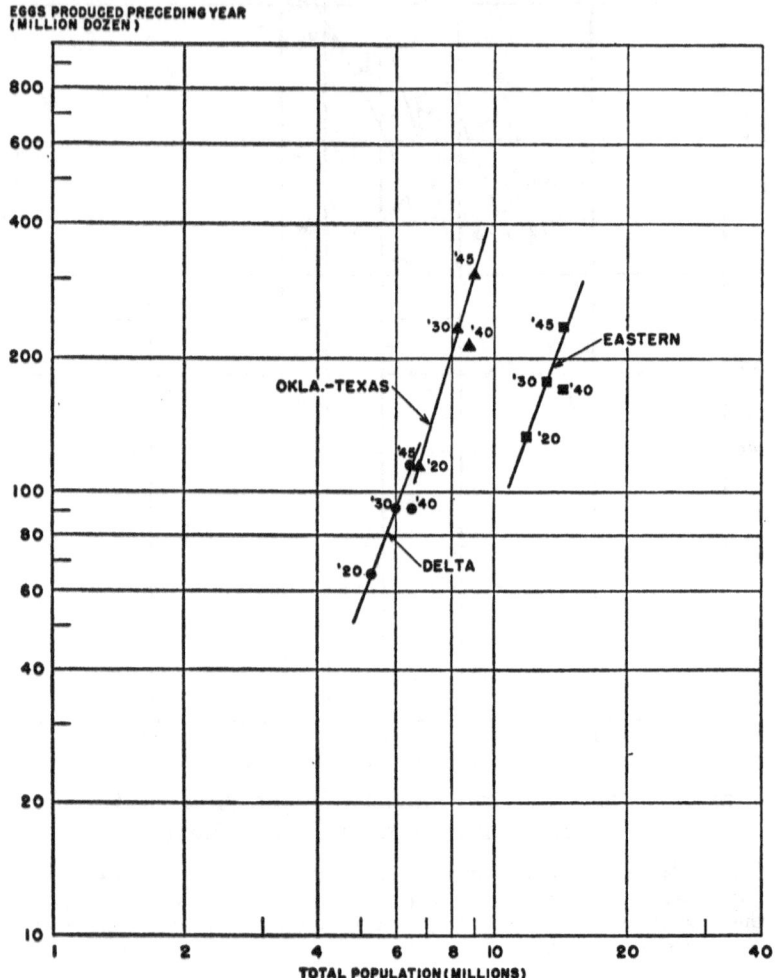

FIGURE 19. RELATION OF TOTAL POPULATION TO EGGS PRODUCED, BY CENSUS DATES

During the period a unit increase in population was associated with an increase in eggs produced of 3.5 to 5.5 times.

explain the more than proportionate increase in eggs relative to the population increase.

The expansion in demand for agricultural products and the contiguous agriculture associated with urban growth cause farmers to shift to dairy, truck, poultry, and similar intensive types of farms. These types increase near the cities, while the more extensive types decrease, and in certain areas close to the urban centers discontinue in the area altogether.

Rising land values is another effect of urbanization. This is caused by the growth in demand for alternative commercial uses and by the increased earnings from the greater intensive use of the land.

EFFECT OF MIGRATION ON AGRICULTURE

Although it affords an outlet for surplus farm population, city growth produces certain unfortunate effects. According to a study by Brunner, "among the 20 to 24-year-olds three out of every five migrants went either to a city or village, only in the ages 30 to 64 did the farm retain more than half of the migrants." On the other hand, the urban-to-farm migration is primarily in the older age groups. "From 25 to 64 years, the older an urban migrant, the greater the chance he will go to the farm. This tendency helps to increase the already high average age of the adult farm population."[21]

Although farming is coming more and more to require a high order of intelligence, even more so than is realized by rural scientists, it is still an occupation where brawn, stamina, and energy pay good dividends. The long-time trends in farm-to-city migration have taken those who from the standpoint of these requirements are most adapted to farming. Both owners and tenants have been affected, as is shown in Table 26. Since the first date shown in the table, 1910, the ratio of both classes in the ages from 34 years down have steadily declined, over 2/3 for the age group among owners under 25 years, and 44 per cent for the age group from 25 to 34 years; in the tenant class the age group under 25 years declined 59 per cent and the age

---

[21] Edmund de S. Brunner, "Internal Migration in the United States, 1935-40," *Rural Sociology*, Vol. 13, No. 1 (March, 1948), pp. 18-19.

group 25-34 years, 28 per cent. On the other hand, the percentage of operators in the age groups of 55 years and over has been increasing in importance almost in an equivalent ratio. Other age classes have shown changes but the big ones have been in the age group extremes.

TABLE 26
SHIFT IN AGE DISTRIBUTION OF FARM OPERATORS IN THE CENSUS SOUTH*

Tenure and age	Percentage of total operators reporting				
	1910	1920	1930	1940	1945
Owners					
Under 25 years....	3.2	3.1	2.0	1.7	1.0
25-34 years........	17.9	15.3	10.9	10.9	10.1
35-44 years........	24.8	24.4	21.9	19.7	21.3
45-54 years........	25.0	25.6	27.1	25.8	26.0
55-64 years........	18.3	18.8	22.2	23.0	22.5
65 years and over..	10.8	12.8	15.9	19.1	19.0
34 years and under.	21.1	18.4	12.9	12.6	11.1
55 years and over..	29.1	31.6	38.1	42.1	41.5
Tenants					
Under 25 years....	14.8	13.6	15.2	9.6	6.1
25-34 years........	31.4	27.8	25.8	27.2	22.7
35-44 years........	24.1	25.0	23.6	24.2	27.9
45-54 years........	16.6	19.8	20.0	19.8	21.4
55-64 years........	9.1	9.2	10.7	12.6	13.8
65 years and over..	4.0	4.7	4.6	6.6	8.1
34 years and under.	46.2	41.4	41.0	36.8	28.8
45 years and over..	29.7	33.7	35.3	39.0	43.3

* Includes the following Census geographic subdivisions: South Atlantic, East South Central, and West South Central. The term "South" in future tables of this section implies the same geographic subdivisions.
Source: *Census of Agriculture, 1945*, Vol. II, Chapter IV (Reprint), p. 252.

The effect of these trends on the number of operators by major age categories is estimated in Table 27.

Thus it appears that while the total number of owner-operators showed little change until 1945 when there was a considerable increase, apparently from tenants becoming owners, the operators 34 years and under were only 58 per cent as great as 35 years earlier but the age class 55 years and older was 57 per cent larger. In other words, a reduction of 135,000 operators in the younger class was associated with an increase of 255,000 operators in the older age groups.

TABLE 27
TREND IN NUMBER OF FARM OPERATORS IN THE CENSUS SOUTH BY AGE GROUPS
(000 omitted)

Year	Owner-operators			Tenant-operators		
	Total	Estimated number 34 years and under	Estimated number 55 years and over	Total	Estimated number 34 years and under	Estimated number 45 years and over
1910............	1,545	325	450	1,537	710	460
1920............	1,597	295	505	1,591	660	540
1930............	1,416	185	540	1,791	730	630
1940............	1,544	195	650	1,449	530	565
1945............	1,703	190	705	1,165	335	505
1945 as per cent of 1910......	.....	58	157	.....	47	110

Source: Total number of operators obtained from *Census of Agriculture, 1945*, Vol. II, Chapter IV (Reprint); p. 252. The number by tenure and age class was computed by applying the percentages shown in Table 26, and rounded for convenience in comparison.

In the case of tenants the total number of units have been on the decrease in the South[22] only since 1930, apparently due to increased size of farms, more favorable economic opportunities outside agriculture, ability to make the step from tenant to owner in the recent war prosperity, and other factors.[23] But in the age classes the changes have been even more striking. Although there has been only a small increase, 10 per cent relative to 1910, in the age group 45 years and over, the age classes of 34 years and under have shrunk quite drastically, so that in 1945 the number of tenants in this group was only 47 per cent of the number in 1910, or 375,000 operators less. It should be emphasized, however, that the absolute change in the tenant age group under 35 years occurred primarily after 1930, but the relative change goes back to 1910, as shown in Table 26.

That the effect of age shifts may be more important for certain unpopular types of farming, such as cotton, is shown in Table 28 which gives data according to the 1946 age of the operator for a sample[24] of cotton farms from the upper Piedmont of South Carolina and Georgia.

[22] See Table 26, footnote, on regions included.   [23] Cf. Chap. IV.

[24] Based on the cooperative study between the University of Virginia and the Bureau of Agricultural Economics on cotton yield variability. The data show that the 1946 age of cotton farmers averaged 51 in the upper Piedmont and 46 in West Texas. The former reflects a contracting cotton economy, the latter, a normal one.

TABLE 28

COMPARISON OF 1946 AGE DISTRIBUTION OF A SAMPLE OF FARM OPERATORS
IN THE UPPER PIEDMONT OF SOUTH CAROLINA AND GEORGIA WITH THE
1945 AGE DISTRIBUTION OF ALL FARMERS IN THE SOUTH AND
UNITED STATES AS REPORTED IN THE
CENSUS OF AGRICULTURE

	Owners			Tenants†		
Item	Total all ages	34 years and under	55 years and over	Total all ages	34 years and under	55 years and over
Upper Piedmont sample of cotton farmers:						
1. Number of operators in sample....	633	57	303	319	51	93
2. Per cent of total..	100	9	48	100	16	29
Per cent of total from Census:						
1. South*..........	100	11	42	100	29	22
2. United States*....	100	11	42	100	30	20

* Census data for 1945.
† The sample study includes only bona fide tenants, whereas the census reports include sharecroppers as well. The percentage distribution for tenants is therefore not strictly comparable.

It appears that the age distribution for cotton farmers is even more unfavorable for a continued high capacity in the industry than for the general run of farms in the South. Cotton farming is an unpopular type for the young farmer with modern outlook, who desires less drudgery in an occupation.

Age is likely therefore to become a more important factor in reducing the number of cotton farms in the future, and probably more quickly than for the general agricultural economy. Undoubtedly some of the reduction in cotton farms and cotton acreage in the recent past has been due to the natural events which come with age.

What all this means for agriculture is difficult to assess at this point because of the paucity of facts on the situation. It is a problem of such importance that it deserves a full-fledged study. However, it is certain that the farmers 55 years and over will to a large extent pass out of the picture in another ten to twenty years. This means that, unless there is a reversal in the direction of migration, considerable adjustments may be expected in the agricultural production of the South. Potentially, this situation holds large possibilities for mechanization and enlargement of farms. But since the cities have been attracting the better-educated,[25] it is not certain that those operators remaining will have the foresight, or ability, to exploit the opportunity. Instead of fewer but larger and more mechanized farms, there may be fewer farms of the same size with widespread farm abandonment. This latter alternative would be a blight upon the agricultural economy of the South, and one to be avoided if possible.

Further decline in number of farms and agricultural labor is desirable in order to relieve population pressure and decrease the ratio of people to resources. But if the more intelligent and better educated males continue to be attracted away from agriculture,[26] it will not be possible to reconstruct Southern agriculture to the extent desired with those left on the land. The alternative is to attract the more intelligent and better educated to remain in farming, and make adjustments toward fewer, larger, and more mechanized farms. In order to bring this about, the farming industry as a way of life must be made more attractive, which might be effected in part by making the road to ownership easier. This could be accomplished to a considerable degree by substituting educational achievement for a large part of the capital security for loans.

SUMMARY

Although urban population growth has been phenomenal in the ten Cotton Belt states since 1890, the percentage of total urban population in 1940 was about the same as for the United States about 1890. Since urban centers fail to reproduce themselves, they afford an outlet for surplus farm population. Assuming a continuation of the 1905-10 to 1935-40 downward trend in net reproduction rates of rural-farm and rural-nonfarm population, it appears on the basis of population projections that urban centers may be sufficiently large by 1970 to absorb normal rural-farm migration without further growth.

Urban centers also afford a demand for perishable farm

[25] Brunner, *op. cit.*, p. 17.
[26] *Ibid.*

products, such as milk, eggs, and vegetables. As urban population increases the demand for these products expands in a geometric ratio, because of the relationship of size of city to level of income.[27] This expansion in demand provides opportunities for farmers to engage in the production of more profitable enterprises, discontinuing cotton and thereby relieving production pressure of the enterprise.

But farm-city migration is not without its harmful effects for agriculture. Since the younger, more alert, and better educated are attracted by city employment opportunities, a class of farmer is left on the land which is ill-equipped to cope with modern farming. The tendency for the young to migrate to cities and the old to retire to farms has caused over the last thirty years an unfavorable age distribution for maximum development and efficiency of agriculture in the South. Rural scientists agree that further reduction in the farm population is in the interest of increased scale and efficiency, but it seems unlikely that the age and educational classes now accumulating on farms will be capable of taking advantage of the situation in terms of recent advances in mechanization. Migration should continue but the alert and more capable should be attracted to remain on farms, or, if already gone, to return, thus enabling Southern agriculture to have fewer but larger farms with appropriate mechanical equipment. A chief means of attracting the *higher types* of farm operators to agriculture as a vocation may be found in making ownership easier. This would seem to indicate the necessity for substituting educational achievement for a large part of capital assets as security for long-term loans at low interest rates.

[27] Average incomes increase significantly with the size of the city. See *Current Population Reports: Consumer Income*, U. S. Dept. of Commerce, Bureau of the Census, Series P-60, No. 1, June 3, 1948.

CHAPTER VII

Other Dynamic Factors Influencing Southern Agriculture

NUMBER OF COTTON FARMS

THE TOTAL NUMBER of cotton farms in any region is a reflection of total land area suitable for cotton production, the relative profitability of the cotton type of farm as compared to other types of farms, degree of mechanization, size of farm, and labor supply.

Considering only the 25-year period, 1919 to 1944, the maximum number of cotton farms in the Eastern states was reached in 1919, in the Delta states in 1929, and in Oklahoma and Texas in 1924; the total number at the peaks being 901, 603, and 544 thousand cotton farms, respectively. From these peaks to 1944 the number of cotton farms decreased 40 per cent in the Eastern states, 33 per cent in the Delta states, and 57 per cent in Oklahoma and Texas.

The steady decline in number of cotton farms from 1919 to 1944 in the Eastern states reflects boll weevil damage; competition of city markets for truck crops, fruit, eggs and poultry, and dairy products; and industrial employment for labor. The increase in cotton acreage in 1947 and 1948 reflects the comparatively high price for cotton, and the return to farming of many veterans and others who had city employment during the war.

The Delta states continued to expand acreage, mainly in the Mississippi Delta proper, even during the years of the boll weevil, and, with drainage and clearing operations, it is probable that considerable cotton land could be added. However, the acreage restriction features of the A.A.A. program tended to discourage further expansion, since land already in cultivation was somewhat limited as to use. Consequently, we find that the number of cotton farms decreased after 1929.

In Oklahoma and Texas, high prices for cotton during the early 1920's, due in part to the greater boll weevil damage in other sections of the Cotton Belt, encouraged an expansion at the expense of other types of farms. However, soon after 1926 the other states began to understand the art of boll weevil control, and the drop in prices which followed the increased production and later the depression put pressure on farmers to shift to other types of farming. This condition also encouraged new areas to be developed with other types of farming.

As shown previously, changes in the number of tractors are *associated* with changes in number of non-cotton farms,[1] which in turn is related to the number of cotton farms. The relation of number of non-cotton farms to the number of cotton farms is shown in Figure 20. In all areas an increase of one non-cotton farm displaced about two cotton farms, this ratio varying from one to 1.7 farms in the Eastern states to one to 2.2 farms in the Delta states. Almost any tendency toward larger farms and a more extensive agriculture would displace one or more sharecroppers. The displacement was less in the Eastern cotton states because as a rule the multiple unit cotton farms were the smallest of any in the regions; and more in the Delta states because of the multiple family displacements on cotton plantations which occurred during the A.A.A. period.

Changes in acreage of cotton per farm would account for changes in number of cotton farms; a tendency toward less average acreage of cotton per farm tending to increase them, and conversely for increases in acreage per farm. Actually, as shown by Figure 21, the tendency has been toward a smaller acreage of cotton per farm, this trend being especially marked during the A.A.A. period. This means that the decrease in cotton farms was less than it otherwise might have been, considering the total decrease in cotton acreage which occurred between 1929 and 1944.

Figure 21 also indicates that a steady upward trend

[1] Cf. Chap. IV, pp. 72-75.

Other Influences on Southern Agriculture   137

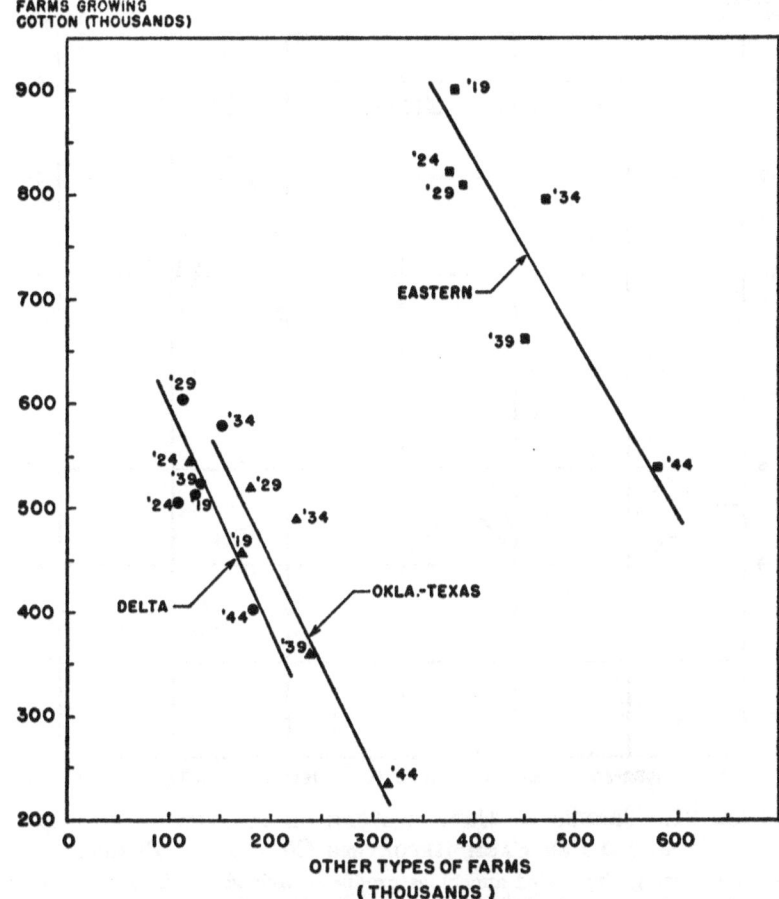

FIGURE 20. RELATION OF NUMBER OF OTHER FARMS TO NUMBER OF COTTON FARMS, BY CENSUS YEARS

When the number of non-cotton farms increases, the number of cotton farms decreases. On the average one non-cotton farm displaces about two cotton farms.

in the output of cotton per farm has occurred, the tendency continuing during the A.A.A. period. This is an important factor in production economics. Greater output on less acres means not only a larger income from more cotton for sale and more other crops for sale grown on the vacated acres but greater profits as a result of the reduced costs per acre of cotton grown. This could occur because of the sharp upward trend in yields, 44 per cent from 1925-29

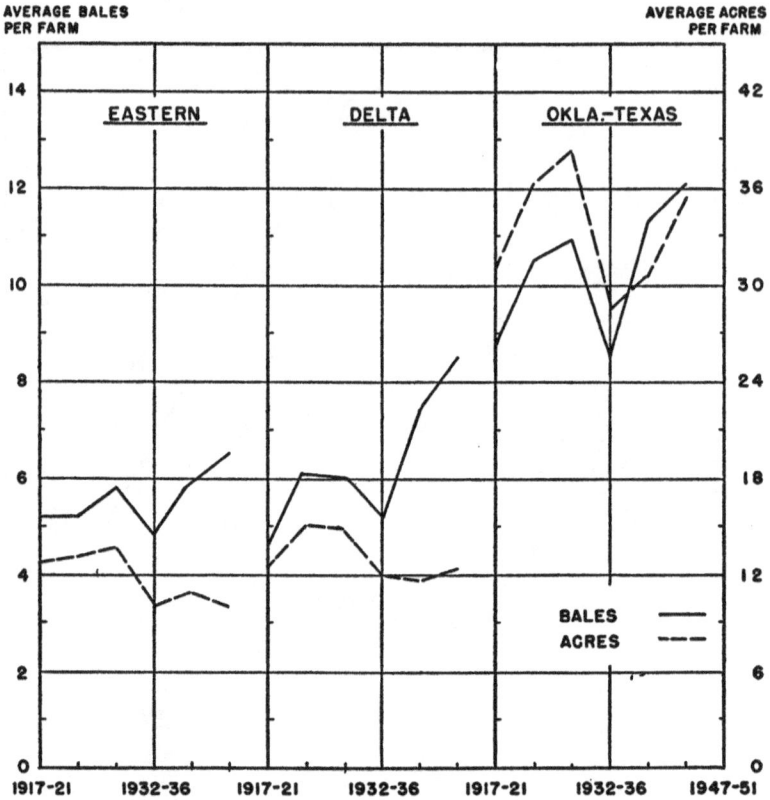

FIGURE 21. TRENDS IN COTTON ACREAGE HARVESTED AND BALES PRODUCED PER FARM REPORTING COTTON, BY PERIODS

(Average acreage harvested and bales produced divided by the census number of cotton farms, as reported for the mid-year in each period.)

Acreage and production of cotton per farm increases from East to West in the Cotton Belt. After 1927-31 acreage dropped off sharply in all regions, with considerable recovery occurring in the Okla.-Texas region during 1937-41 and 1942-46. However, except for the dry period 1932-36 production per farm shows a strong upward trend, reflecting the influence of new techniques on yield.

to 1940-46. The conclusion is that cotton farms increased both in efficiency and size during the period, but changed in both respects at a much faster pace during the A.A.A. period.

FARM POPULATION

Because of the high birth rate and limited land area, there is normally population pressure in the Cotton Belt.

Other Influences on Southern Agriculture 139

Given the opportunity, industrial and other types of city jobs, this excess population leaves the farms eagerly. As a result, except during a severe depression period when there is widespread unemployment in cities, there is a net movement out of agriculture. Prior to World War II, only in 1932 was the returning stream of migrants large enough to exceed the farm exodus.[2] In 1932 and for a few years during the period when there was low net migration to cities, a large population excess developed, and, along with the relatively low net migration from then until the outbreak of the war, formed a very large labor pool for war industries and general industrial expansion. As shown above,[3] this excess, and some more perhaps, responded to these job openings in an unprecedented manner, 3.6 million persons leaving farms in the five-year period from 1940 to 1945. The farm population was reduced 28 per cent by this record movement. However, 48 per cent of the war loss in farm population was regained by January 1, 1947 in the cotton states as a whole, and in the Eastern cotton states the percentage regained was apparently 65 per cent.[4]

As to the relation of farm population change to cotton production, there are both cause and effect relationships. If there is free mobility from agriculture, a reduction in farm population will reduce the labor supply and hence the acres of a given intensity which can be cultivated and harvested. On the other hand, if profitability of cotton drops to the point where other types of farming are more favorable, shrinkage in acreage will occur without any change in population, but not as much shrinkage as with free movement of farm population. In the period from 1940 to 1948 and to a lesser extent from 1920 to 1930 reduced farm population was the factor, while from 1930 to 1940 both the A.A.A. and greatly reduced relative returns from cotton operated to decrease cotton acreage and production. Labor scarcity characterizes the former two periods but farm population pressure the latter period. Since the entrepreneur operates primarily to maximize his capital and manage-

[2] *Farm Population Estimates, 1910-1942,* U. S. Dept. of Agri., Bur. of Agri. Econ., Nov., 1942, pp. 8-10.
[3] Cf. Chap. I, pp. 17-18.
[4] Cf. Chap. II, pp. 38-40.

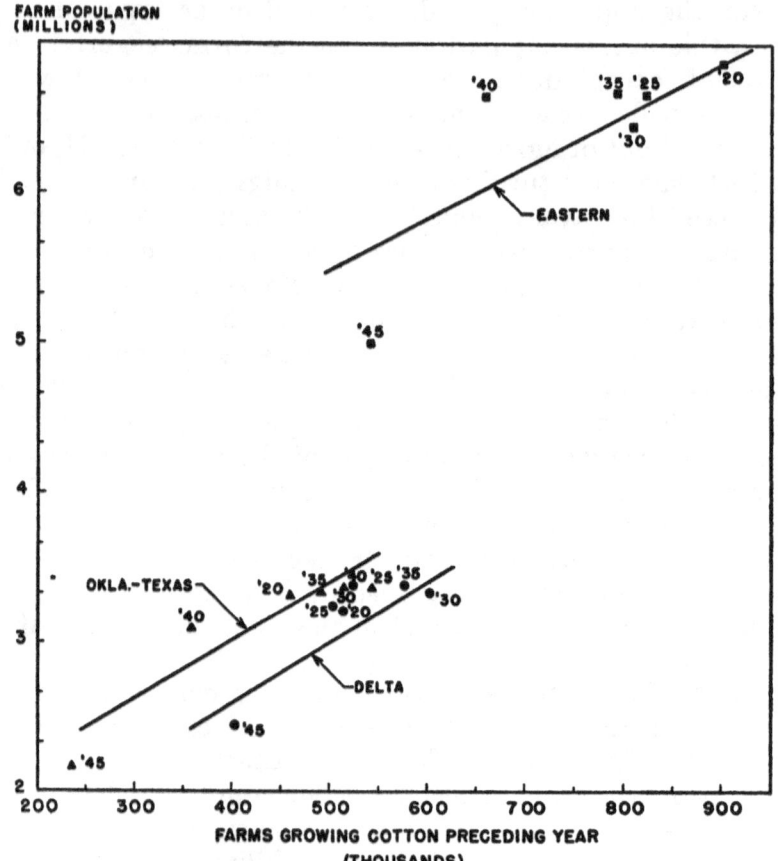

FIGURE 22. RELATION OF FARMS GROWING COTTON TO TOTAL FARM POPULATION, BY CENSUS YEARS

When the number of cotton farms decreases, farm population shrinks also if there is some place for the farm population to go. During the period (1920 to 1945) a decrease of one farm showed a *tendency* to displace about 3.5 farm persons in the Eastern cotton states and about four in the Delta states and in Oklahoma and Texas.

ment returns, he will select that system of farming and the size of farm which is most profitable under the circumstances. Therefore, it will be taken that the cause and effect chain runs predominantly from the entrepreneur to type and size of farms, thence to farm population change.

In Figure 22, number of cotton farms is related to farm population. It is there shown that the relationship tends to be direct, although the scatter about the regression line is rather large for accurate forecasting. Many factors influence farm population movement and it has not been possible to eliminate them. Nevertheless, the regression lines show that on the average four farm persons are displaced by each cotton farm taken out of production in the Delta states and in Oklahoma and Texas, and about 3.5 farm persons for each reduction of one cotton farm in the Eastern states. If the excess remains on farms, we have to this extent unemployment, or only partial employment, in agriculture. If the excess is fortunate enough to find employment in cities, a healthy relationship between the factors of production in agriculture is established. The former condition prevailed during the depression, while the latter is more typical of World Wars I and II and of their postwar periods.

CHANGE IN WORKSTOCK

To a great extent, in areas other than West Texas, cotton culture has generally been a man and mule combination—more frequently, one man, one mule. Since the harvest labor requirements are of the same nature as the hoeing and picking operations, the need for family labor has held cotton to a family enterprise. The acreage of cotton which can be hoed and picked is generally the acreage which can be cultivated by the head of the family. A multiple team upsets the balance because more acreage can be cultivated than can be picked and harvested by the family labor. To depend upon importing transient labor[5] is risky and not entirely satisfactory. Furthermore, since the cost per man hour and per mule hour is often highly associated, not much incentive exists for economizing in the use of man power.

Census data for the period indicate that the number of mules (and horses) on farms varies with the total number of cotton farms. (See Figure 23.) Since farms are smaller in the Eastern states and the Delta states, except where plantations prevail, the ratio of the change in number of cotton farms to the change in number of horses and mules

[5] Migratory labor is relied on to a considerable extent for cotton snapping in West Texas; and usually the ability to hire pickers locally from the towns in the Delta plays an important role in the agriculture there.

varies greatly between regions. In the Eastern states the ratio is one farm to 1.8 work animals; in the Delta states, one cotton farm to one work animal; and in Oklahoma and Texas, a decrease of one cotton farm is associated with a decrease of 5.4 workstock, reflecting the much larger farms and a more direct connection between tractors and workstock displacement. If this analysis is correct, the connection between number of tractors on farms and the number of workstock displaced is not so direct in the Cotton Belt, except perhaps in Oklahoma and Texas and on the large Delta plantations. Cause and effect appear to run from an increase in tractors to an increase in non-cotton farms, to a decrease in number of cotton farms, thence to a decline in number of workstock.

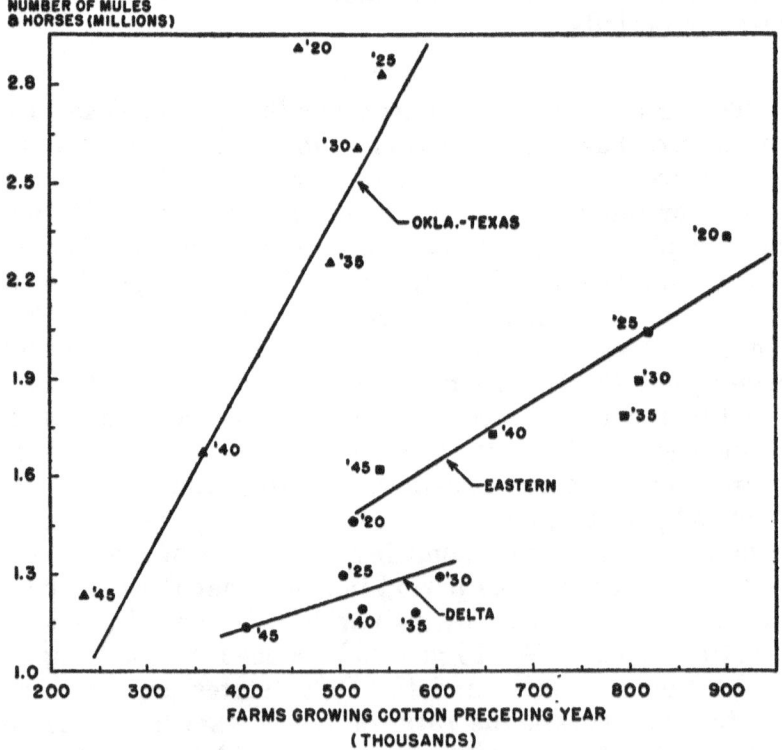

FIGURE 23. RELATION OF NUMBER OF COTTON FARMS TO THE NUMBER OF HORSES AND MULES ON FARMS

The number of horses and mules on farms decreased with the number of cotton farms in all regions, but more strongly in Oklahoma and Texas.

It should be emphasized that the discussion does not center around how many work animals the tractor displaces but around the intermediate stages of the apparent causation. Unfortunately, few farmers move as promptly in displacing work animals when a tractor is purchased as they should. There is a wide difference between the number of work animals it is possible to replace technically and those actually displaced. Inertia, rough topography, rotations or systems of farming causing short rows, and maladjustments in the labor supply tend to hold more work animals on tractor farms than are necessary both from the standpoint of need or security in certain operations and of greatest efficiency in the utilization of farm resources. Cooper and others have investigated the work animals displaced by tractors on *tractor farms* in different regions of the United States.[6] Their results are shown in Table 29 for the Southern geographic regions, which are only roughly comparable to our Cotton Belt subregions.

According to the calculations,[7] the displacements have

TABLE 29

Tractor Farms: Average Acreage of Land, Cropland Harvested, Tractors, and Horses and Mules Three Years or More of Age on Farms Reporting Tractors and Workstock on January 1, 1943

State group	Land per farm in 1942	Cropland harvested per farm in 1942	Tractors per farm as of Jan. 1, 1943	Work animals per farm as of Jan. 1, 1943	Work animals displaced per farm tractor
	Acres	*Acres*	*Number*	*Number*	*Number*
Corn Belt*	237	152	1.25	3.1	3.4
Southeast†	381	143	1.18	4.1	2.1
Delta states‡	600	309	1.80	10.5	5.8
Oklahoma-Texas	894	294	1.31	3.8	8.6
United States	522	202	1.27	3.8	4.4

* Ohio, Indiana, Illinois, Iowa; and Missouri.
† Virginia, North Carolina, South Carolina, Georgia, Florida, and Alabama.
‡ Mississippi, Arkansas, and Louisiana.

[6] U. S. Dept. of Agri., Misc. Pub. No. 630, October, 1947, pp. 33-36.

[7] "It was assumed that if there were no tractors the work stock needed in each State group would be the same per 100 acres of cropland as was reported for horse or mule farms. From the calculated number of needed work animals on tractor farms the actual number of workstock on tractor farms

been very large in the Delta states and Oklahoma and Texas but comparatively small in the Southeast states. However, in view of the tendency for farms to become more extensive after tractors are introduced,[8] it is apparent that their method overestimates the number of work animals displaced per tractor. Even their calculations show a ratio of displacement for the Southeast below that possible on technical grounds.[9]

EFFECT OF LAND CONSERVATION

A dynamic force of tremendous importance in remaking the Cotton Belt's agriculture has been the effect of better land use on crop yields. The heavy reduction in acreage of cotton and other soil-depleting crops permitted production on higher quality lands and the practice of some sort of a rotation system. It was no longer necessary to plant cotton on the same land year after year. A rotation with grain and some leguminous hay crop, often Lespedeza, gives the land a rest and improves its physical condition and fertility for the cotton crop.

The effect of the conservation program on land use, acreage of crops, yields and production, and change in livestock is shown in Table 30. These data have been compiled by the Soil Conservation Service, U. S. Department of Agriculture, from records of nearly 5,000 cooperating farms in the soil conservation districts in the different regions of the Cotton Belt. It is seen that idle land was almost entirely eliminated on these cooperating farms in all regions, and pasture land increased by nearly 50 per cent in

---

was deducted and this figure divided by the average number of tractors gives the work animals displaced per tractor." Quoted from U. S. Dept. of Agri., Misc. Pub. No. 630, p. 34.

[8] Greene and others of the North Carolina Agricultural Experiment Station have found that farmers using tractor power had a lower percentage of cropland in row crops and a higher percentage in grains than those using animal power. Cited by G. W. Forster, in "Impact of Technology on Southern Agriculture," *Journal of Farm Economics*, XXIX (May, 1947), p. 524.

[9] B. T. Lanham, Jr., of the Alabama Agricultural Experiment Station, found in a study of power and equipment costs in Northern Alabama that each tractor displaced an average of 4.5 work animals, but on the basis of work performed in 1945 each tractor should have displaced 5.0 work animals. The actual displacement is therefore less by 0.5 work animals than that technically possible. See Bul. 260, p. 6, of the Ala. Agri. Expt. Station, Auburn, Ala., March, 1947.

Other Influences on Southern Agriculture 145

the Eastern and Delta states. The acreage of both cotton and corn was reduced, but the increase in yield of each crop was sufficient to cause an absolute increase in the production of both crops in all regions.

Increases in acreage of hays of 40 to 75 per cent in the Eastern and Delta states and from 4 to 45 per cent in Oklahoma and Texas, coupled with an increase in pasture land, left considerable latitude for the development of livestock farming. This is shown by the fact that the largest increase in livestock occurred in the regions (Eastern and

TABLE 30
EFFECT OF SOIL CONSERVATION ON LAND USE, YIELDS, PRODUCTION, AND LIVESTOCK ON COOPERATING FARMS IN THE DIFFERENT REGIONS OF THE COTTON BELT
(based on 4,934 farms)

Item	Percentage change*			
	Eastern states	Delta states	Oklahoma and Texas	10 cotton states
Land use change:				
Idle land	−88	−98	−89	−92
Grazing land	44	56	6	11
Cropland	2	− 2	− 7	− 4
Acreage change:				
Cotton	−24	−16	−20	−20
Corn	−26	−14	− 5	−15
Wheat	21	−39	−14	−13
Legume hay	70	75	45	68
Nonlegume hay	40	47	4	12
Yield increase:				
Cotton	40	41	25	33
Corn	46	45	28	39
Wheat	36	22	46	46
Production increase:				
Cotton	6	18	1	7
Corn	7	24	21	18
Wheat	64	−26	26	28
Livestock increase:				
Dairy cattle	44	44	33	38
Beef cattle	126	127	23	60
Brood sows	94	39	55	61
Chickens	78	49	49	55

* The minus shows a decrease.
Source: *Cotton*, Hearings before the Subcommittee of the Committee on Agriculture, House of Representatives, Seventy-Eighth Congress, Second Session, Dec. 4 to 9, 1944, pp. 405-8.

Delta states)[10] which also had the largest percentage increase in pasture land and hay acreage.

Beginning with the Agricultural Adjustment Act of 1938, the national agricultural programs have to a considerable extent been based upon the conservation approach. Incentive payments were made to farmers to encourage them to increase seeding of leguminous crops, lime and superphosphate applications, terracing, etc. This program reached all classes of farmers. That they benefited is shown by the fact that cotton yields increased 17 per cent from 1933-39 to 1940-46 in the Eastern states and Delta states, and 11 per cent in Oklahoma and Texas. These increases are less than one-half those obtained by farmers who were in a cooperative program with the Soil Conservation Service (see Table 30), but the increases are significant and help to explain why cotton production has been maintained at a comparatively high level despite the large decrease in acreage harvested.

It is apparent that a class, a large group, of farmers have been reached by the A.A.A. program who were never touched by the Extension Service and other agricultural informational services. Through the A.A.A. incentive programs, they have been encouraged to try some of the simpler recommendations of the experiment stations. They have gotten results, as shown by the production figures, and the chances are that this new knowledge has become somewhat habitual with this class of farmer; and irrespective of what happens to the A.A.A. program in the future it is expected that the residual effects will continue to influence Southern agriculture for many years.

SUMMARY

Three of the dynamic forces considered in this chapter are the introduction of farm machinery, change in type of farms, and displacement of men and workstock. The sequence of events in the chain of cause and effect are considered to run from the increase in number of tractors on farms, to the increase in number of non-cotton farms, to the decrease in cotton farms and number of workstock, to the

[10] Cf. Chap. II, pp. 31-36.

decrease in farm population. During the period 1920 to 1945 the following relationships were evident:

1. An increase of one tractor was *associated* with an increase of 2.5 non-cotton farms in the Eastern states, 1.3 in the Delta states, and 3/4 of a non-cotton farm in Oklahoma and Texas.[11]

2. An increase in one non-cotton farm was associated with a decrease of 1.7 cotton farms in the Eastern states, 2.2 cotton farms in the Delta, and 2.0 cotton farms in Oklahoma and Texas.

3. A decrease of one cotton farm was associated with a decrease of about four farm persons in Oklahoma and Texas and the Delta states, and with 3.5 farm persons in the Eastern states. During a long period, 1925 to 1940, only small changes occurred in farm population; however, from 1940 to 1945 a rapid decline occurred, which released much population pressure that had developed as a result of fundamental changes occurring in the Cotton Belt's agriculture—mainly, reduced cotton acreage and increased mechanization. The regression line, therefore, is based on a series of observations that are closely clustered and one observation (1945), which largely gives the slope to the line. The degree of reliability is, therefore, low.

4. A decrease of one cotton farm was associated with a decrease of 1.8 workstock in the Eastern states, one in the Delta states, and 5.4 in Oklahoma and Texas.

5. The decrease in cotton farms was accompanied by a decrease in acreage per farm in all regions after 1929 but an increase in the production of cotton per farm. The result is a great increase in efficiency of production of cotton and a better balanced farm organization, permitted by the acreage made available for other crops.

Another dynamic force of great effect has been the conservation programs. Records kept on about 5,000 cooperating farms by the Soil Conservation Service indicate that idle land was practically eliminated and pasture increased. Soil-depleting crops were decreased but the very large in-

---

[11] Cf. pp. 72-74. The increase in tractors in the latter region was more closely connected with mechanization of cotton farms than in the other two regions.

crease in yields caused an increase in production. The increase in hays and pasture land resulted in very large increases in livestock in all regions, the largest changes occurring in the Eastern and Delta states.

While the average increase in yields of all farmers who were touched by the A.A.A. conservation programs was not as large as that achieved by the farmers cooperating with the Soil Conservation Service, the increase in cotton yields from 1933-39 to 1940-46 is very significant because it shows that there is a method (incentive payments of A.A.A.) by which the mass of farmers can be, and were, encouraged to improve their farming, which they are unable or do not have the vision to do alone. It is believed that the good work done by the A.A.A. in establishing habits of production among the general run of farmers may continue for a long time to maintain Southern agriculture at its present level, in part at least, in better farm practices.

CHAPTER VIII

Income Shifts

FARM INCOME

THE FINAL MEASURE of whether the shifts from cotton to other crops, to more livestock, to fewer cotton farms and more other farms, to larger farms and more mechanization, and to fewer farm people on farms have been beneficial is the effect on farm income. This is shown in the following tabulation:

Average for	Index of prices received by farmers (1910-14 = 100)	Cash farm receipts (million dollars)	
		10 cotton states	38 other states
1924-29................	148	$2,589	$ 8,228
1935-39................	107	1,766	6,207
1941-45................	174	3,658	13,709
1947...................	278	6,378	23,808
Percentage increase:			
1924-29 to 1941-45......	18	41	67
1935-39 to 1941-45......	63	107	121
1924-29 to 1947.........	88	146	189

Source: Compiled from *The Farm Income Situation*, various issues; *Cotton*, Hearings before the Subcommittee of the Committee on Agriculture, House of Representatives, Seventy-Eighth Congress, Second Session, Dec. 4 and 9, 1944, pp. 600-607; *Agricultural Statistics, 1944*, and *The Agricultural Situation*.

The tabulation indicates that the average cash farm receipts in the ten cotton states during the period 1941-45 was 41 per cent above the 1924-29 level and 107 per cent above the 1935-39 level, while cash farm receipts in 1947 were 146 per cent above those in 1924-29. But the relative changes are less than those which occurred in the thirty-eight other states, which indicates that farm income improved more rapidly outside the cotton states during the period. Since the increase in farm prices was from 44 to 60 per cent of the changes in income between all periods in the ten cotton states, the change in farm balance and increase in volume of production, but more particularly volume,[1] were importantly associated with the income increases.

Table 31 shows that the yearly average per capita cash farm receipts in the period 1941-45 varied from $252 in the Eastern states to $547 in Oklahoma and Texas, representing increases in all three regions that varied from 58 to 76 per cent from 1924-29 to 1941-45 and from 119 to 169 per cent from 1935-39 to 1941-45. In 1947 per capita cash farm receipts varied from $398 to $1,024, being from 156 to 208 per cent higher than the 1924-29 average. Considering the ten cotton states together, it is found that per capita cash receipts increased 64 per cent from 1924-29 to 1941-45, 141 per cent from 1935-39 to 1941-45, and 174 per cent from 1924-29 to 1947. Remarkable as these increases were, they were less than occurred in the thirty-eight other states, which exceeded all regions of the Cotton Belt, except Oklahoma and Texas from 1935-39 to 1941-45, both in absolute and relative increases between all three periods. During the three periods and 1947 the Eastern and Delta states received from 26 to 35 per cent as much per capita farm income as the thirty-eight other states, and Oklahoma and Texas from 58 to 70 per cent as much. From 1935-39 to 1947 by periods, the Eastern and Delta states lost ground in the ratio to the thirty-eight other states, while Oklahoma and Texas gained. In general, per capita cash receipts[2] were slightly higher in the Delta states than in the Eastern states, and from 90 to 157 per cent higher than either region in Oklahoma and Texas.

Certain interesting, and startling, contrasts may be drawn between government payments in the different regions. Average per capita government payments amounted to nearly 50 per cent more in the Delta states and around 150 per cent more in Oklahoma and Texas than in the Eastern states. Per capita figures for the thirty-eight other

---

[1] The Census South increased total volume of output 15 per cent from 1935-39 to 1941-45, while all other geographic divisions as an average increased total output 26 per cent. The percentage increases were computed by averaging the index numbers of farm output by divisions and years, from data given in *Agricultural Statistics, 1947*, p. 534.

[2] Excludes government payments.

Income Shifts

TABLE 31
AVERAGE YEARLY PER CAPITA CASH FARM RECEIPTS AND GOVERNMENT PAYMENTS BY PERIODS AND REGIONS

Type of receipt by periods	Eastern cotton states	Delta states	Oklahoma and Texas	10 cotton states	38 other states
Cash farm receipts					
1. Per capita					
1924-29	$143	$168	$ 333	$197	$ 474
1935-39	107	121	203	134	348
1941-45	252	265	547	323	860
1947*	398	430	1024	540	1517
2. Per cent increase in per capita cash farm receipts from:					
1924-29 to 1941-45	76	58	64	64	81
1935-39 to 1941-45	136	119	169	141	147
1924-29 to 1947	178	156	208	174	220
3. Per capita cash farm receipts as percentage of per capita cash farm receipts for 38 other states					
1924-29	30	35	70	42	100
1935-39	31	35	58	38	100
1941-45	29	31	64	38	100
1947	26	28	68	36	100
Government payments					
1. Per capita					
1935-39	$ 9.69	$13.99	$25.61	$14.66	$17.37
1941-45	11.46	16.86	28.48	16.74	32.38
1947	5.09	7.39	12.79	7.34	14.48
2. Per capita government payments as percentage of per capita government payments for 38 other states					
1935-39	56	81	147	84	100
1941-45	35	52	88	52	100
1947	35	51	88	51	100

* The average annual population for 1947 was estimated by applying percentage changes from 1940 to the Jan. 1; 1947 and 1948 average, for the South Atlantic, East South Central, and West South Central regions to the corresponding Cotton Belt regions.
Source: *Farm Population Estimates*, U. S. Dept. of Agri., Bur. of Agri. Econ., current issues; and official U. S. Dept. of Agri. estimates of farm income.

states illustrate a real inconsistency. For while the Cotton Belt states have a per capita farm income considerably lower than the rest of the United States, only three-tenths of it in the Eastern and Delta states and two-thirds in Oklahoma and Texas, the government payments were distributed more heavily outside the cotton states, about 20 per cent higher than the ten-state average during 1935-39, and nearly double it during 1941-45 and 1947. While some increase occurred in per capita government payments between 1935-39 and 1941-45 in the ten cotton states, less than 15 per cent, an increase of over 80 per cent occurred in the thirty-eight other states. However, because of a national agricultural policy of reduced agricultural subsidies and many other benefits in 1946 and 1947, per capita government payments declined over 50 per cent from 1941-45 to 1947. A large part of the payments during 1941-45 originated in connection with the subsidy programs to stimulate the production of certain scarce agricultural products during the war, and for that reason alone would be expected to be larger than during other periods; but it seems obvious that the agricultural benefit payments have not been, and are not being, made on the basis of need or disparities in farm income.

As to approximately how much of this improvement in per capita farm incomes in each region was due to farm price increases and to farm population decreases may be roughly estimated from the data in Table 32. In the Cotton Belt the relative percentage changes indicate that the price increases were from 20 to 30 per cent of the increases in cash receipts from 1924-29 to 1941-45, from 40 to 50 per cent from 1935-39 to 1941-45, and from 40 to 55 per cent of the increases from 1924-29 to 1947. Farm population decreases were from 15 to 35 per cent of the increases in cash receipts from 1924-29 to 1941-45; about 10 per cent from 1935-39 to 1941-45; and from 3 to 10 per cent of the increases from 1924-29 to 1947. It appears, therefore, that price increases were more highly associated with the increases in per capita cash farm receipts by a wider margin than population decreases, and price increases and population decreases combined probably were associated with between one-half and two-thirds of the increases in per capita cash farm receipts. Consequently, it appears that the other shifts, affecting volume of product per capita primarily (decrease in cotton acreage and increase in other crops, increase in livestock and livestock products, increase in size of farms, etc.) considered compositely have been at least

TABLE 32
RELATION OF PERCENTAGE CHANGES IN FARM PRICE AND FARM POPULATION TO PERCENTAGE INCREASES IN PER CAPITA CASH FARM RECEIPTS BY PERIODS AND REGIONS

Item	Eastern cotton states	Delta states	Oklahoma and Texas	10 cotton states	38 other states
Percentage change:					
1924-29 to 1941-45:					
Farm price*................	18	18	18	18	18
Farm population...........	−11†	− 9	−23	−14	− 8
Per capita cash farm receipts.	76	58	64	64	81
1935-39 to 1941-45:					
Farm price................	63	63	63	63	63
Farm population...........	−12	−12	−20	−14	−11
Per capita cash farm receipts.	136	119	169	141	147
1924-29 to 1947:					
Farm price................	88	88	88	88	88
Farm population‡..........	− 5	− 5	−24	−10	−10
Per capita cash farm receipts.	178	156	208	174	220

* Based on the BAE index number of the price of all farm products (1910-14=100) for the United States.
† The minus sign denotes a decrease.
‡ See Table 31 for description of method employed in estimating farm population for 1947 by Cotton Belt regions.
Source: Changes in farm population and per capita cash farm receipts were computed from data in Table 31; percentage increases in farm prices were computed from basic data found in various issues of *Agricultural Statistics*.

one-half as important in raising per capita farm cash receipts as changes in farm prices and farm population.

In the thirty-eight other states, on the basis of data in Table 32, a greater absolute and relative increase in per capita cash farm receipts occurred between all periods than in the ten cotton states; this despite a much smaller farm population decrease outside the ten cotton states between all periods except the last—40 per cent less from 1924-29 to 1941-45, 20 per cent less from 1935-39 to 1941-45, and an equal decrease from 1924-29 to 1947. Accordingly, the changes were associated with population and price changes by probably less than 50 per cent, and the forces producing a better farm balance and a more prosperous agriculture otherwise, and consequently a greater volume of output per capita, were evidently operating more strongly elsewhere in the United States than in the Cotton Belt. It was claimed above that improved balance in the Cotton Belt's agriculture (reduced cotton acreage, increased acreages of other crops, increased livestock and livestock products, and increased size of farms and mechanization) contributed importantly. These same forces are also at work in the thirty-eight other states, particularly size of farms, mechanization, and greater production of the higher-priced products which due to inflated city incomes readily found outlets during the war years and are finding them at present.

The improvements in Southern agriculture which we have been studying—increase in size of farm, more mechanization, decrease in number of farm people, and various technological gains—are reflected in changes in farm efficiency, which in turn have a bearing on the trend in per capita farm income and shifts in per capita farm income between regions. In order to relate these improvements directly to per capita income changes, some measure of the output per worker in agriculture by regions is needed. Unfortunately, such data are not available for the Cotton Belt subdivisions employed in this discussion. The nearest comparable data available are by geographic divisions.[3] These do not afford a good comparison, as discussed previously in other connections, but they do enable us to determine roughly some of the important trends and relationships. It would be preferable to compute such an index of output per worker for the geographic areas under discussion, but it would be time-consuming, and much too expensive for the scope of this study.

In Figure 24 are shown index numbers of output per worker in agriculture by geographic divisions since 1919. It is seen that in 1946 the average worker was producing vastly more than the average worker in 1919, twenty-seven years before. The increase in productivity per worker from 1919-23 to 1942-46 was 43 per cent for the United States as a whole, but varied from 20 per cent in the Middle Atlantic division and 25 per cent in the West South Central division (comparable to Oklahoma and Texas) to 64 per cent in the South Atlantic division and 61 per cent in the Pacific division. Thus it is seen that the South Atlantic

[3] S. E. Johnson, *Changes in Farming*, p. 107.

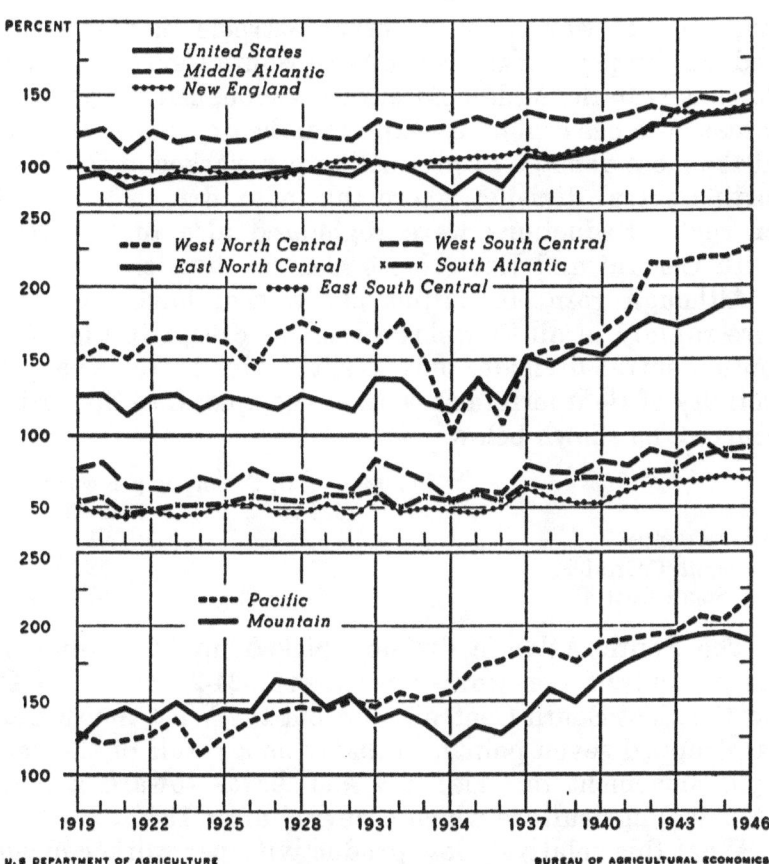

FIGURE 24. TRENDS IN GROSS FARM PRODUCTION PER WORKER BY GEOGRAPHIC DIVISIONS, 1919-46

(Index numbers: U. S. 1935-39 average = 100)

During the period, farm production per worker was lowest in the Southern regions and highest in the Central and Western divisions, being in the ratio of almost 1 to 3 in recent years. Since 1919 all regions have shown improvement in gross output per worker; but the West South Central and Middle Atlantic divisions gained the least in this respect and the South Atlantic and Pacific divisions the most. High gains in efficiency have been registered also in the Mountain and New England divisions. The East North Central and West North Central divisions showed the highest gain in gross output per worker during the war years.

division made the greatest gain between the two periods, although exceeding the Pacific division only slightly in this respect; furthermore, the gain in the West South Central division (46 per cent) was the third largest of the nine divisions. However, at the other extreme in the rise in productivity per worker is the West South Central division which, next to the Middle Atlantic division, had the smallest increase (25 per cent). As expected, the dry years, 1934-36, did the most damage to production per worker in the West North Central division where the index dropped over 40 per cent. Reductions were registered also in the West South Central and East North Central divisions.

Although gains in output per worker have increased more rapidly in all Southern divisions except in the West South Central division, only a slight rise in relative productivity of Southern farm workers compared to the nation occurred, as shown below:

	Per cent of U. S. output per worker	
	1924-29	1941-45
South Atlantic	58	61
East South Central	51	52
West South Central	74	67

The South Atlantic division picked up two points in relative output per worker between 1924-29 and 1941-45, and the East South Central, one; but the West South Central dropped seven points, probably as a result of the very rapid movement in Oklahoma and Texas toward a more extensive[4] agriculture which occurred after 1930.

What this relatively low productivity per worker means for per capita farm incomes on Southern farms is obvious. With only one-half to two-thirds as much production per worker, it is apparent that per capita incomes are doomed to a disparity with other farming regions. As a matter of fact, as shown in Table 33, the Southern divisions had in 1941-45 from three-tenths to four-tenths as much output per worker as in the West North Central and Pacific divisions, and from four-tenths to five-tenths that in the Mountain and East North Central divisions. These differences go a long way toward explaining why per capita cash farm receipts in 1947 were less than three-tenths of that of 38 other states in the Eastern and Delta cotton states and two thirds as much in Oklahoma and Texas. From this discussion it should not be inferred, however, that the South-

[4] Cf. Chap. III, pp. 47-50.

ern farm gains referred to in preceding pages have not been important—far from it—but it does appear that they have done no more than keep the farm income disparity between Southern agriculture and the rest of the country from becoming much greater.[5] The increases in size of farms, mechanization, loss of farm population, and improved yields, etc., have also been vital to maintaining the spirit of progress in the Cotton Belt, and will perhaps form the basis for the advances needed to bring the regions to the desired parity with other regions.

TABLE 33

COMPARISON OF INDEX NUMBERS OF GROSS PRODUCTION PER WORKER IN SPECIFIED GEOGRAPHIC DIVISIONS OF THE UNITED STATES WITH SOUTHERN DIVISIONS FOR PERIOD 1941-45

Geographic divisions	Average 1941-45 index of production per worker (U. S. 1935-1939 = 100)	Southern divisions as a percentage of specified geographic divisions			
		South Atlantic	East South Central	West South Central	Percentage range for Southern divisions
United States.............	*129*	*61*	*52*	*67*	*52-67*
New England...........	130	61	51	66	51-66
Middle Atlantic.........	141	56	47	61	47-61
East North Central......	177	45	38	49	38-49
West North Central......	210	38	32	41	32-41
Mountain...............	188	42	36	46	36-46
Pacific.................	198	40	34	44	34-44
Southern Divisions:					
South Atlantic..........	79	100	85	109	.....
East South Central......	67	118	100	129	.....
West South Central.....	86	91	78	100	.....

Source: Computed from annual data supplied through the courtesy of the Bureau of Agricultural Economics.

TOTAL INCOME

Since agriculture interdependently with industry and other segments of the national economy is affected importantly by general business conditions, it can neither be analyzed efficiently nor accurately in isolation. The interplay of forces and the interactions of the segments on each other make it imperative that agriculture as an industry be

[5] However, the Eastern and Delta states have lost some ground since 1935-39 in this regard relative to the rest of the United States; Oklahoma and Texas have gained since then but were, even in 1947, below agriculture outside the Cotton Belt. See Table 31.

studied in conjunction with the national economy, the whole of which it is a part.

One of the best indicators of general economic conditions is national income. From 1939 to 1946 national income increased 105.7 billion dollars, or 146 per cent. The 1946 national income was over twice that of 1929. In fact the increase alone in national income from 1939 to 1946 was 1.2 times the 1929 figure.[6]

Since farm income is a component part of national income it is directly affected by the magnitude of the latter; although most segments of farm income often increase proportionately more than national income, and vice versa. Economists have in recent years considered that national income determines farm income and not the other way around. This undoubtedly holds a high measure of truth because of the direct dependence of high prices in agriculture on a high level of consumer demand, which is in turn dependent on a high national income.[7]

Black, et al., in their book, *Farm Management*, show that the correlation between gross national income and gross agricultural income is $+.956$.[8] According to the regression line which they fit, a billion dollar increase in national income is associated with an increase in gross agricultural income of about 100 million dollars. Calculations for the ten Cotton Belt states for the period 1935-45 indicate that a billion dollar change in national income was associated with about a 13.5 million dollar increase in farm income, or nearly one-seventh the effect on the nation's agriculture as a whole.

It has been shown above that while farm income increased rather sharply in the ten cotton states, the improvement has been less in cash farm receipts both in the percentage increase and in the actual amount of increase than in the thirty-eight other states. Increases in per

[6] *National Income Supplement to Survey of Current Business*, July, 1947, p. 19.

[7] But for a discussion of how changes in agricultural income might cause fluctuations in industrial activity, followed by some unemployment, and then by a reduction in national income, see Chap. IX, pp. 180-81.

[8] John D. Black, et al., *Farm Management* (New York: The Macmillan Co., 1947), pp. 1040-41.

capita cash farm receipts have likewise been less in the Cotton Belt. But how do the cotton states stack up with the rest of the United States in changes in the general, or over-all, per capita income? Table 34 gives per capita incomes by regions and for the rest of the country for selected years from 1929 to 1946. Comparisons of changes are shown for three periods: 1929 to 1946, 1939 to 1946, and 1933 to 1946; and while the actual increases in per capita incomes for the rest of the nation exceeded those for the ten cotton states, or either of its three subregions, during all three periods, the *percentage* increases were higher in the Cotton Belt regions, being in fact from 20 to 120 per cent greater.

TABLE 34

COMPARISON OF PER CAPITA INCOME PAYMENTS IN REGIONS OF THE COTTON BELT WITH THAT OF THE REST OF THE UNITED STATES,* SELECTED YEARS, 1929 TO 1946

Year	Cotton regions by states			10 Cotton Belt states	Rest of the United States*
	Eastern states	Delta states	Oklahoma-Texas		
1929	$312	$332	$461	$361	$ 769
1933	187	170	249	202	416
1939	183	270	385	311	606
1940	302	274	398	324	648
1941	385	353	476	405	778
1942	505	472	647	540	967
1945	774	691	944	807	1280
1946	802	691	936	819	1319
Increase in per capita income:					
1929 to 1946	$490	$359	$475	$458	$550
1939 to 1946	519	421	551	508	713
1933 to 1946	615	521	687	617	903
Percentage increase in per capita income:					
1929 to 1946	157	108	103	127	72
1939 to 1946	183	156	143	163	118
1933 to 1946	329	306	276	305	217

* In agricultural comparisons heretofore the term "38 other states" was sufficiently accurate because the District of Columbia is of no significance, but in general comparisons with population and incomes it is of sufficient importance to be included with "the 38 other states." It has been thus handled in the discussion which follows in the next few pages.

Source: Computed from population and income data obtained from current issues of *Population Estimates;* Bureau of the Census, and from *Survey of Current Business*, August, 1947, U. S. Dept. of Commerce.

Figure 25 shows per capita incomes of the different regions expressed as a percentage of per capita income for the thirty-eight other states plus the District of Columbia. Several important tendencies are apparent from the graphed lines. First, per capita incomes in all three regions have risen relative to that of the rest of the nation. Second, the Eastern states began the relative rise from 1933, the Delta states from 1934, and Oklahoma and Texas from 1937. Third, the Eastern cotton states made the largest relative increase in per capita income of the three regions. But fourth and finally, despite the comparatively large gains

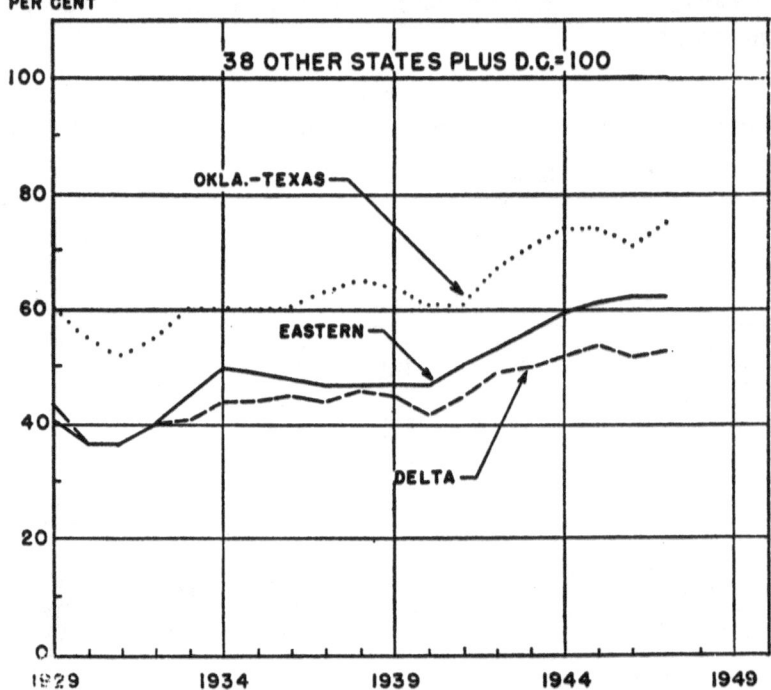

FIGURE 25. PER CAPITA INCOMES OF THE EASTERN, DELTA, AND OKLAHOMA-TEXAS COTTON PRODUCING REGIONS EXPRESSED AS A PERCENTAGE OF PER CAPITA INCOME OF THE 38 OTHER STATES PLUS THE DISTRICT OF COLUMBIA, 1929-47

Since 1929 all three cotton regions have gained in per capita income relative to the rest of the United States but the relative gain in the Eastern cotton states was greater and more consistent than in the other two cotton regions, although Oklahoma and Texas continue to show the highest ratio to the per capita income of the rest of the nation.

which have occurred in the per capita incomes of the three regions, they are still far short of a parity with the rest of the United States. This is especially true of the Eastern states and the Delta states, which in 1947 had 61 and 53 per cent respectively of the per capita income of the thirty-eight other states plus the District of Columbia. Oklahoma and Texas were compositely somewhat better in this regard with 75 per cent.

The extent of the disparity between total income payments and total population in various regions of the Cotton Belt, relative to the rest of the United States, is shown in Figure 26. The Eastern cotton states with about 14 per cent as many people received during the period (1929 to 1947) from 6 to 8 per cent as much total income as the thirty-eight other states and the District of Columbia; relative income showed a very sharp rise after 1940 and relative population an almost equally sharp drop after 1942, although the tendency prior to this date was for population to increase more rapidly than in the thirty-eight other states and the District of Columbia. In the Delta states, in contrast, the gains to the region's economy from relative income increase and relative population decrease were much less perceptible. The income rise after 1940 relative to the thirty-eight other states and the District of Columbia was not nearly so rapid as in the Eastern states, being more of a continuation of the trend which began in 1932. Population, likewise, continued to increase more rapidly than in the thirty-eight other states and the District of Columbia until 1943, after which it lost ground relatively, declining more in this sense than the Eastern cotton states.

In Oklahoma and Texas, however, no change in the position of population compared to the thirty-eight other states plus the District of Columbia occurred until 1943 and 1944, after which a moderate decline relative to the rest of the nation is detectable. The relative change in total income was intermediate between the comparatively large gain in the Eastern states and the comparatively low gain in the Delta states. From 1929 to 1936 the Oklahoma-Texas region barely improved its position[9] in total income

---

[9] The greatest improvement by far has occurred in Texas.

162   *Agricultural Progress in the Cotton Belt*

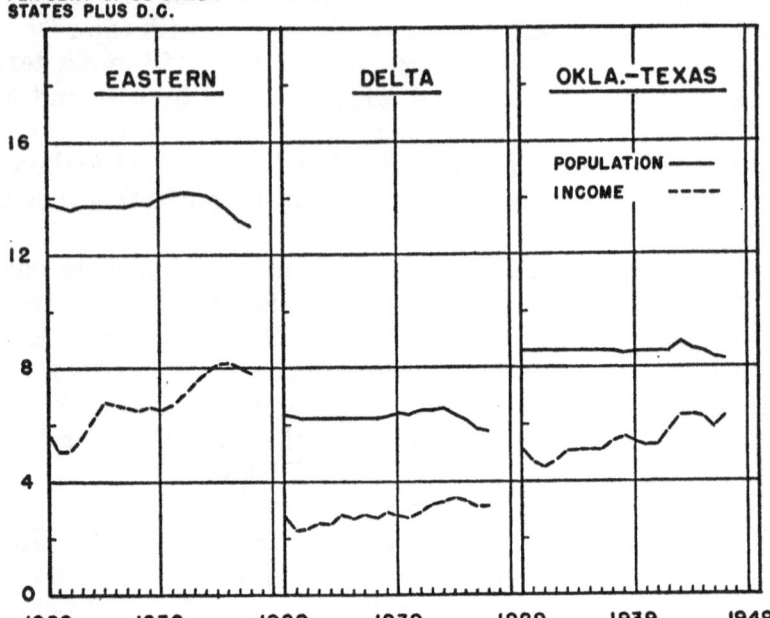

FIGURE 26. TOTAL POPULATION AND TOTAL INCOME PAYMENTS IN DIFFERENT REGIONS OF THE COTTON BELT EXPRESSED AS PERCENTAGES OF 38 OTHER STATES PLUS THE DISTRICT OF COLUMBIA, 1929 TO 1947

Income payments are generally around 40 per cent as great comparatively as total population in the Delta, 45 per cent in the Eastern states, and 60 per cent in Oklahoma and Texas. All regions maintained a stable population relative to the rest of the country until 1938 when gains occurred in the Eastern cotton states to 1942, in the Delta states to 1943, and Oklahoma and Texas in 1943 only. After 1942 in the Eastern cotton states and 1943 in the other two regions the respective population ratios declined to the lowest point for the period.

relative to the thirty-eight other states and the District of Columbia, gaining less in this period than either of the other two cotton regions. Although some gains were registered between 1936 and 1941, they were greatest from 1941 to 1944. Throughout the nineteen-year period, however, this region appears to have ranked second, next to the Eastern cotton states, in total income gain relative to the rest of the country.

The more sustained and greater relative gain in income of the Eastern cotton states is undoubtedly associated with the higher degree of industrialization and better balanced economy found in this region. The T.V.A. has been a factor in accelerating industrialization in these states.[10] Also, war demand for textiles, which industry looms very large in the industrial economy of the region, was undoubtedly an important factor in the relatively greater gain in the region's total income. Some part of the comparatively greater gain in total income experienced during the war years by the three regions relative to the rest of the United States is due to very large government payments going to military personnel and Federal civilian employees resident in these states,[11] which force was of sufficient strength in the income flow to more than overcome the comparatively fewer contracts for war supplies in the Southeast[12] and Southwest.[13] The two regions did, however, obtain a higher percentage of the war facilities but in total cost these were minor compared to the supply contracts.[14] Another factor contributing to the gain in income in excess of the trend rate during the war was the improvement in Southern wage differentials. For seven major industries (covered by state unemployment compensation) average wages rose from $1,016 in 1939 to $1,798 in 1944, an increase of 77 per cent; in the country as a whole the rise was from $1,360 in 1939 to $2,302 in 1944, or an increase of 69 per cent.[15] Hence, the average worker in the South gained in wages relatively but not absolutely during the period.

So far as the postwar period is concerned, it appears that in 1947 as in 1946, the South's income, although reflecting the tendency of national income to increase, failed to make as rapid relative gain as the country as a whole. This means that the slump in position from 1945 to 1946, shown in Figure 26, apparently more or less continued in

[10] *A Study of Agricultural and Economic Problems of the Cotton Belt*, p. 687.

[11] *Labor in the South*, U. S. Dept. of Labor, Bur. of Labor Statistics, Bul. No. 898, 1947, p. 55.

[12] Alabama, Arkansas, Florida, Georgia, Kentucky, Louisiana, Mississippi, North Carolina, South Carolina, Tennessee, and Virginia.

[13] Arizona, New Mexico, Oklahoma, and Texas.

[14] *State and Regional Market Indicators, 1939-1945*, U. S. Dept. of Commerce, Economic Series No. 60, pp. 28-30.

[15] *Labor in the South*, pp. 44-45.

1947. The smaller relative gain in income in 1946 and 1947 is due to the shrinkage in government payments,[16] most notably those going to military personnel, and to the shift in the structure of the region's industrial economy, which returned, to some extent, to the prewar low-wage industries.[17] During the period 1942 to 1945, war contracts, limited though they were, tended to skew the industrial distribution somewhat toward the higher wage-earning industries, such as iron and steel, transportation and equipment, and other durable types of industries, but these gains were to a considerable extent lost in the early postwar period.[18] However, Schwartz and Graham, writing in August, 1948, *Survey of Current Business,* state that "it is not particularly significant, therefore, that income payments rose at less-than-average rates from 1944 to 1947 in the far West, Southeast, and Southwest. Over the 1940-44 period, when the upsurge of total income in these regions far outpaced the national average the stimulus to income growth provided by the war was greatest in these areas. Hence, the impact of readjustment from war to peace on the income flows of the far West, Southeast, and Southwest was comparatively severe.

"What is significant, however, and of striking importance, is that income expanded in each of these regions after the end of the war at a rate not far below that of the country as a whole. Since 1944 the far West, Southeast, and Southwest have retained and carried into the second full postwar year most of the substantial relative gains in total income which they achieved during the war.... The fact that after the war the far West, Southeast, and Southwest retained most of their war-period relative income gains is evidence of considerable strength in their postwar income flows. This strength contributed materially to these regions' long-term upward income trends."[19]

So much for the South's relative income gains in the war and postwar periods. These were by and large super-

[16] *Survey of Current Business,* U. S. Dept. of Commerce, August, 1948, p. 12.
[17] *Labor in the South,* p. 29.
[18] *Ibid.*
[19] *Survey of Current Business,* August, 1948, pp. 16-17.

imposed on the long-period trends. The extent to which these gains persist will determine their contribution to the long-term gain in the South's[20] income position, which is related to the gradual changing character of the Southern economy. The fundamental change in it is the trend toward more industrial and less agricultural employment. According to a recent U. S. Department of Labor Report, "industrialization . . . has increased significantly. In 1880, less than 8 per cent of the wage earners employed in manufacturing in the United States were in the 13 Southern states. By 1939 this percentage had risen to 17.2. Moreover, while the absolute level of factory employment declined sharply in the country as a whole between 1929 and 1939, there was a small increase in the level of manufacturing employment in the southern region."[21] Although manufacturing employment increased sharply during the war years, the gains were for the most part in war-induced industries which were temporary and did not contribute to the permanent industrial gains of the region.[22] However, the employment growth which has occurred since the war through expansion of established industries and newly located industries has contributed permanently not only to the South's industrial growth but also to its industrial pattern. During the war the South's proportion of workers increased significantly in the manufacture of the following durable products: iron and steel and their products, electrical machinery, non-electrical machinery, transportation equipment (except automobiles), automobiles, non-ferrous metals and their products; and in the following high-wage non-durable products: chemicals and allied products, and rubber products. All of these industries had employment in 1946 greatly above prewar levels, except iron and steel and their products, whose importance in the postwar contraction cannot be minimized, since it is the largest durable industry group. Consequently, the South's industry has become more diversified and favorable not only for a higher

[20] Alabama, Florida, Georgia, Mississippi, North Carolina, South Carolina, Tennessee, Virginia, Kentucky, Arkansas, Louisiana, Oklahoma, and Texas.
[21] *Labor in the South*, p. 2.
[22] *Ibid.*, pp. 28-29.

level of income but also somewhat less vulnerable to economic disturbances.

That the South has made even more rapid progress toward industrialization since 1946 is supported by an Associated Press digest of government and private research reports in the *Richmond Times-Dispatch*, September 5, 1948.[23] Extracts from this highly informative digest follow:

"Government reports and private surveys indicate that the industry of New England and the Middle Atlantic states is no longer growing so fast as it once did. But in the Southeast, Texas and California new factories are being built at an ever increasing rate.

". . . industry is spreading out into less developed areas . . . chiefly to be closer to the source of supplies, closer to markets, to be in regions where labor and other costs are cheaper."

More specifically the digest (from a study by the Territorial Information Department, Chicago) shows, for the period May, 1945, to October, 1947, that while the Southeast had only 14 per cent of all government-financed plant construction during the war, its share had increased to 19 per cent of all construction in the nation by October, 1947, a relative gain in position of over a third in the first twenty-nine months after the war.[24]

Further excerpts indicate that "The Southwest's share jumped from 8 per cent during the war to 15 per cent since V-E Day. Texas was far ahead of any other State in the value of new plants constructed . . .

"New England got 5 per cent of government construction in war-time but since V-E Day has gotten only 3 per cent of the national industrial building.

"The Middle East had 22 per cent, dropped after the war to 19 per cent.

"The Central region had 33 per cent and fell to 30 per cent (yet still led all other regions)."[25]

Factors which have been important in shifting the industrial axis, according to the digest (based on a Commerce

[23] Page 8-B.
[24] *Richmond Times-Dispatch*, September 5, 1948, p. 8-B.
[25] *Loc. cit.*

Income Shifts

Department study) are, first, government-built plants were deliberately located inland in uncongested areas, which gave industry no choice of location when these plants were taken over; second, recent extensions of electric power lines; third, new pipe lines carrying natural gas; fourth, better highways; fifth, development of air freight; sixth, ironing out of freight rate differentials; and seventh, the development of semi-automatic machine tools, which have made industry less dependent on highly skilled labor.[26]

SUMMARY AND CONCLUSIONS

From 1935-39 to 1947 per capita cash farm receipts have improved in the ten cotton states but less rapidly than in the thirty-eight other states, although Oklahoma and Texas had a greater percentage increase from 1935-39 to 1941-45. Even though per capita cash receipts during 1941-45 were in the Eastern and Delta states less than a third, and in Oklahoma and Texas hardly two-thirds, of per capita cash receipts in the thirty-eight other states, average per capita government payments during the period were to the thirty-eight other states nearly three times those to the Eastern cotton states, twice those to the Delta states, and about 14 per cent more than those to Oklahoma and Texas. A large part of the differential in per capita cash farm receipts between the South and other geographic divisions is explained by differences in output per worker. During 1941-45 output per worker in the Southern geographic divisions was 50 to 60 per cent of the United States average and from 30 to 40 per cent of the productivity per worker in some of the leading agricultural regions.

In total income the ten cotton states gained relative to the rest of the United States from 1929 to 1946, although not absolutely. The Eastern cotton states showed the greatest relative gain and the Delta states the least, but both had a less rapid gain in total population from 1942 relative to the rest of the nation than did Oklahoma and Texas. During the war years the gains in total income were relatively inflated with respect to the long-time trends by the comparatively large government payments, most nota-

[26] *Loc. cit.*

bly to military personnel stationed in the Southern states, and by a relative rise in wages. But at the end of the war the shrinkage in military payments, which ordinarily would have had serious effects on Southern incomes relatively, was counteracted to a large extent by an increase in private income payments larger than for the country as a whole. So that while Southern income showed some relative loss in the postwar period, the underlying changes were healthy, being a continuation of those changes, more industrialization and more high-wage industries, both of which over the long pull have been important in the rise of income in the South relative to the rest of the country.

The conclusion is that the Cotton Belt has made progress in both the agricultural and non-agricultural aspects of its economy in recent years, but more rapidly and favorably in the latter.

Although farmers in the ten cotton states have made important strides in recent years toward a better balanced and more progressive agriculture, further progress must be made in raising yields, increasing the size of farms, and improving the efficiency of labor, and all at a much more rapid pace, if Southern agriculture is to pull abreast of agriculture elsewhere in the nation. But the real hope for Southern agricultural and Southern economic progress is in attaining such a balance in the general economy of the region, in the form of more industry and less agriculture, that full employment can be afforded locally for all excess farm population arising from high birth rates and from under-employment on farms.

CHAPTER IX

Summary and Conclusions

THE FACTS PRESENTED in the foregoing chapters make it apparent that the Cotton Belt's agriculture is currently more prosperous and in a more healthy condition than it has been in the last twenty-five years. The significant trends which brought about this condition began, by and large, about 1930. Cotton acreage began to decline after the peak acreage in 1926, was much accelerated during the depression, and rapidly adjusted to much lower levels during the A.A.A. programs from 1933 to date. The significant shifts from cotton to other crops, accompanied by increases in livestock and livestock products occurred primarily during the A.A.A. era of production control, 1933 to 1942, although there was considerable additional development in this direction during the war years.

Of prime significance is the shift in the constitution of the farm income stream which has changed radically during the last twenty years. Cotton and cottonseed as a source of gross farm income declined from 45 per cent of the total on the average in the six-year period, 1924-29, to 25 per cent on the average in the five-year period, 1941-45; and as a source of cash farm receipts, from 56 per cent in the former period to 30 per cent in the latter period. Thus cotton and cottonseed declined in emphasis nearly 45 per cent in the gross income stream and nearly one-half in cash farm receipts. The enterprise lost most emphasis between these two periods as a source of cash farm receipts in Oklahoma and Texas and least in the Delta states, losing nearly three-fifths of its position in the former, one-fourth in the latter, and nearly one-half in the Eastern cotton states.

The enterprises which gained in emphasis as cotton and cottonseed declined were tobacco, truck crops, peanuts, pecans, hogs, and chickens, all of which more than doubled in relative contribution to cash farm receipts from 1924-29 to 1941-45; and cattle and calves, dairy products, and eggs which increased in emphasis from 40 to 66 per cent. The enterprises which have been strongest in replacing cotton in the different regions are as follows:

Eastern cotton states: tobacco, truck crops, dairy products, hogs, peanuts, cattle and calves, eggs, and chickens.

Delta states: cattle and calves, rice, dairy products, hogs, chickens, and eggs.

Oklahoma and Texas: cattle and calves, dairy products, wheat, hogs, eggs, and truck crops.

FACTORS INFLUENCING PROGRESS

1. *The reduction in cotton acreage.* This made available large acreages for the production of feed crops and increased pasturage for livestock. The reduced cotton area also left wide choice for selecting the better lands for cotton production, thereby having an important bearing on crop rotations and yields, not only of cotton but of all crops.

2. *The increase in number of tractors.* The number of tractors on farms increased 264 per cent from 1930 to 1945, 82 per cent from 1940 to 1945, and there was a further increase of 42 per cent from January 1, 1945 to May 1, 1948. However, despite the comparatively large increase which occurred in the fifteen years ending in 1945, the region was still greatly in arrears of the rest of the country in relative numbers. In that year the ten cotton states had only 4.6 tractors per thousand acres of cropland harvested compared to 7.6 tractors per thousand acres harvested in the rest of the United States. Oklahoma and Texas had the most tractors per 1,000 acres of cropland harvested and the Eastern cotton states the least, although the latter showed the highest percentage increase in number of tractors on farms from 1940 to 1945.

Farmers are attracted to the purchase of a tractor by the possibilities of removing drudgery from farm work, by timeliness and flexibility in farm operations, etc. But in the case of a cotton farmer, inefficiency appears in the use of work animals, and difficulties with the customary (sharecropper) labor arrangements arise. Consequently work animals will be eliminated over time but sharecroppers even more quickly. When this latter occurs, in addition to eliminating one or more sharecropper units, the operator is likely to reduce sharply the cotton acreage or may eliminate it altogether. Therefore the tractor is a great force in reducing cotton acreage and cotton farms, especially in the Eastern cotton states. During the period 1920 to 1945 an increase of one tractor was associated with an increase of 2.5 non-cotton farms in the Eastern cotton states, 1.3 non-cotton farms in the Delta states, and 3/4 of a non-cotton farm in Oklahoma and Texas.

The increase in number of tractors affected farm balance in still another way. The work animals thus displaced saved feed, which permitted an additional increase in livestock and livestock products.

3. *The decline in tenancy.* The turning point in relative tenancy in the South was reached about 1930 and in total number of tenants around 1935. And the largest decrease by far occurred in sharecroppers, which began declining both absolutely and relatively about 1930. As pointed out above, tractors and sharecroppers do not go together because of inefficiency in labor use. Either the tractor or the sharecropper must go. If the latter goes, cotton acreage is also greatly curtailed; if the tractor remains, the farm organization is in for serious modification, as a rule.

The other force, in addition to tractors, which tends to reduce the number of sharecropper farms, is the upward trend in cotton yields in recent years which has resulted from a more complete and effective application of known technology. Under the conventional sharing arrangements in a system of sharecropper labor, any improvement in yield above that yield level which is just sufficient to return the cropper a current wage tends to cause the operator to shift to hired labor in order that he, the operator, may reap the benefit of the high land productivity.

Calculations for South Carolina show that the limit of

profitable use of sharecropper labor (compared to hired labor) is *about* 250 pounds of lint cotton per acre. Average yields in the state have been above this level since 1930, and this increased yield level has been operative in reducing the number of sharecroppers.

The yield limit of profitable use of sharecroppers will vary from state to state, depending upon hours of labor required per acre and conventions concerning sharecropper arrangements. However, the rapid improvement in cotton yields which has occurred in the Cotton Belt since the A.A.A. has undoubtedly carried many state average yields beyond the point where sharecroppers would be profitable.

From this argument it is seen that hours of labor required per acre in relation to yield per acre holds the answer to the employment of sharecropper labor. Consequently, any force which upsets this equilibrium influences this type of tenancy. The equilibrium may be destroyed either by changes in the technology of production, which raises yield, or by mechanization of the production operation, which reduces labor requirements per acre. In the latter case, tractors and other labor-saving devices have been and are playing their parts in reducing sharecropper units, and hence tenancy, in the Cotton Belt.

4. *The reduction in number of farms.* From 1930 to 1945 the number of cotton farms decreased 39 per cent but other types of farms increased 59 per cent, which resulted in a net reduction of 13 per cent in the number of all farms. These changes were associated with the increase in number of tractors and reduction in number of sharecropper units during the period.

The 13 per cent reduction in number of all farms, coupled with a 9 per cent increase in the land in farms, caused an average increase in farm size of 26 per cent in the ten cotton states, but a 12 per cent increase in the Eastern states, 34 per cent increase in the Delta states, and 42 per cent increase in Oklahoma and Texas.

In 1944 the average farm in Oklahoma and Texas exceeded the average farm in the other regions by four times in land area and three times in cropland harvested.

In all regions the acreage of intensive crops per farm

has been declining since 1929, giving way primarily to extensive crops. Medium intensive crops per farm showed some increase until 1939 but since have declined in the Eastern and Delta states. In 1944 the acreage of extensive crops per farm exceeded the acreage of intensive crops in the Eastern states by 1.5 acres per farm and were in a ratio of three to one in Oklahoma and Texas; however, in the Delta states the acreage of intensive crops per farm exceeded the acreage of extensive crops by nearly 2 acres as an average. In 1944 the acreage of medium intensive crops per farm was greater than that of either the extensive or the intensive crops in the Eastern and Delta states but was below the acreages of either extensive or intensive crops by a wide ratio in Oklahoma and Texas. In this latter region in 1944 the acreage of extensive crops per farm was four times the acreage of medium intensive crops and three times the acreage of intensive crops, and was 65 per cent greater than the acreage of both combined.

5. *The increase in yields, most notably in cotton production.* From 1925-29 to 1940-46 yield of cotton per acre harvested increased nearly one-fourth in Oklahoma and Texas, and one-half in the Eastern cotton states and Delta states. The improvement in cotton yield has been due to production on better lands (made possible by the acreage reduction program), improved seed, more adequate crop rotations, unusually favorable weather, and an increased rate of fertilizer application. Total fertilizer used in the ten cotton states increased 33 per cent from 1929 to 1944, with a further increase of 15 per cent from 1944 to 1948. In spite of the reduced acreage of cotton harvested per farm, total production per farm expanded from 1920 to 1944 at every census report except 1934, when very unfavorable weather prevailed. From 1927-31 to 1942-46 cotton farms became smaller in terms of cotton acreage harvested but larger in production, which means, if the trend persists, lower costs per unit of cotton produced and greater farm profitability due to the comparatively larger acreages in other enterprises.

6. *The soil conservation programs.* A dynamic factor of great import in remaking the Cotton Belt's agriculture

has been the conservation programs associated with the A.A.A. While the large acreage of cotton taken out of cultivation was perhaps the outstanding cause of improved farm balance, and higher yields (because of the improvement in land quality and production techniques) were next in importance, the conservation practices associated with the program made important contributions both in land management and improved yields. This is shown by records kept by the Soil Conservation Service on about 5,000 cooperating farms in the Southern states. Cotton yield increased 25 to 40 per cent; other crops showed large increases in yield. The net effect was an increase in production of all crops, even soil-depleting crops which had large acreage decreases. The indications are that the mass of farmers hardly got one-half of the yield increases which farmers who cooperated with the Soil Conservation Service obtained, primarily because the latter were better farmers. Additionally, the mass of farmers have formed conservation habits as a result of the A.A.A. program which are likely to have a carry-over effect for many years.

7. *The decline in farm population.* From 1940 to 1945 this decline was 28 per cent, 48 per cent of which was restored by the back-to-the-farm movement during 1945 and 1946; however, the farm-to-city migration was again resumed in 1947 at a rate greatly in excess of the 1930-39 rate and about equal to the 1920-29 rate. A reduction in farm population has been long advocated by agricultural economists as a means of reducing population pressure and increasing per capita farm incomes. The 1947 rate was sufficient to cause a small decline in farm population during the year, but most notably in the Eastern cotton states. For quick adjustment in Southern agriculture an even more rapid rate is needed. This is dependent on the rate of Southern industrialization, which since the war shows an increase over the prewar rate. Even without much pick-up in the rate of Southern industrialization, the current rate of migration from farms to the cities would be sufficient to maintain the recent net loss in farm population, while the continued growth of cities would bring the needed balance from another direction—in the form of increased demand

for farm products and expanded outlets for surplus farm population.

8. *Progress of urbanization.* From 1890 to 1940 total population in the ten cotton states increased from 13.9 million persons to 29.6 million, or 113 per cent. During the same period, however, urban population increased from 1.7 million persons to 10.0 million, or 488 per cent. Stated another way, one person in eight lived in an urban center in 1890 and one person in three in 1940. However, despite the rapid relative growth of urban population in the ten cotton states in the last fifty years, the region was about as urbanized in 1940 as the United States was in 1890. Even though the South falls far short of the rest of the country in urbanization, urban growth has been relatively more rapid in the last fifty years, and this has influenced the region in many beneficial ways. Most important, since urban centers fail to reproduce themselves, they afford, even to maintain a given urban population, an outlet for surplus farm population; and to promote urban growth, considerable absorption of outside population becomes necessary. This means that where a healthy urban growth is present a very large outlet exists for the surplus farm population locally, or at least in the region. During 1941-45, about 75 per cent of all types of migration was confined to the limits of the South, and 82 per cent from 1935 to 1940.

As to when population will be in balance (between urban and rural replacement rates) depends upon the trend in net reproduction rates. If the downward trend in net reproduction rates which occurred between 1905-10 and 1935-40 persists, the urban centers in the region should be of sufficient size around 1970 to absorb farm migration without further growth. At this date urban population would be about double the rural-farm population, and 70 per cent larger than the rural-nonfarm, if previous population trends can be reliably projected. As to whether this sort of balance in population would be good for the South depends upon the point of view. It would apparently provide a more ready and stable outlet for excess farm population than occurred when the excess farm population was dependent upon additional growth in city jobs and opportunities. It would also require a much higher proportion of the rural population to supply perishable products, including milk, eggs, fruits, and vegetables, thus permitting a reduction in cotton production and making for a much healthier regional economy. For the farmers transferring to the production of such articles, a better organized farm business, higher labor efficiency, and higher farm incomes would be the rewards. However, the balance in population here envisioned has its disadvantages also. In a mature economy, social and economic mobility is most difficult for the individual, and yet that is the kind of economy the region will probably have if population becomes balanced.

9. *Migration of farm population.* The tendency of farm population to reproduce at a rate greatly in excess of replacement needs, coupled with improvements in farm technology without a corresponding increase in demand for farm products, causes a surplus of population to develop which must find an escape. Without an outlet, the human element becomes superabundant relative to land and capital resources, and population pressure develops. Since 1900, and even before, Southern agriculture has found such an outlet in the cities within or outside the region. However, in the early years of the great depression there was a backwash and a rate of migration for the remainder of the 1930's too low to permit the reduction of farm population needed in the interest of efficiency. This is shown for the Census South by the following rates of net reproduction and net migration, respectively, in thousands: 1920-29, 318 and 382; 1930-39, 263 and 228; 1940-46, 239 and 424; and 1947, 283 and 338. Consequently, the rate of migration from 1920 to 1929 was 20 per cent in excess of the rate of net reproduction; 1930-39, 13 per cent deficit; 1940-46, 77 per cent excess; and 1947, 19 per cent excess. Thus a healthy farm population situation existed during the periods of 1920-29 and 1940-46, but an unhealthy one during 1930-39. The rate of excess migration during 1947 was about the same as existed during 1920-29, which, superimposed on the large farm population losses during the war,

should give the South a favorable farm population for some time even if the rate drops, but especially if there is no decline in the migration excess.

But farm-city migration is not without its harmful effects. Since the younger, more alert, and better-educated are attracted by city employment opportunities, a class of farmers ill-equipped to cope with modern farming is left on the land. The tendency for the young to migrate to cities and for the old to retire to farms, coupled with the aging of the population because of increased length of life, has caused over the last thirty years an unfavorable age distribution for continued high production capacity and efficiency in Southern agriculture. Further reduction in farm population is in the interest of increased scale and efficiency, but it seems unlikely that the age and educational classes now accumulating on farms will be capable of taking advantage of the situation in terms of recent mechanization advances. Migration should continue, but the alert and more capable should be attracted to remain on farms, or, if already gone, to return, thus enabling Southern agriculture to have fewer but larger farms equipped with appropriate machinery. A chief means of attracting the higher types to agriculture as a vocation may be found in making ownership easier. This would seem to indicate the necessity for substituting educational achievement for a large part of capital assets as security for long-term loans at low interest rates.

10. *Farm income changes.* The composite effect of the various shifts which occurred in the ten cotton states, including the improvement in general economic conditions, is reflected in the farm income changes. Total cash receipts during 1941-45 averaged 41 per cent above the 1924-29 level and 107 per cent above the 1935-39; per capita cash receipts in 1941-45 were 64 per cent above the 1924-29 average and 141 per cent above the 1935-39 average. During 1941-45, per capita cash receipts in Oklahoma and Texas averaged $547, twice that of the Delta states and over twice that of the Eastern states, but were $313 less, or 36 per cent lower, than the 38 other states.

From 1924-29 to 1941-45 and from 1935-39 to 1941-45,

the percentage increase in per capita cash receipts of the thirty-eight other states exceeded the increase in the ten cotton states as a whole, although the percentage increase of Oklahoma and Texas was greater from 1935-39 to 1941-45. Therefore, the farm income increase in the rest of the country was larger by a good margin, both absolutely and relatively, which means that, despite the recent agricultural progress in the Cotton Belt, more rapid gains were being made in the rest of the country.

Even though per capita cash farm receipts during 1941-45 were, in the Eastern and Delta states, less than a third, and in Oklahoma and Texas hardly two-thirds, of per capita cash receipts in the thirty-eight other states, average per capita government payments during the period were to the thirty-eight other states nearly three times those to the Eastern cotton states, twice those to the Delta states, and about 14 per cent more than those to Oklahoma and Texas. Consequently, it is apparent that government subsidy payments were not being dispensed according to income needs or to the income disparity between the states. The justification for making payments according to income need is obvious, but disbursements on some such basis would hardly be feasible politically.

From the standpoint of total income changes, the picture is more favorable. From 1929 to 1946 the ten cotton states gained $458 in average annual per capita income as compared to $550 for the rest of the country; the percentage increases were 127 per cent and 72 per cent respectively. Therefore, the ten cotton states during the period gained more relatively but less absolutely than the rest of the nation. The Eastern cotton states showed the greatest relative gain and the Delta states the least, but both showed a greater relative decline in population from 1942, compared to the rest of the country, than did Oklahoma and Texas.

The greater relative gain in Southern income during the period is a reflection of the long-term basic changes in the economic structure of the region, such as more industry and less agriculture and a modest shift in the industrial pattern toward more high-wage industries.

Summary and Conclusions

CONSIDERATIONS PERTINENT TO FURTHER AGRICULTURAL
PROGRESS IN THE COTTON BELT

1. *A cotton program of about twenty million acres but with considerable flexibility permitted in regional adjustments in the enterprise.* Since 1920 there has been a tendency for cotton production to shift to the West. The areas of increasing production, partly through acreage increases but more largely from increased yields, are the Mississippi Delta, High Plains areas of West Texas, Eastern Hilly areas, and the irrigated cotton areas—mainly in New Mexico, Arizona, and California. Even before the A.A.A. these shifts were apparent through acreage changes; during the A.A.A., however, despite the inflexible acreage policy, the increase in relative production in these areas continued primarily through improved yields, except in Arizona and California where acreage continued to increase during that era. In 1947 and 1948, larger increases in acreage occurred in the irrigated states, and apparently to some extent in the other areas, than had previously occurred in these regions.

During the war years, mainly from 1943 to 1945, and the postwar years, 1946 to 1948, cotton acreage was permitted to seek its own level under the forces of free competition. Yet, because of labor scarcity, in no year did total acreage harvested exceed the 1939 acreage, although the 1948 acreage indicated for harvest is about 1.3 million acres short of it. The October estimate of cotton for harvest in 1948 indicates a crop in excess of 15 million bales, the seventh largest crop on record, caused primarily by an unusually high average yield. Because of cyclical changes in solar radiation and other associated factors, not definable at the present stage of scientific progress, such crops have been occurring with considerable regularity since 1909 at five- to six-year intervals, with somewhat larger crops at eleven-year intervals, and with an occasional large crop out of phase, as in 1911, 1933, and 1944, but still in some multiple of eleven years.

It appears, therefore, that the carry-over from this 1948 crop will be in the vicinity of 5 to 6 million bales, becoming once again a drug on the cotton market and a burden on the government in storage costs, etc. These cyclical crops have a habit of upsetting normal adjustments in the cotton economy of the South. They have always given more than a normal carry-over; but subsequent adjustments in production have generally been able to bring supply back to normal, except in 1931, when the cotton surplus was coupled with a major depression. The 1931 crop gave cotton farmers an unusually troublesome surplus because carry-over had previously reached burdensome proportions. At the beginning of the cotton year, August 1, 1929, the carry-over was 2.3 million bales; and continued to mount with each succeeding crop-year, being, on August 1, 1930, 4.5 million bales, and on that date the following year, 6.4 million bales. None of the accompanying crops, 1928, 1929, and 1930, was large, so that unfavorable business conditions which reduced domestic consumption and somewhat lowered exports, were responsible for the large carry-over of cotton August 1, 1931. But the 1931 crop was a cyclical crop (five years from 1926), and dumped about 17 million bales on the cotton market, and by the end of the year (August 1, 1932) carry-over was increased further by 3.3 million bales. At that point carry-over was 9.7 million bales, and the situation was critical because the supply was almost sufficient for the next year without further production. Those are the years that really put the cotton farmer in the hole from the standpoint of supply, and poor business conditions did very little to remove the surplus prior to the second cyclical crop in the depression, the 1937 crop, which raised carry-over still further, to 11.5 million bales.

Faced with a carry-over at the end of the crop season 1948-49 of around 6 million bales, the Southern cotton grower is wondering if he will have controls again. The current cotton situation, however, is not analogous to that of 1931 or even of 1926; it is more nearly analogous to 1920, when a large crop of cotton occurred (again a cyclical crop). The postwar recession began in June of that year in agricultural prices and in September in other prices. The large crop of cotton (along with large crops of corn, wheat, and apples which occurred that year) reduced, as a result of the over-supply in agriculture, farm income

Summary and Conclusions

more than proportionately; and more importantly, it reduced farm purchasing power. This was a factor in the recession beginning in 1920. Farm prices of farm products began declining in June, 1920, and reached a low twelve months later. The wholesale prices of all commodities except farm products began declining in August, 1920, but did not reach the first postwar low until eighteen months later. The fact that recessions in both price series began in 1920 and that agricultural prices began the decline two months prior to non-agricultural prices suggests probable relationship or at least a chain of events initiated perhaps by the large agricultural crops. The impact of large crops on the economic system would run the sequence from large supply; to lower farm prices; to reduced farm income and purchasing power; to reduced farmer demand for food, household goods, farm machinery, fertilizer and other supplies, and automobiles; to reduced output in industry; thence to unemployment. Agricultural surpluses of the sort here decribed may not have much effect on the economic system, but it appears to be a serious error to overlook the fact that they may be the initiating force in some of the cyclical swings to which the economy is subjected at intervals of varying duration.

The answer to the question as to what should be the agricultural policy with respect to cotton in 1950 depends greatly upon what happens to cotton acreage and production in 1949. If a very large increase in acreage occurs and also another large crop, the surplus may rise to burdensome proportions. During the last forty years a large production of cotton has always been followed by a reduction in acreage. This happened after the following large crops: 1914, 1920, 1926, 1931, 1933, 1937, 1942, and 1944. Likewise, since such crops are cyclical, occurring generally every five to six years or in submultiples of eleven years, yields are expected to drop 30 to 40 pounds in 1949. If both production functions act according to past behavior, there would be without doubt a decrease in production. But since the government-loan program has kept the price of cotton near 30 cents and above 90 per cent of parity for the 1948-49 crop through March, 1949, the necessary price discount to reduce acreage will be absent. In fact because of this policy, cotton, in comparison with other unstabilized products in the Cotton Belt produced in competition with it, should show a price advantage, and hence have a profit incentive sufficient to increase acreage. As to whether the acreage increase will be sufficient to overcome the cyclical reduction in yield depends upon the relative sizes of the acreage increase and the yield decrease. The former must exceed 10 per cent and probably be near 20 per cent if the yield decrease is as much as 50 pounds, as it was after the 1920 cyclical crop. If a production of 14 to 15 million bales comes in 1949, the carry-over would again become burdensome. It would then become necessary to reimpose acreage control in order to reduce supply to manageable limits.

The objections to operating an important segment of the economy under rigid controls are well-known and detested. But the alternatives, 5-cent cotton and chaos in the cotton South, are to be abhorred even more. Yet if it becomes apparent that the country is again facing a cotton situation similar to the one in the 1930's, there is no doubt as to the course of action which would be adopted.

In preceding pages the contributions of the A.A.A. program to Southern agriculture, not only when it was in operation but also during the war and after, have been repeatedly emphasized. Consequently, if such a program again becomes necessary, provided it is adequately safeguarded with accepted principles of scientific agriculture and especially with those of soil conservation, it can be expected to continue to be of great benefit to Southern agriculture. However, in view of the trend toward more specialized and large-scale production in the Delta, West Texas, and the irrigated areas, it is apparent that if the program is revived it should be provided with sufficient flexibility to permit normal shifts to the areas possessing efficiency and other advantages in production. If this becomes an accepted procedure, the Eastern cotton states may be expected to continue to decline in both acreage and production, which is in line with recent trends in the region relative to its economic and agricultural development. These states have had a comparatively greater growth in diversified agriculture, which trends in industrialization have helped, and are expected to continue to show progress, although further assistance to both agricultural and industrial development is needed. A shrewd use of subsidies would do much to encourage needed improvements and changes in the region's agriculture and to accelerate the desirable shifts already under way.

Tremendous aid to agricultural adjustments not only in the Eastern cotton states but in the entire Cotton Belt can be given by developing a market organization, or set-up at almost every whistle stop, which will provide the accessibility, ease, and liquidity in marketing the new products that exist for cotton. The well-nigh perfect marketability of cotton is a force of tremendous import in maintaining the *status quo* in Southern agriculture. It has been too long ignored by those who hope, and by those who work, for a better Southern agriculture. It is high time that this factor be recognized and steps be taken to remedy the deficiency, emphasized again by repetition, of a marketing organization for other products truly competitive with cotton.

2. *Inducements to the agriculturally trained and capable young men to enter agriculture.* Although the Smith-Hughes Act, enacted in 1917, established vocational agricultural education in the public schools, and agricultural instruction in state institutions at the college level had been provided much earlier (Morrill Land Grant Act, 1862), with many thousand young men receiving some form of agricultural training at one or both of these set-ups, a recent sample survey of farm operators of cotton farms in the Piedmont of South Carolina and Georgia showed that only 8 per cent had had any agricultural training. It is probable that other types of farms would show a higher percentage of trained operators, for it would be easier for such operators to succeed with other enterprises. Furthermore, this type of operator would be more attracted to the non-cotton type of farm because of the greater possibility for mechanization and the elimination of drudgery from farm work. It is common observation that too few of the trained and more capable farm youths enter the business of

farming, and studies cited previously tend to support this view. Yet modern farming is a challenge, for to be highly successful as a farmer one must have both intelligence and energy, as well as plenty of stamina.

Where one has the necessary capital and personal attributes to succeed at farming, the compensations are great—not alone in money, which, once a certain income is reached, may be one of the lesser advantages; but in the pride and thrill which comes with taking part in and becoming a part of nature's great scheme of things. Study of agricultural subjects increases appreciation of the "living occupation," that calling which not only provides a living but a way of life.

The crux of the matter is that the average farm youth with agricultural training does not have the capital to farm on the scale necessary to obtain a living equal to what he might earn elsewhere. In order to farm at all, a majority of them would have to begin as tenants and laborers. With a price situation such as prevailed prior to World War II, the struggle to obtain farm ownership would be long, but that to obtain a size of farm necessary for a reasonably adequate level of earnings, even longer. Consequently, they drift into professional work, some into professions with agricultural aspects, others into wholly non-agricultural occupations. But if they, along with the vocational agricultural students, could farm in accordance with their capabilities, they would be more successful financially and better citizens of the community and nation as well.

Farm management surveys and studies of various kinds have demonstrated that operators with agricultural training make more money proportionately than other educated classes of operators. They obtain higher yields of both crops and livestock, higher labor efficiency, higher capital and power efficiency, and conserve and rebuild the soil more nearly according to recommendations. These attributes produce extra income not only immediately but even more so in the long run. This extra income-earning ability has capital value. It will, in fact, retire a larger loan. The big difficulty is the initial capital requirements. Banks and other lending institutions have conventional security requirements, one of the most important of which, and one which limits, or eliminates, the capable farmer here being considered, is the capital equity requirement. It is that part of the capital value of the farm which the borrower must have in his own right, or have on a second mortgage, which is very difficult to obtain except occasionally from a relative. The proportion of equity varies with the bank and the type of agency, but in any event is fairly large, or otherwise under conventional loaning procedures, the little equity that the borrower has is subject to very great risk of total loss.

G. F. Warren in his volume, *Farm Management*, published in 1914, estimated on the basis of farm surveys in New York State that a high school course increased annual earnings by an amount equal to an investment of $6,000 in five per cent bonds, and concluded that an agricultural college education increased it as much more. If a high school education had that much capital value about 1914, a high school education today has undoubtedly a greater capital worth, that of the high school graduate with vocational agricultural training would be even higher, and that of the farm operator trained in an agricultural college, still higher. Recent studies support the argument; however, the current capital value which may be attributed to the extra earnings at these different levels of education is not known, but it should not be difficult to estimate reasonably accurately. If this cannot be done, studies should be initiated which would make these data available.

The thought is that, in order to encourage capable farm boys with proper training to enter agriculture on a favorable basis, some plan should be devised by which the capital worth of a man's education can be substituted for equity as security in farm loans. Until the plan becomes established and proved, banks would very likely be adverse to making this substitution, because, high as the capital value might be from the additional earning power of farm persons with various levels of education, such capital value would have no market value in foreclosure proceedings. This objection may be partially overcome by character and ability certifications from friends and teachers. Even so, it may be necessary for some federally sponsored loan agency to undertake the development of this form of credit, at least in the earlier stages, until it is proved sound experimentally.

3. *A farm labor program.* There are two aspects to the problem. The first concerns those farm persons who migrate and become laborers in some city industry or other occupation. If these laborers are to be of maximum benefit to society and to earn reasonably decent wages and consequently an adequate standard of living, they must have some form of training. Training provided by the prospective employer will be exceedingly narrow and will leave the employee without choice in alternative lines of work; or the employer may not trouble to give any training and rely instead on interregional migrant labor. War-located factories in the South imported some labor from other regions. This may and likely will happen again, especially in the case of high-wage industries requiring skilled labor. We should ask ourselves this question: Of what value will industrialization be to the South if a part of the labor is imported? If this happens, would population pressure on Southern farms be relieved? The answer may be "no" to both questions. Even if only a part of the skilled labor is imported, local labor would not be participating in high-wage industries to the extent desired, neither to the extent it is due nor to that necessary for raising Southern incomes and the standard of living to the highest possible maximum. If these points are pondered long and well, it will be obvious that some sort of labor training program is needed in urban centers to better prepare farm migrants for industrial and other jobs. Such training need not be elaborate or intricate. It should include certain basic courses of instruction in industrial safety, hygiene, discipline, and standard mechanical routines, with a fair offering of vocational lines. Whether a training center of this sort should be operated by the state, city, or private interests will not be answered here because an answer is not available. A reliable answer would seem to be dependent on a thoroughgoing study of the problem, followed by a period of experimentation with alternative solutions.

The second aspect of the farm labor program needing solution is that of the training of farm labor for farming. In farm management studies it has been found that a three-man farm is highly desirable because it will supply an adequate income for all farm labor. Some operators are able to organize more than a three-man farm. But the vast majority of operators fall below a three-man farm. As a matter of fact, the typical American farm, the family farm, is a one-man farm plus. Obviously, the more highly trained farm labor becomes, the greater the number of laborers for which the operator has capacity. If he has the capacity to manage three laborers of the run-of-the-mill type, his capacity may be increased twofold with trained labor, and perhaps even threefold. The volume of production would expand in an even greater ratio, and consequently the operator's net income would rise. Farm labor also would be paid more, since its productivity would be greatly enhanced.

The conditions which suggest that training of farm labor may be a new frontier in agricultural productivity, not only in the Cotton Belt but in the rest of the country, are the degree and complexity of mechanization, the great variety of jobs which the laborer must do in agriculture, the real need for a dependable and alert type of labor, and the hazardous nature of farming which causes heavy losses from farm accidents. Basic training in farm safety precautions, farm discipline and behavior, mechanical techniques, the management of livestock, and the handling of certain crops would seem to be the minimum required. But again, as in the case of city migrants, a careful study of farm labor deficiencies, followed by a period of experimentation in types and methods of training, is all that can be suggested. However, it is a subject of tremendous import, for a high level of agricultural productivity directly affects the standard of living of everyone, and is therefore of vital interest to national health and national welfare.

4. *Formulation of a national land use policy for the Cotton Belt.* The region is noted for its small farms and in some regions for the serious erosion which has occurred as a result of the one-crop system. National welfare, as

well as continued national survival, has a first interest in preserving this greatest resource, the soil. The limitations on how far the public should go in regulating the use of a natural resource, such as land, has not been determined. Movement in this direction by statutory regulations has been delayed undoubtedly by confusion in the public mind as to: (1) What the policy should be, and (2) the philosophy of freedom of enterprise, which has permitted exploitation, not only of natural resources but of human resources, for the benefit almost entirely of the individual and to the detriment of the national future. It should not be difficult to formulate limits of land use with respect to certain external characteristics of the soil (such as soil type, slope, and degree of erosion), which would permit setting by legal statute the percentage of land of given characteristics which could be devoted to specified erosive crops; sequence of production, that is, how often the seriously erosive crops might be grown; and restrictions as to mechanical procedures in cultivating the land, such as terracing or strip farming and contour tillage. In certain counties a very high percentage of the land might be removed from the main cash crop, which would eliminate most or all of the support for rural social institutions. In that event the effective period of complete compliance might be adjusted over a period of time, say a generation, coupled with a purchase program and the government acting as sole buying agent in all land transfers. The land might then be returned to forests and the public domain, or reorganized as larger and more extensive farms and leased for very long terms under rigidly defined conditions of land use. In the meantime the long period involved would permit a systematic relocation and consolidation of the rural social institutions. There are undoubtedly legal bars to this approach, but, if the public welfare is shown to be sufficiently involved, a method of amendment or other legal process with necessary enabling procedures should be forthcoming.

5. *Discovery of a method by which the more important, practical, and simple agricultural research findings of the experiment stations and other research workers can be*

Summary and Conclusions 189

quickly applied by the mass of farmers. Present methods leave much to be desired, for only a small percentage of the farmers, and primarily those who least need assistance, become the early recipients of the advantages of new technology. In applying the results of agricultural research to farming, it's the early bird who gets the worm, for once this new knowledge becomes the property of all, and when it is universally applied, the additional supply, because of the relative inelasticity of the demand curve for agricultural products, probably brings less total income. The greatest individual gain goes to those farmers who obtain the increased production before the total supply is affected appreciably. However, the complete application of research findings contributes greatly to social gain and raises the standard of living of the entire population through increased specialization and expanded volume of production. Since society's gain is greater and comes more quickly, it is socially profitable for the public to finance not only the research in the first place but also the educational expense required to induce the mass of farmers to adopt quickly the new production knowledge. The best approach to this problem to date has been the A.A.A. subsidy payments for certain land use and cropping and conservation practices. This program made a great difference in the rebuilding of worn-out soils and conservation of resources, resulting in increased yields almost immediately but in even higher yields five to ten years later, during World War II, when the nation had the greatest need for large volume. If the A.A.A. program could be further extended in this respect, or perhaps an even more effective program of education developed, it would continue to make a great difference to the conservation of our soil resources and to the cheap production of large volumes of food and fiber. It would make a great difference to the success of millions of farmers, but would mean even more to the health and survival of present and future Americans. This problem of our national existence is deliberately or unknowingly taken much too lightly; it is a mistake to make political capital out of the comparatively modest appropriations required for such incentive programs. The attitude of a people toward the conservation and proper use of this universal natural resource, soil, is as necessary for survival as any philosophy of foreign policy, national defense, industrial and labor relations, and domestic welfare, because of the effect of a plentiful supply of healthful food on physical development, stamina, and mental capability of the masses.

Statistical Appendix

Statistical Appendix

TABLE I
STATISTICS FOR MAJOR AGRICULTURAL ENTERPRISES IN 10 COTTON BELT STATES* BY CENSUS YEARS

Item	Unit	1920†	1925†	1930‡	1935†	1940‡	1945†
Farm population	Thousand	13,367	13,240	13,180	13,393	13,022	9,546
Number of farms	Thousand	2,550	2,470	2,612	2,714	2,367	2,260
Total land area	Million acres	453	453	453	453	453	454
Land in farms	Million acres	289	267	287	317	311	314
Farms with electricity	Thousand	n.a.	n.a.	90	n.a.	410	703
Motor trucks on farms	Thousand	21	n.a.	177	n.a.	225	349
Tractors on farms	Thousand	29	59	112	n.a.	223	407
Horses and mules on farms	Thousand head	6,698	6,153	5,759	5,149	4,590	3,982
All cattle on farms	Thousand head	15,797	13,526	12,440	18,053	15,267	21,316
Cows and heifers milked	Thousand head	n.a.	3,796	3,953	5,014	4,498	4,402
Hogs and pigs on farms	Thousand head	14,648	8,691	6,094	9,376	8,719	10,036
Sows and gilts for spring farrowing	Thousand head	2,461	1,228	790	1,222	1,230	1,342
Chickens on farms	Million head	82	88	78	85	78	100
Land in orchards§	Thousand acres	n.a.	n.a.	1,059	1,142	1,133	1,043
Produced, grown or used in—		*1919*	*1924*	*1929*	*1934*	*1939*	*1944*
Chickens raised	Million head	131	131	150	134	151	228
Chicken eggs produced	Million dozen	314	294	505	356	480	663
Turkeys raised	Thousand head	n.a.	n.a.	5,426	n.a.	5,596	3,014
Milk produced	Million gallons	1,022	1,179	1,571	1,626	1,774	1,637
Whole milk sold	Million gallons	74	120	270	n.a.	389	615
Total cropland harvested	Million acres	n.a.	88	95	87	89	88
Number of farms growing cotton	Thousand	1,872	1,868	1,931	1,863	1,544	1,180
Cotton	Thousand acres	33,263	38,048	41,995	25,817	21,723	17,993
Cotton production	Thousand bales	11,154	13,159	13,758	8,703	10,369	10,815
Corn	Thousand acres	n.a.	24,948	24,635	28,298	27,800	22,655
Wheat	Thousand acres	8,926	5,571	8,289	7,940	8,004	10,800
Oats	Thousand acres	4,453	3,897	3,376	4,306	4,536	6,192
Barley	Thousand acres	163	392	297	262	782	783
All hay, excluding grain sorghums	Thousand acres	6,462	5,877	5,465	9,192	9,666	8,473
Lespedeza hay	Thousand acres	n.a.	394#	323#	1,096	2,440	3,157
Soybeans and cowpeas:							
Grown alone	Thousand acres	n.a.	n.a.	997	2,844	3,986	2,573
Grown with other crops	Thousand acres	n.a.	n.a.	1,250	3,203	6,011	2,220
Sorghums for all purposes except syrup	Thousand acres	5,199	4,428	5,306	6,213	7,194	10,489
Peanuts grown alone for all purposes	Thousand acres	n.a.	n.a.	1,284	1,764	2,178	3,254
Tobacco	Thousand acres	732	646	1,019	715	1,139	952
Tobacco production	Million pounds	478	403	733	581	1,039	1,002
Rice	Thousand acres	778	670	657	611	747	1,162
Vegetables harvested for sale	Thousand acres	206	n.a.	623	1,006	787	1,099
Irish potatoes	Thousand acres	209	209	299	398	389	388
Sweet potatoes and yams	Thousand acres	637	362	517	806	583	558
Fertilizer	Thousand tons	3,937	3,838	4,202	2,789	3,487	5,575
Lime	Thousand tons	n.a.	n.a.	460	139	1,163	4,327

* Includes North Carolina, South Carolina, Georgia, Alabama, Tennessee, Mississippi, Arkansas, Louisiana, Oklahoma and Texas.
† Inventory date as of January 1.
‡ Inventory date as of April 1.
§ Includes vineyards and planted nuts.
# Includes sweet clover.
n.a. means the data are not available.

Source: Sixteenth Census of the United States, 1940, *Agriculture*, Vol. I, pts. III, IV and V; and *Census of Agriculture: 1945*. Lime consumption was compiled from *Agricultural Statistics;* fertilizer consumption for the most part came from the Census reports cited above but the data for 1919 were compiled from the *Yearbook of Agriculture*, 1925, and data for 1944 from *Agricultural Statistics*.

TABLE II
Statistics for Major Agricultural Enterprises in the Eastern Cotton States* by Census Years

Item	Unit	1920†	1925†	1930‡	1935†	1940‡	1945†
Farm population	Thousand	6,869	6,635	6,491	6,672	6,562.4	4,992
Number of farms	Thousand	1,282	1,196	1,196	1,264	1,111	1,119
Total land area	Million acres	147.8	147.8	147.8	147.8	148.2	148.2
Land in farms	Million acres	97.0	85.8	86.1	96.3	91.4	90.2
Farms with electricity	Thousand	n.a.	n.a.	45	n.a.	220	374
Tractors on farms	Thousand	8.5	22.2	32.3	n.a.	46.3	109.4
Horses and mules on farms	Thousand head	2,330	2,042	1,877	1,723	1,732	1,623
All cattle on farms	Thousand head	4,438	3,593	2,957	4,528	3,617	4,961
Cows and heifers milked,	Thousand head	n.a.	1,565	1,456	1,836	1,593	1,712
Hogs and pigs on farms	Thousand head	7,517	4,542	2,868	4,620	4,087	5,176
Sows and gilts for spring farrowing	Thousand head	1,156	616	384	559	598	647
Chickens on farms	Million head	35.8	38.0	29.1	36.8	30.5	40.3
Land in orchards§	Thousand acres	n.a.	n.a.	575	603	555	537
Produced, grown or used in—		*1919*	*1924*	*1929*	*1934*	*1939*	*1944*
Chickens raised	Million head	63	61	61	62	65	109
Chicken eggs produced	Million dozen	133	117	178	138	171	237
Turkeys raised	Thousand head	n.a.	n.a.	671	n.a.	556	700
Milk produced	Million gallons	475	501	591	637	651	730
Whole milk sold	Million gallons	34	48	106	n.a.	144	247
Total cropland harvested	Million acres	n.a.	30.9	31.5	32.4	32.5	30.1
Number of farms growing cotton	Thousand	901	820	810	794	660	541
Cotton	Thousand acres	12,162	10,354	11,632	7,297	6,351	5,048
Cotton production	Thousand bales	5,042	4,079	4,762	3,625	3,422	3,848
Corn	Thousand acres	n.a.	13,252	12,261	15,099	14,486	12,225
Wheat	Thousand acres	1,564	752	734	1,248	1,066	1,266
Oats	Thousand acres	757	1,025	996	1,194	1,365	2,152
Barley	Thousand acres	7	15	32	39	76	177
All hay, excluding grain sorghums	Thousand acres	3,179	2,966	2,862	5,029	5,130	4,090
Lespedeza hay	Thousand acres	n.a.	171¢	179¢	933	1,766	1,995
Soybeans and cowpeas:							
Grown alone	Thousand acres	n.a.	n.a.	654	1,690	1,948	1,351
Grown with other crops	Thousand acres	n.a.	n.a.	730	1,859	3,260	1,281
Sorghums for all purposes except syrup	Thousand acres	139	134	97	244	123	155
Peanuts grown alone for all purposes	Thousand acres	n.a.	n.a.	917	1,194	1,593	2,329
Tobacco	Thousand acres	730	645	1,019	714	1,138	951
Tobacco production	Million pounds	476	402	732	580	1,039	1,002
Rice	Thousand acres	11.8	6.4	2.8	5.8	2.1	....
Vegetables harvested for sale	Thousand acres	101	n.a.	287	434	340	402
Irish potatoes	Thousand acres	104	123	155	209	216	209
Sweet potatoes and yams	Thousand acres	376	240	314	461	341	308
Fertilizer	Thousand tons	3,613	3,278	3,462	2,448	2,898	4,465
Lime	Thousand tons	n.a.	n.a.	450	136	1,067	2,694

* Includes North Carolina, South Carolina, Georgia, Alabama, and Tennessee.
† Inventory date as of January 1.
‡ Inventory date as of April 1.
§ Includes vineyards and planted nuts.
¢ Includes sweet clover.
n.a. means the data are not available.
Source: Same as for Table I.

TABLE III
STATISTICS FOR MAJOR AGRICULTURAL ENTERPRISES IN THE DELTA COTTON STATES* BY CENSUS YEARS

Item	Unit	1920†	1925†	1930‡	1935†	1940‡	1945†
Farm population	Thousand	3,204	3,249	3,313	3,372	3,370	2,427
Number of farms	Thousand	640	612	716	735	658	592
Total land area	Million acres	92.4	92.4	92.4	92.4	92.9	92.9
Land in farms	Million acres	45.7	40.5	42.7	47.8	47.2	47.1
Farms with electricity	Thousand	n.a.	n.a.	14	n.a.	68	125
Tractors on farms	Thousand						
Horses and mules on farms	Thousand head	5.3	8.8	16.2	n.a.	32.6	65.2
All cattle on farms	Thousand head	1,457	1,287	1,285	1,179	1,190	1,130
Cows and heifers milked₅	Thousand head	3,128	2,430	2,141	3,670	3,174	4,390
Hogs and pigs on farms	Thousand head	n.a.	855	899	1,200	1,099	1,067
Sows and gilts for spring farrowing	Thousand head	3,602 681	2,063 332	1,502 192	2,591 392	2,354 323	2,520 349
Chickens on farms	Million head	17.1	16.9	15.6	17.9	16.6	19.6
Land in orchards§	Thousand acres	n.a.	n.a.	222	239	312	238
Produced, grown or used in—		*1919*	*1924*	*1929*	*1934*	*1939*	*1944*
Chickens raised	Million head	25	24	29	28	34	44
Chicken eggs produced	Million dozen	65	51	92	65	92	115
Turkeys raised	Thousand head	n.a.	n.a.	168	n.a.	178	163
Milk produced	Million gallons	209	226	318	337	378	390
Whole milk sold	Million gallons	14	24	56	n.a.	80	128
Total cropland harvested	Million acres	n.a.	15.4	17.2	17.2	17.6	16.0
Number of farms growing cotton	Thousand	514	504	603	578	524	404
Cotton	Thousand acres	6,846	7,223	9,401	5,878	5,595	4,874
Cotton production	Thousand bales	2,134	2,713	4,072	2,438	3,602	3,810
Corn	Thousand acres	n.a.	5,279	5,054	6,994	6,825	5,126
Wheat	Thousand acres	263	37	17	61	35	62
Oats	Thousand acres	260	295	141	234	409	956
Barley	Thousand acres	1	1	....	1	11	18
All hay, excluding grain sorghums	Thousand acres	1,390	1,235	1,115	2,067	2,379	2,492
Lespedeza hay	Thousand acres	n.a.	202‡	135‡	155	663	1,095
Soybeans and cowpeas:							
Grown alone	Thousand acres	n.a.	n.a.	214	870	1,283	900
Grown with other crops	Thousand acres	n.a.	n.a.	411	1,121	2,416	858
Sorghums for all purposes except syrup	Thousand acres	102	118	78	206	142	121
Peanuts grown alone for all purposes	Thousand acres	n.a.	n.a.	54	174	119	58
Tobacco	Thousand acres	3	1	....	1	1	....
Tobacco production	Million pounds	1.2	.4	.2	.2	.5	.2
Rice	Thousand acres	601	518	549	495	557	817
Vegetables harvested for sale	Thousand acres	45	n.a.	120	168	121	181
Irish potatoes	Thousand acres	53	45	66	100	101	114
Sweet potatoes and yams	Thousand acres	176	87	142	263	173	167
Fertilizer	Thousand tons	278	428	579	280	504	862
Lime	Thousand tons	n.a.	n.a.	10	3	86	1,206

* Includes Mississippi, Arkansas and Louisiana.
† Inventory date as of January 1.
‡ Inventory date as of April 1.
§ Includes vineyards and planted nuts.
‡ Includes sweet clover.
n.a. means the data not available.
Source: Same as for Table I.

TABLE IV
STATISTICS FOR MAJOR AGRICULTURAL ENTERPRISES IN OKLAHOMA AND TEXAS BY CENSUS YEARS

Item	Unit	1920*	1925*	1930†	1935*	1940†	1945*
Farm population	Thousand	3,295	3,356	3,376	3,349	3,090	2,128
Number of farms	Thousand	628	663	699	714	598	550
Total land area	Million acres	212.3	212.3	212.3	212.4	213.0	213.0
Land in farms	Million acres	146.0	140.5	158.5	172.9	172.5	177.5
Farms with electricity	Thousand	n.a.	n.a.	31	n.a.	122	204
Tractors on farms	Thousand	15.3	27.7	63.3	n.a.	144.3	232.8
Horses and mules on farms	Thousand head	2,912	2,825	2,597	2,248	1,668	1,230
All cattle on farms	Thousand head	8,231	7,503	7,343	9,855	8,476	11,966
Cows and heifers milked	Thousand head	n.a.	1,376	1,598	1,978	1,806	1,623
Hogs and pigs on farms	Thousand head	3,530	2,086	1,725	2,165	2,278	2,340
Sows and gilts for spring farrowing	Thousand head	624	280	214	271	308	346
Chickens on farms	Million head	29.2	32.7	33.0	30.2	30.8	40.3
Land in orchards‡	Thousand acres	n.a.	n.a.	262	300	267	268
Produced, grown or used in—		*1919*	*1924*	*1929*	*1934*	*1939*	*1944*
Chickens raised	Million head	43	46	60	44	53	74
Chicken eggs produced	Million dozen	116	126	235	153	217	311
Turkeys raised	Thousand head	n.a.	n.a.	4,587	n.a.	4,862	2,151
Milk produced	Million gallons	339	452	662	652	745	718
Whole milk sold	Million gallons	27	48	108	n.a.	165	241
Total cropland harvested	Million acres	n.a.	41.6	46.2	37.8	38.8	41.6
Number of farms growing cotton	Thousand	457	544	519	490	360	235
Cotton	Thousand acres	14,256	20,471	20,962	12,642	9,777	8,070
Cotton production	Thousand bales	3,978	6,368	4,924	2,640	3,245	3,157
Corn	Thousand acres	n.a.	6,416	7,320	6,205	6,488	5,305
Wheat	Thousand acres	7,098	4,782	7,538	6,631	6,902	9,472
Oats	Thousand acres	3,436	2,577	2,239	2,878	2,761	3,085
Barley	Thousand acres	155	376	265	221	696	588
All hay, excluding grain sorghums	Thousand acres	1,893	1,677	1,488	2,097	2,157	1,891
Lespedeza hay	Thousand acres	n.a.	20§	9§	9	12	68
Soybeans and cowpeas:							
Grown alone	Thousand acres	n.a.	n.a.	129	284	754	322
Grown with other crops	Thousand acres	n.a.	n.a.	109	222	334	81
Sorghums for all purposes except syrup	Thousand acres	4,958	4,175	5,131	5,764	6,930	10,213
Peanuts grown alone for all purposes	Thousand acres	n.a.	n.a.	312	396	466	867
Tobacco	Thousand acres	....	....	....	....	....	....
Tobacco production	Million pounds	....	....	....	....	....	....
Rice	Thousand acres	164	146	106	110	186	345
Vegetables harvested for sale	Thousand acres	61	n.a.	216	405	326	516
Irish potatoes	Thousand acres	53	40	78	89	71	66
Sweet potatoes and yams	Thousand acres	85	34	61	83	70	82
Fertilizer	Thousand tons	46	132	161	61	85	248
Lime	Thousand tons	n.a.	n.a.	....	....	11	426

* Inventory date as of January 1.
† Inventory date as of April 1.
‡ Includes vineyards and planted nuts.
§ Includes sweet clover.
n.a. means the data are not available.
Source: Same as for Table I.

Statistical Appendix

TABLE V
COMPARISON OF PERCENTAGE CHANGE OF AGRICULTURAL FACTORS BY REGIONS FOR SIGNIFICANT PERIODS

Item	Period	Percentage change*				Region showing largest percentage change
		Eastern states	Delta states	Oklahoma & Texas	Ten cotton states	
Land use:						
Land in farms........	1930 to 1945	5	10	12	9	Oklahoma and Texas
Pasture land.........	1930 to 1945	22	59	26	28	Delta states
Cropland harvested...	1929 to 1944	−4*	−7	−10	−8	Oklahoma and Texas
Acreage:						
Cotton..............	1929 to 1944	−57	−48	−62	−57	Oklahoma and Texas
Corn................	1929 to 1944	..	1	−28	−8	Oklahoma and Texas
Oats................	1929 to 1944	116	578	38	83	Delta states
Wheat..............	1929 to 1944	72	265	26	30	Delta states
Lespedeza hay.......	1929 to 1944	1,015	711	n.c.	877	Eastern states
Sorghum............	1929 to 1944	n.c.	n.c.	99	98	Oklahoma and Texas
Peanuts grown alone..	1929 to 1944	154	n.c.	178	153	Oklahoma and Texas
Rice................	1929 to 1944	n.c.	49	225	77	Oklahoma and Texas
Vegetables for sale....	1929 to 1944	40	51	139	76	Oklahoma and Texas
Cotton yield...........	1925-29 to 1940-46	49	48	24	44	Eastern states
Livestock:						
All cattle...........	1915-19 to 1940-46	11	32	14	17	Delta states
	1925-29 to 1940-46	35	60	38	41	Delta states
Hogs................	1915-19 to 1940-46	−14	−10	−12	−12	Eastern states
	1925-29 to 1940-46	32	45	31	35	Delta states
Chickens............	1925-29 to 1940-46	16	20	22	19	Oklahoma and Texas
Livestock products:						
Milk produced.......	1919 to 1944	54	87	112	80	Oklahoma and Texas
	1929 to 1944	24	23	8	17	Eastern states
Milk sold............	1919 to 1944	626	814	793	731	Delta states
	1929 to 1944	133	129	123	128	Eastern states
Eggs produced.......	1919 to 1944	78	77	168	111	Oklahoma and Texas
	1929 to 1944	33	25	32	31	Eastern states
Number of tractors......	1930 to 1945	239	302	268	264	Delta states
	1940 to 1945	136	100	61	83	Eastern states
Number of other farms...	1930 to 1945	50	66	75	59	Oklahoma and Texas
Number of cotton farms..	1929 to 1944	−33	−33	−55	−39	Oklahoma and Texas
Number of all farms.....	1930 to 1945	−6	−17	−21	−13	Oklahoma and Texas
Number of farm population...........	1930 to 1945	−23	−27	−37	−28	Oklahoma and Texas
	1924-29 to 1941-45	−11	−9	−23	−14	Oklahoma and Texas
	1935-39 to 1941-45	−12	−12	−20	−14	Oklahoma and Texas
Number of workstock....	1920 to 1945	−30	−22	−58	−41	Oklahoma and Texas
	1930 to 1945	−14	−12	−53	−31	Oklahoma and Texas

* The minus means a decrease.
n.c. means the percentage was not calculated but the change is insignificant in every case.
Source: Computed from Appendix, Tables I-IV, and IX-XV.

TABLE VI
COMPARISON OF ACREAGE AND NUMBER PER FARM IN 1944 BY REGIONS WITH PERCENTAGE CHANGES BETWEEN PERIODS

Item	Period	Eastern states		Delta states		Oklahoma and Texas		10 cotton states		38 other states		Region having largest number or acreage; also showing greatest percentage change
		Acres or No.	Per cent	Acres or No.	Per cent	Acres or No.	Per cent	Acres or No.	Per cent	Acres or No.	Per cent	
Acreage per farm:												
Land area............	1945	80.6		79.6		322.7		138.9		230		Oklahoma and Texas
Per cent change*.....	1930 to 1945		12		34		42		26		21	Oklahoma and Texas
Cropland harvested...	1944	26.9		27		75.6		38.9		74		Oklahoma and Texas
Per cent change......	1929 to 1944		2		12		14		7		3	Oklahoma and Texas
Intensive crops†.....	1944	6.7		9.4		16.4		9.7		n.c.		Oklahoma and Texas
Per cent change......	1929 to 1944		−43		−32		−47		−44		n.c.	Oklahoma and Texas
Medium intensive crops‡	1944	13.0		10.1		11.8		12.0		n.c.		Eastern states
Per cent change......	1929 to 1944		18		28		6		18		n.c.	Delta states
Extensive crops§.....	1944	8.2		7.7		46.5		17.4		n.c.		Oklahoma and Texas
Per cent change......	1929 to 1944		82		250		94		91		n.c.	Delta states
Cotton (per cotton farm)	1944	9.3		12.1		34.3		15.2		n.c.		Oklahoma and Texas
Per cent change......	1929 to 1944		−35		−22		−15		−30		n.c.	Eastern states
Bales of cotton per cotton farm	1942 to 1946	6.47		8.52		12.10		8.3		n.c.		Oklahoma and Texas
Per cent change......	1927-31 to 1942-46		12		42		11		15		n.c.	Delta states
Number per farm:												
All cattle.............	1942 to 1946	4.4		7.3		21.5		9.3		17.0		Oklahoma and Texas
Per cent change......	1917-21 to 1942-46		29		43		35		35		24	Delta states
Per cent change......	1927-31 to 1942-46		52		103		85		72		37	Delta states
Hogs.................	1942 to 1946	5.7		5.5		6.5		5.8		15.2		38 other states
Per cent change......	1917-21 to 1942-46		−2		−4		5		−2		30	38 other states
Per cent change......	1927-31 to 1942-46		42		77		67		57		17	Delta states
Chickens.............	1943 to 1946	46		44		91		56		112		38 other states
Per cent change......	1927-31 to 1942-46		33		47		55		42		15	Oklahoma and Texas

* Per cent change with a minus shows a decrease. † Includes tobacco, cotton, orchards, vegetables, Irish potatoes, and sweet potatoes.
‡ Rice, corn, and peanuts. § Wheat, oats, barley, hay, cowpeas, soybeans, and sorghums.
n.c. means not calculated. Source: Same as for Table V.

Statistical Appendix

TABLE VII
COMPARISON OF ACREAGE AND NUMBER PER 100 ACRES OF CROPLAND HARVESTED* IN 1944, OR 1942-46 BY REGIONS WITH PERCENTAGE CHANGES BETWEEN PERIODS

Item	Period	Eastern states		Delta states		Oklahoma and Texas		10 cotton states		38 other states		Region in lead
		Acres or No.	Per cent	Acres or No.	Per cent	Acres or No.	Per cent	Acres or No.	Per cent	Acres or No.	Per cent	
Acreage per 100 acres of cropland harvested:												
Intensive crops†	1944	24.8		34.8		21.6		25.0		n.c.		Delta states
Per cent change‡	1929 to 1944		−44		−40		−54		−48			Oklahoma and Texas
Medium intensive crops§	1944	48.4		37.5		15.7		30.8		n.c.		Eastern states
Per cent change	1929 to 1944		16		14		−6		10			Eastern states
Extensive crops‡	1944	30.5		28.4		61.5		44.7		n.c.		Oklahoma and Texas
Per cent change	1929 to 1944		78		212		69		79			Delta states
Cotton	1944	16.8		30.5		19.4		20.4		n.c.		Delta states
Per cent change	1929 to 1944		−54		−44		−57		−54			Oklahoma and Texas
Number per 100 acres of cropland harvested plus pasture:												
All cattle	1942 to 1946	9.2		12.6		7.0		8.2		8.5		Delta states
Per cent change	1927-31 to 1942-46		35		38		27		30		12	Delta states
Number per 100 acres of cropland harvested:												
Hogs	1942 to 1946	21		20		9		15.0		20.6		Eastern states
Per cent change	1927-31 to 1942-46		42		56		46		47		14	Delta states
Chickens	1942 to 1946	172		161		120		145		152		Eastern states
Per cent change	1927-31 to 1942-46		30		30		36		33		13	Oklahoma and Texas
Workstock	1945	5.4		7.1		3.0		4.5		n.c.		Delta states
Per cent change	1930 to 1945		−10		−5		−46		−26			Oklahoma and Texas
Tractors	1945	.36		.41		.56		.46		.76		38 other states
Per cent change	1930 to 1945		260		356		300		283		145	Delta states

* Except all cattle which are shown on the basis of each 100 acres of cropland harvested plus pasture land.   n.c. means not calculated.
† Includes tobacco, cotton, orchards, vegetables, Irish potatoes, and sweet potatoes.
‡ Rice, corn, and peanuts.   § Wheat, oats, barley, hay; cowpeas and soybeans grown alone, and sorghum.
The minus indicates a percentage decrease.
Source: Same as for Table V.

TABLE VIII
Changes in Sources of Gross Farm Receipts, 10 Cotton Belt States

Source	Five year average (000,000)			1947 (000,000)
	1924-29	1935-39	1941-45	
Cotton and cottonseed	$1,453.9	$ 685.0	$1,103.4	$1,946.5
Tobacco	127.4	172.0	359.4	596.6
Rice	32.4	28.5	82.1	140.3
Wheat	83.8	56.8	119.5	429.3
Truck crops	56.7	48.8	195.9	141.2
Peaches	19.6	13.0	31.9	33.6
Peanuts	24.6	29.0	109.1	175.1
Pecans	7.4	4.0	20.2	25.2
White potatoes	17.9	13.8	30.1	31.7
Sweet potatoes	15.4	14.4	28.3	36.7
Total of all crops*	2,010.4	1,207.5	2,311.6	4,160.1
Cattle and calves	180.2	184.9	428.0	884.9
Dairy products	135.5	142.9	279.7	419.4
Hogs	81.4	82.0	231.8	379.0
Eggs (chicken)	92.0	62.4	183.5	236.3
Chickens	46.6	31.0	114.3	166.4
Total of all livestock*	578.9	558.3	1,346.7	2,218.2
Total receipts from farm marketings	2,589.3	1,765.8	3,658.3	6,378.3
Government payments	.....	193.4	189.9	86.7

* Includes the enterprises listed plus all others from which receipts were obtained during the period.

Source: 1. *Cotton:* Hearings before the Subcommittee of the Committee on Agriculture, House of Representatives, Seventy-Eighth Congress, Second Session, Dec. 4 to 9, 1944, pp. 600-7.
2. *Cash Receipts from Marketings by States and Commodities, Calendar Years, 1924-44*, U. S. Dept. of Agri., Bur. of Agri. Econ., Washington, D. C., January, 1946, pp. 83-121.
3. *The Farm Income Situation*, U. S. Dept. of Agri., Bur. of Agri. Econ., current issues.
4. *Agricultural Statistics, 1946*, U. S. Dept. of Agri.

Statistical Appendix

TABLE IX
COTTON ACREAGE HARVESTED BY REGIONS, 1910-1948
(Thousand acres)

Year	Eastern states	Delta states	Oklahoma and Texas	10 cotton states
1910	12,372	6,167	12,536	31,075
1911	13,684	6,399	14,317	34,400
1912	12,762	5,680	13,721	32,163
1913	12,844	6,341	15,594	34,779
1914	13,790	6,449	14,870	35,109
1910-14	13,090	6,207	14,208	33,505
1915	11,778	5,402	12,391	29,571
1916	12,490	6,603	13,482	32,575
1917	11,426	6,180	14,121	31,727
1918	12,458	7,002	15,022	34,482
1919	12,041	6,647	13,752	32,440
1915-19	12,039	6,367	13,754	32,160
1920	11,582	6,776	15,370	33,728
1921	9,701	5,841	12,776	28,318
1922	9,426	6,548	14,794	30,768
1923	9,827	6,924	17,985	34,736
1924	10,325	7,194	20,852	38,371
1920-24	10,172	6,657	16,355	33,184
1925	11,813	8,730	22,624	43,167
1926	12,193	8,910	22,360	43,463
1927	10,719	7,500	19,290	37,509
1928	11,424	9,016	20,894	41,334
1929	11,585	9,412	20,989	41,986
1925-29	11,547	8,714	21,231	41,492
1930	11,536	9,593	20,067	41,196
1931	10,380	9,111	18,130	37,621
1932	9,642	8,854	16,442	34,938
1930-32	10,519	9,186	18,213	37,918
1933	7,814	6,662	13,929	28,405
1934	7,290	5,886	12,744	25,920
1935	7,440	6,145	12,975	26,560
1936	7,750	6,889	13,848	28,487
1937	9,090	7,772	14,911	31,773
1938	6,900	5,777	10,440	23,117
1939	6,611	5,785	10,304	22,700
1933-39	7,556	6,417	12,736	26,709
1940	6,674	5,691	10,294	22,659
1941	6,212	5,398	9,376	20,986
1942	6,116	5,363	9,829	21,308
1943	5,941	5,370	9,280	20,591
1944	5,275	5,029	8,660	18,964
1945	4,728	4,544	6,885	16,157
1946	4,850	4,705	7,100	16,655
1940-46	5,685	5,157	8,775	19,617
1947	5,204	5,221	9,323	19,748
1948	5,616	5,792	10,030	21,438

Source: 1910-1927: *Cotton—Acreage, Yield, and Production, 1866-1938, by States, and Related Data*, U. S. Dept. of Agri., Agriculture Marketing Service, September, 1940.
1928-1944: *Farm Production, Farm Disposition, and Value of Cotton and Cottonseed and Related Data, 1928-1944*, U. S. Dept. of Agri., Bur. of Agri. Econ., October, 1945.
1945-1948: *Cotton Production*, Crop Reporting Board, U. S. D. A., current issues.

TABLE X
COTTON YIELD PER HARVESTED ACRE BY REGIONS, 1910-1948
(Pounds of lint per acre)

Year	Eastern states	Delta states	Oklahoma and Texas	10 cotton states
1910.........	199	181	151	176
1911.........	268	189	170	212
1912.........	204	186	206	201
1913.........	237	213	147	192
1914.........	254	201	188	216
1910-14......	233	194	172	200
1915.........	205	187	149	178
1916.........	165	173	161	165
1917.........	188	195	138	167
1918.........	219	191	104	163
1919.........	196	154	143	165
1915-19......	195	180	138	168
1920.........	204	176	177	186
1921.........	158	155	100	131
1922.........	166	171	124	147
1923.........	155	110	133	134
1924.........	184	178	148	163
1920-24......	174	158	138	153
1925.........	203	246	124	170
1926.........	222	229	158	190
1927.........	189	185	134	160
1928.........	172	181	144	160
1929.........	197	211	116	159
1925-29......	197	211	135	168
1930.........	216	152	116	153
1931.........	238	239	174	207
1932.........	181	168	162	169
1930-32......	212	186	149	176
1933.........	241	192	195	207
1934.........	238	203	102	163
1935.........	241	208	130	179
1936.........	252	275	111	189
1937.........	294	351	190	259
1938.........	240	309	167	224
1939.........	251	309	156	223
1933-39......	252	266	151	207
1940.........	287	269	187	237
1941.........	228	280	172	216
1942.........	299	361	182	261
1943.........	289	330	165	244
1944.........	358	376	181	282
1945.........	319	315	144	243
1946.........	294	257	129	213
1940-46......	294	312	168	243
1947.........	295	307	194	250
1948.........	371	420	172	291

Note: The period average is weighted according to the quantity produced each year.
Source: Same as for Table IX.

TABLE XI
Production of Cotton by Regions, 1910-1948
(Thousand bales)

Year	Eastern states	Delta states	Oklahoma and Texas	10 cotton states
1910	5,162	2,330	3,972	11,464
1911	7,659	2,528	5,278	15,465
1912	5,441	2,214	5,901	13,556
1913	6,359	2,828	4,785	13,972
1914	7,314	2,711	5,854	15,879
1910-14	6,387	2,522	5,118	14,027
1915	5,063	2,111	3,867	11,041
1916	4,319	2,389	4,550	11,258
1917	4,493	2,519	4,084	11,096
1918	5,717	2,801	3,278	11,796
1919	4,934	2,143	4,115	11,192
1915-19	4,905	2,393	3,978	11,276
1920	4,947	2,497	5,681	13,125
1921	3,197	1,889	2,679	7,765
1922	3,268	2,344	3,849	9,461
1923	3,184	1,594	4,996	9,774
1924	3,970	2,686	6,460	13,116
1920-24	3,713	2,202	4,733	10,648
1925	5,017	4,501	5,854	15,372
1926	5,657	4,262	7,401	17,320
1927	4,237	2,901	5,389	12,527
1928	4,122	3,409	6,310	13,841
1929	4,767	4,155	5,083	14,005
1925-29	4,760	3,846	6,007	14,613
1930	5,209	3,049	4,891	13,149
1931	5,159	4,558	6,581	16,298
1932	3,656	3,111	5,584	12,351
1930-32	4,675	3,573	5,685	13,933
1933	3,935	2,680	5,694	12,309
1934	3,632	2,496	2,722	8,850
1935	3,751	2,668	3,523	9,942
1936	4,077	3,967	3,223	11,267
1937	5,595	5,700	5,927	17,222
1938	3,459	3,729	3,649	10,837
1939	3,477	3,740	3,372	10,589
1933-39	3,989	3,569	4,016	11,574
1940	4,003	3,207	4,036	11,246
1941	2,970	3,167	3,370	9,507
1942	3,831	4,046	3,746	11,623
1943	3,589	3,702	3,207	10,498
1944	3,952	3,951	3,280	11,183
1945	3,158	2,989	2,079	8,226
1946	2,980	2,530	1,910	7,420
1940-46	3,498	3,370	3,090	9,958
1947	3,205	3,350	3,767	10,322
1948	4,350	5,075	3,600	13,025

Source: Same as for Table IX.

TABLE XII
ALL CATTLE ON FARMS JANUARY 1 BY REGIONS, 1910-1948
(Thousand head)

Year	Eastern states	Delta states	Oklahoma and Texas	10 cotton states
1910	3,715	2,540	8,697	14,952
1911	3,709	2,588	8,325	14,622
1912	3,696	2,590	8,173	14,459
1913	3,706	2,543	8,006	14,255
1914	3,817	2,669	8,502	14,988
1910-14	3,729	2,586	8,341	14,656
1915	3,970	2,766	9,036	15,772
1916	4,067	2,952	9,744	16,763
1917	4,162	3,156	10,205	17,523
1918	4,335	3,300	10,135	17,770
1919	4,459	3,411	9,660	17,530
1915-19	4,199	3,117	9,756	17,072
1920	4,442	3,273	9,874	17,589
1921	4,321	3,151	10,100	17,572
1922	4,247	3,122	10,300	17,669
1923	4,039	2,932	10,000	16,971
1924	3,860	2,774	9,250	15,884
1920-24	4,182	3,050	9,905	17,137
1925	3,671	2,678	8,795	15,144
1926	3,485	2,588	8,077	14,150
1927	3,354	2,525	7,895	13,774
1928	3,362	2,482	7,679	13,523
1929	3,363	2,559	8,069	13,991
1925-29	3,447	2,566	8,103	14,116
1930	3,435	2,646	8,415	14,496
1931	3,632	2,788	8,624	15,044
1932	3,900	3,071	9,090	16,061
1930-32	3,656	2,835	8,710	15,201
1933	4,233	3,424	10,075	17,732
1934	4,437	3,698	11,160	19,295
1935	4,529	3,713	9,855	18,097
1936	4,230	3,361	9,283	16,874
1937	3,955	3,395	9,799	17,149
1938	3,844	3,472	9,405	16,721
1939	3,980	3,514	9,264	16,758
1933-39	4,173	3,511	9,834	17,518
1940	4,111	3,615	9,328	17,054
1941	4,207	3,709	9,818	17,734
1942	4,415	3,860	10,752	19,027
1943	4,711	4,168	11,831	20,710
1944	5,114	4,396	12,210	21,720
1945	5,142	4,563	12,359	22,064
1946	4,984	4,509	11,892	21,385
1940-46	4,669	4,117	11,170	19,956
1947	4,980	4,350	11,478	20,808
1948	4,841	3,942	11,057	19,840

Source: 1920-1935: *Livestock on Farms, January 1, 1867-1935: Revised Estimates—Number, Value per Head, Total Value by States and Divisions*, U. S. Dept. of Agri., Bur. of Agri. Econ., January, 1938.
1935-1940: *Crops and Markets*, Vol. 19, No. 2, February, 1942, p. 33.
1940-1945: *Livestock and Poultry on Farms January 1, Number, Value per Head, and Total Value: Livestock and Poultry by Classes, Rev. Estimate, 1940-1945 by States*, U. S. Dept. of Agri., Bur. Agri. Econ., Crop Reporting Board, February, 1947.
1946-1947: *Livestock on Farms January 1*, U S. Dept. of Agri., Bur. of Agri. Econ., Crop Reporting Board, February, 1947.
1948: *Ibid.*, February, 1948.

Statistical Appendix

TABLE XIII
MILK COWS ON FARMS JANUARY 1 BY REGIONS, 1910-1948
(Thousand head)

Year	Eastern states	Delta states	Oklahoma and Texas	10 cotton states
1910	1,535	987	1,430	3,952
1911	1,548	1,020	1,440	4,008
1912	1,559	1,042	1,450	4,051
1913	1,562	1,048	1,452	4,062
1914	1,567	1,047	1,475	4,089
1910-14	1,554	1,029	1,449	4,032
1915	1,584	1,071	1,510	4,165
1916	1,625	1,091	1,519	4,235
1917	1,662	1,105	1,535	4,302
1918	1,707	1,132	1,535	4,374
1919	1,744	1,139	1,521	4,404
1915-19	1,664	1,108	1,524	4,296
1920	1,768	1,145	1,494	4,407
1921	1,750	1,104	1,484	4,338
1922	1,738	1,115	1,551	4,404
1923	1,717	1,075	1,568	4,360
1924	1,682	1,059	1,568	4,309
1920-24	1,731	1,100	1,533	4,364
1925	1,664	1,060	1,567	4,291
1926	1,612	1,031	1,640	4,283
1927	1,596	1,028	1,699	4,323
1928	1,596	1,032	1,728	4,356
1929	1,601	1,048	1,791	4,440
1925-29	1,614	1,040	1,685	4,339
1930	1,632	1,062	1,852	4,546
1931	1,716	1,112	1,913	4,741
1932	1,821	1,206	2,042	5,069
1930-32	1,723	1,127	1,935	4,785
1933	1,951	1,324	2,169	5,444
1934	2,016	1,407	2,299	5,722
1935	2,042	1,415	2,186	5,643
1936	1,923	1,322	2,154	5,399
1937	1,847	1,317	2,130	5,294
1938	1,817	1,323	2,162	5,302
1939	1,821	1,342	2,178	5,341
1933-39	1,917	1,350	2,183	5,450
1940	1,843	1,348	2,188	5,379
1941	1,862	1,346	2,226	5,434
1942	1,951	1,408	2,354	5,713
1943	2,034	1,482	2,459	5,975
1944	2,117	1,494	2,490	6,101
1945	2,122	1,535	2,479	6,136
1946	2,070	1,498	2,337	5,905
1940-46	2,000	1,444	2,362	5,806
1947	2,042	1,424	2,218	5,684
1948	2,012	1,330	2,055	5,397

Source: Same as for Table XII.

TABLE XIV
Hogs on Farms January 1 by Regions, 1910-1948
(Thousand head)

Year	Eastern states	Delta states	Oklahoma and Texas	10 cotton states
1910	6,060	3,464	3,681	13,205
1911	6,719	3,819	4,140	14,678
1912	6,997	3,812	3,580	14,389
1913	6,500	3,410	3,450	13,360
1914	6,235	3,215	3,700	13,150
1910-14	6,502	3,544	3,710	13,756
1915	6,335	3,160	3,850	13,345
1916	7,153	3,430	4,030	14,613
1917	7,160	3,600	4,000	14,760
1918	7,550	4,081	4,040	15,671
1919	8,183	3,857	3,785	15,825
1915-19	7,276	3,626	3,941	14,843
1920	7,516	3,602	3,884	15,002
1921	6,947	3,177	3,873	13,997
1922	6,709	3,070	3,794	13,573
1923	6,535	2,829	3,541	12,905
1924	5,759	2,358	3,015	11,132
1920-24	6,693	3,007	3,621	13,321
1925	4,694	2,114	2,569	9,377
1926	4,433	2,071	2,196	8,700
1927	4,619	2,200	2,523	9,342
1928	5,253	2,479	2,904	10,636
1929	4,788	2,315	2,975	10,078
1925-29	4,757	2,236	2,633	9,626
1930	4,449	2,201	2,726	9,376
1931	4,522	2,013	2,467	9,002
1932	4,978	2,570	3,095	10,643
1930-32	4,650	2,261	2,763	9,674
1933	5,413	2,966	3,766	12,145
1934	5,148	2,866	3,300	11,314
1935	4,667	2,591	2,199	9,457
1936	4,756	2,517	2,279	9,552
1937	5,243	2,870	2,358	10,471
1938	5,182	2,937	2,272	10,391
1939	5,821	3,361	2,747	11,929
1933-39	5,176	2,873	2,703	10,752
1940	6,384	3,586	3,518	13,488
1941	5,607	2,968	2,882	11,457
1942	5,840	2,995	3,141	11,976
1943	6,762	3,437	4,150	14,349
1944	7,715	3,820	4,541	16,076
1945	6,232	3,145	3,051	12,428
1946	5,492	2,808	2,912	11,212
1940-46	6,290	3,251	3,456	12,997
1947	5,880	2,845	2,447	11,172
1948	5,979	2,725	2,484	11,188

Source: Same as for Table XII.

TABLE XV
ALL CHICKENS ON FARMS BY REGIONS, 1925-1948
(Thousand head)

Year	Eastern states	Delta states	Oklahoma and Texas	10 cotton states
1925.........	40,826	18,452	34,798	94,076
1926.........	40,497	19,512	33,942	93,951
1927.........	42,983	21,570	39,422	103,975
1928.........	45,854	22,196	43,676	111,726
1929.........	39,714	20,610	40,704	101,028
1925-29.....	41,975	20,468	38,508	100,951
1930.........	40,509	22,058	41,640	104,207
1931.........	38,853	19,865	39,860	98,578
1932.........	38,800	20,462	39,915	99,177
1930-32.....	39,387	20,795	40,472	100,654
1933.........	40,669	21,039	41,480	103,188
1934.........	38,883	19,155	37,194	95,232
1935.........	38,226	18,591	31,708	88,525
1936.........	39,152	18,645	32,866	90,663
1937.........	41,780	21,105	35,132	98,017
1938.........	38,353	20,130	33,573	92,056
1939.........	41,007	22,193	37,755	100,955
1933-39.....	39,724	20,123	35,673	95,520
1940.........	41,992	22,080	40,335	104,407
1941.........	39,972	21,050	38,255	99,277
1942.........	45,838	24,317	45,098	115,253
1943.........	51,936	27,265	52,816	132,017
1944.........	57,439	29,066	55,621	142,126
1945.........	51,477	24,256	48,603	124,336
1946.........	51,782	24,119	48,595	124,496
1940-46.....	48,634	24,593	47,047	120,274
1947.........	46,862	21,127	40,510	108,499
1948.........	43,187	19,634	39,611	102,432

Source: 1925-1935: *Farm Production and Disposition of Chickens and Eggs; 1925-1937: Chickens on Farms January 1 by States*, U. S. Dept. of Agri.; Dec., 1938.
1935-1940: *Crops and Markets*, Vol. 19, No. 2, Feb.; 1942; p. 40.
1940-1945: *Livestock and Poultry on Farms, January 1; Number, Value per Head, and Total Value: Livestock and Poultry by Classes; Rev. Estimates, 1940-1945; by States*, U. S. Dept. of Agri.; Bur. of Agri. Econ.; Crop Reporting Board; Feb., 1947.
1946-1947: *Livestock on Farms January 1, Ibid.*; Feb.; 1947.
1948: *Ibid.*; Feb.; 1948;

TABLE XVI

STOCK SHEEP ON FARMS IN THE UNITED STATES AND TEXAS BY PERIODS

Period	Average number of head (in thousands)		Per cent Texas is of United States
	United States	Texas	
1915-19	36,567	2,323	6
1925-29	38,485	4,673	12
1933-39	46,222	8,124	18
1940-46	44,390	9,823	22
1947	32,542	8,308	26

Source: Same as for Table XII.

TABLE XVII

PROPORTION OF THE UNITED STATES COTTON ACREAGE AND PRODUCTION IN VARIOUS PRODUCTION AREAS FOR SPECIFIED PERIODS

Production area	Acreage			Production		
	1928-32 average per cent	1935-39 average per cent	1941-43 average per cent	1928-32 average per cent	1935-39 average per cent	1941-43 average per cent
Delta	13.2	14.4	16.3	17.4	22.8	26.5
Eastern Hilly	10.7	10.9	11.5	11.7	12.8	13.7
Coastal Plains	13.6	14.0	13.6	14.5	16.8	12.8
Low Plains	12.9	11.7	11.8	9.9	6.3	8.7
Piedmont	7.8	7.5	7.6	9.8	8.7	8.1
Texas Blackland	13.7	12.7	11.6	11.7	8.7	6.7
Irrigated	1.4	2.6	3.3	3.1	6.2	6.1
High Plains	3.6	4.9	5.5	2.7	3.8	4.7
Sandy Lands	10.6	9.3	7.9	8.7	5.6	4.6
Gulf Coastal Prairies	3.4	3.7	3.5	3.7	3.4	3.2
Ozark-Ouachita Mountains and Valleys	3.4	2.9	2.8	2.9	2.2	2.2
Texas Grazing	2.5	2.4	2.2	1.5	1.2	1.2
Oklahoma Prairie	1.4	1.4	1.1	1.2	.6	.7
Cross Timbers	1.8	1.6	1.3	1.2	.9	.7

Source: E. L. Langsford, *Changes in Cotton Production in War and Peace*, U. S. Dept. of Agri., Bur. of Agri. Econ., F. M. 45, Dec., 1944, p. 14.

TABLE XVIII
YIELD OF COTTON AS A PERCENTAGE OF 1928-32 AVERAGE BY PRODUCTION AREAS FOR SPECIFIED PERIODS

Production area	1928-32 average per cent	1935-39 average per cent	1941-43 average per cent
Delta	100	155	178
Eastern Hilly	100	138	160
Coastal Plains	100	130	129
Low Plains	100	90	136
Piedmont	100	119	122
Texas Blackland	100	104	98
Irrigated	100	141	122
High Plains	100	127	161
Sandy Lands	100	128	103
Gulf Coastal Prairie	100	108	120
Ozark-Ouachita Mountains and Valleys	100	119	121
Texas Grazing	100	93	120
Oklahoma Prairie	100	97	106
Cross Timbers	100	105	111

Source: Langsford, *op. cit.*, p. 31.

TABLE XIX
CHANGE IN RANK OF STATES IN COTTON PRODUCTION BY SELECTED YEARS

State	1948 production (000 bales)	Rank in cotton production					
		1948	1937–1946	1938	1928	1920	1910
Texas	3,250	1	1	1	1	1	1
Mississippi	2,300	2	2	2	2	7	3
Arkansas	2,050	3	3	3	3	5	7
Alabama	1,250	4	4	4	5	8	4
California	950	5	11	10	11	13	14
South Carolina	940	6	6	7	8	2	5
Georgia	780	7	5	5	6	3	2

Source: Compiled from *Agricultural Statistics*, various issues, and from other U. S. Dept. of Agri. official reports; data for 1948 are from *Cotton Production*, U. S. Dept. of Agri., Crop Reporting Board, October 8, 1948.

TABLE XX

LIST OF URBAN PLACES IN 10 COTTON STATES WITH 10,000-50,000 PERSONS IN 1940 WITH PERCENTAGE INCREASE IN THE POPULATION IN THE DECADES 1930 TO 1940 AND 1920 TO 1930

State and city	1940 population (000)	Per cent increase from 1930 to 1940	Per cent increase from 1920 to 1930	State and city	1940 population (000)	Per cent increase from 1930 to 1940	Per cent increase from 1920 to 1930
NORTH CAROLINA				ALABAMA			
1. 25,000 to 50,000				1 25,000 to 50,000			
a. High Point	38.5	5	157	a. Anniston	25.5	14	26
b. Raleigh	46.9	26	53	b. Gadsden	37.0	54	63
c. Rocky Mount	25.6	19	68	c. Tuscaloosa	27.5	33	72
d. Wilmington	33.4	4	− 3	2. 10,000 to 25,000			
2. 10,000 to 25,000				a. Bessemer	22.8	10	11
a. Burlington	12.2	25	64	b. Decatur	16.6	6	228
b. Concord	15.6	32	19	c. Dothan	17.2	7	60
c. Elizabeth City	11.6	15	12	d. Fairfield	11.7	6	121
d. Fayetteville	17.4	34	47	e. Florence	15.0	28	11
e. Gastonia	21.3	25	33	f. Huntsville	13.0	13	44
f. Goldsboro	17.3	15	33	g. Phenix City	15.4	11	155
g. Greenville	12.7	38	59	h. Selma	19.8	10	16
h. Hickory	13.5	83	45	TENNESSEE			
i. Kinston	15.4	35	16	1. 25,000 to 50,000			
j. Lexington	10.6	9	84	a. Johnson City	25.3	1	102
k. New Bern	11.8	− 1	− 2	2. 10,000 to 25,000			
l. Reidsville	10.4	52	28	a. Bristol	14.0	17	49
m. Salisbury	19.0	12	22	(Bristol, Va.)	9.8	10	31
n. Shelby	14.0	30	199	b. Clarksville	11.8	28	14
o. Statesville	14.4	9	33	c. Cleveland	11.4	24	40
p. Thomasville	11.0	9	78	d. Columbia	10.6	34	43
q. Wilson	19.2	52	19	e. Dyersburg	10.0	15	36
SOUTH CAROLINA				f. Jackson	24.3	8	18
1. 25,000 to 50,000				g. Kingsport	14.4	21	109
a. Greenville	34.7	19	26	MISSISSIPPI			
b. Spartanburg	32.2	12	27	1. 25,000 to 50,000			
2. 10,000 to 25,000				a. Meridian	35.5	11	37
a. Anderson	19.4	35	36	2. 10,000 to 25,000			
b. Florence	16.1	9	35	a. Biloxi	17.5	18	36
c. Greenwood	13.0	18	27	b. Clarksdale	12.2	21	33
d. Orangeburg	10.5	20	20	c. Columbus	13.6	27	2
e. Rock Hill	15.0	33	28	d. Greenville	20.9	41	28
f. Sumter	15.9	35	24	e. Greenwood	14.8	33	43
GEORGIA				f. Gulfport	15.2	21	54
1. 25,000 to 50,000				g. Hattiesburg	21.0	13	40
a. Rome	26.3	20	65	h. Laurel	20.6	14	38
2. 10,000 to 25,000				i. Natchez	15.3	14	6
a. Albany	19.1	31	26	j. Vicksburg	24.5	7	27
b. Athens	20.6	14	9	ARKANSAS			
c. Brunswick	15.0	7	− 3	1. 25,000 to 50,000			
d. Dalton	10.4	28	56	a. Fort Smith	36.6	16	9
e. Decatur	16.6	25	116	2. 10,000 to 25,000			
f. East Point	12.4	30	82	a. Blytheville	10.7	6	57
g. Gainesville	10.2	19	38	b. El Dorado	15.9	− 3	322
h. Griffin	13.2	28	25	c. Hot Springs	21.4	6	73
i. La Grange	22.0	9	18	d. Jonesboro	11.7	14	10
j. Moultrie	10.1	26	18	e. North Little Rock	21.1	9	38
k. Thomasville	12.7	8	43	f. Pine Bluff	21.3	3	8
l. Valdosta	15.6	16	25	g. Texarkana	11.8	10	30
m. Waycross	16.8	8	−14	(Texarkana, Tex.)	17.0	2	45

TABLE XX (continued)

State and city	1940 population (000)	Per cent increase from 1930 to 1940	Per cent increase from 1920 to 1930	State and city	1940 population (000)	Per cent increase from 1930 to 1940	Per cent increase from 1920 to 1930
LOUISIANA				**TEXAS**			
1. 25,000 to 50,000				1. 25,000 to 50,000			
a. Alexandria	27.1	18	32	a. Abilene	26.6	15	126
b. Baton Rouge	34.7	13	41	b. Laredo	39.3	20	44
c. Monroe	28.3	9	105	c. Lubbock	31.9	55	406
2. 10,000 to 25,000				d. Port Arthur	46.1	−9	129
a. Bogalusa	14.6	4	70	e. San Angelo	25.8	2	152
b. Gretna	10.9	14	33	f. Tyler	28.3	65	42
c. Lafayette	19.2	31	86	g. Wichita Falls	45.1	3	9
d. Lake Charles	21.2	34	21	2. 10,000 to 25,000			
e. New Iberia	13.7	72	28	a. Big Spring	12.6	−8	221
OKLAHOMA				b. Borger	10.0	53	..
1. 25,000 to 50,000				c. Brownsville	22.1	*	87
a. Enid	28.1	6	59	d. Brownwood	13.4	5	56
b. Muskogee	32.3	1	6	e. Bryan	11.8	52	24
2. 10,000 to 25,000				f. Cleburne	10.6	−8	−10
a. Ada	15.1	34	41	g. Corsicana	15.2	*	34
b. Ardmore	16.9	7	11	h. Del Rio	13.3	14	10
c. Bartlesville	16.3	10	2	i. Denison	15.6	12	−19
d. Chickasha	14.1	*	38	j. Denton	11.2	17	26
e. Durant	10.0	34	2	k. Greenville	14.0	13	*
f. El Reno	10.1	7	21	l. Harlingen	13.3	10	580
g. Guthrie	10.0	5	−18	m. Highland Park	10.3	22	263
h. Lawton	18.1	49	36	n. Longview	13.8	173	−12
i. McAlester	12.4	5	11	o. McAllen	11.9	31	70
j. Norman	11.4	19	92	p. Marshall	18.4	14	14
k. Okmulgee	16.1	−6	−2	q. Palestine	12.1	6	4
l. Ponca City	16.8	4	129	r. Pampa	12.9	23	961
m. Sapulpa	12.2	16	−10	s. Paris	18.7	19	4
n. Seminole	11.5	1	1242	t. Sherman	17.2	9	4
o. Shawnee	22.1	−5	52	u. Sweetwater	10.4	−4	152
p. Stillwater	10.1	44	49	v. Temple	15.3	−†	39
q. Wewoka	10.3	−1	584	w. Terrell	10.5	19	5
				x. Texarkana	17.0	2	45
				(Texarkana, Ark.)	11.8	10	30
				y. University Park	14.5	244	..
				z. Victoria	11.6	56	25

* Less than 0.5 per cent increase.
† A decrease of only one person from 1930 to 1940.
Source: Sixteenth Census of the United States, 1940, *Population*: Vol. I; *Number of Inhabitants*.

TABLE XXI
TOTAL POPULATION AND URBAN POPULATION IN THE UNITED STATES
(Urban population in places of 2,500 or over)

Census year	Total population		Urban population		Per cent of total urban
	Number of persons (000,000)	Per cent increase over preceding census	Number of persons (000,000)	Per cent increase over preceding census	
1790.....	3.9	....	0.2	....	5.1
1800.....	5.3	35.1	0.3	59.9	6.1
1810.....	7.2	36.4	0.5	63.0	7.3
1820.....	9.6	33.1	0.7	31.9	7.2
1830.....	12.9	33.5	1.1	62.6	8.8
1840.....	17.1	32.7	1.8	63.7	10.8
1850.....	23.2	35.9	3.5	92.1	15.3
1860.....	31.4	35.6	6.2	75.4	19.8
1870.....	38.6	22.6	9.9	59.3	25.7
1880.....	50.2	30.1	14.1	42.7	28.2
1890.....	62.9	25.5	22.1	56.5	35.1
1900.....	76.0	20.7	30.2	36.4	39.7
1910.....	92.0	21.0	42.0	39.3	45.7
1920.....	105.7	14.9	54.2	29.0	51.2
1930.....	122.8	16.1	69.0	27.3	56.2
1940.....	131.7	7.2	74.4	7.9	56.5

Source: Sixteenth Census of the United States, *Population;* Vol. II: *Characteristics of the Population,* pt. 1, p. 18.

Selected Bibliography

Selected Bibliography

ARTICLES AND BOOKS

Abrahamsen, Martin A. "Cotton Mechanization: Its Probable Influence on Marketing," *Journal of Farm Economics*, 31 (February, 1949), 410-14.

Aull, George H. "Employment Prospects in Southern Agriculture," *Southern Economic Journal*, 13 (April, 1947), 378-85.

Bachman, Kenneth L. "Capital-Labor Substitution in Cotton Farming," *Journal of Farm Economics*, 31 (February, 1949), 370-73.

Black, John D. "Coming Readjustments in Agriculture—Domestic Phases," *Journal of Farm Economics*, 31 (February, 1949), 1-15.

――――; Clawson, Marion; Sayre, Charles R.; Wilcox, Walter F. *Farm Management*. New York: The Macmillan Co., 1947, Chaps. I-IX, XXXVII, and XLVIII.

Bertrand, Alvin L. "The Social Processes and Mechanization of Southern Agricultural Systems," *Rural Sociology*, 13 (March, 1948), 31-39.

Bromfield, L. "Go South, Young Man!" *Atlantic Monthly*, 182 (November, 1948), 57-62.

――――. "The Rebirth of the South," *The Reader's Digest*, 55 (July, 1949), 19-22.

Brunner, Edmund de S. "Internal Migration in the United States, 1935-40," *Rural Sociology*, 13 (March, 1948), 9-22.

Cates, J. S. "Revolution in Southern Agriculture," *The Reader's Digest*, 39 (August, 1941), 94-97.

Cole, William E. "Urban Development in the Tennessee Valley," *Social Forces*, 26 (October, 1947), 67-75.

Drucker, P. F. "Exit King Cotton," *Harper's Magazine*, 192 (May, 1946), 473-80.

"Effect of Industrialization on Agriculture," *Monthly Review*, Federal Reserve Bank of Richmond (March, 1948), 3-7.

Ezekiel, Mordecai. "Agriculture and Industry in the Post-war South," *The South: America's Opportunity Number One*. Southern Regional Council, Atlanta, Ga., 1945, pp. 3-8.

Forster, G. W. "Impact of Technology on Southern Agriculture," *Journal of Farm Economics*, 29 (May, 1947), 520-30.

———. "Southern Agricultural Economy in the Postwar Era," *Southern Economic Journal*, 13 (July, 1946), 65-71.

Fulmer, J. L. "Relationship of the Cycle in Yields of Cotton and Apples to Solar and Sky Radiation," *Quarterly Journal of Economics*, 56 (May, 1942), 385-405.

Gee, Wilson. "The Effects of Urbanization on Agriculture," *Southern Economic Journal*, 2 (May, 1935), 3-15.

———. "The 'Drag' of Talent Out of the South," *Social Forces*, 15 (March, 1937), 343-46.

———, and Terry, Edward Allison. *The Cotton Cooperatives in the Southeast*. New York and London: D. Appleton-Century Company, 1933.

Hoover, Calvin B. "What Changes in National Policy Does the South Need?" *Journal of Farm Economics*, 22 (February, 1940), 206-12.

Jones, Phillip E. "Postwar Adjustments in Cotton Production in the Southeastern United States," *Journal of Land and Public Utility Economics*, 21 (November, 1945), 339-51.

McEvoy, J. P. "Bill Bailey and the Four Pillars: What Country Bankers Can Do for Their Communities," *The Reader's Digest*, 44 (April, 1944), 45-47.

Miley, D. Gray. "The Size of Farm in the South," *Journal of Farm Economics*, 31 (February, 1949), 582-87.

Nelson, D. M. "South's Economic Opportunity," *American Mercury*, 59 (October, 1944), 422-27.

Pritchett, W. M. "Crop Yields—A Measure of Farming Efficiency," *Monthly Business Review*, Federal Reserve Bank of Dallas, 33 (December, 1948), 189-99.

Raper, Arthur. *Machines in the Cotton Fields*. Southern Regional Council, Atlanta, Ga., 1946.

Sayre, Charles R. "Technology and Cost Structure on Southern Farms," *Journal of Farm Economics*, 31 (February, 1949), 454-57.

Simkins, Francis Butler. *The South Old and New, A History 1820-1947*. New York: Alfred A. Knopf, 1947, Chaps. XVI and XVII.

Smith, T. Lynn, and Roberts, Ralph W. "Sources and Distribution of the Farm Population in Relation to Farm Benefit Payments," *Journal of Farm Economics*, 23 (August, 1941), 607-18.

Special Committee of Farm Economic Association. "Adjustments in Southern Agriculture with Special Reference to Cotton," *Journal of Farm Economics*, 28 (February, 1946), 341-79.

Study of Industrial Expansion. Territorial Information Department, Chicago, Ill., Sept., 1948.
Taylor, Charles T. "Some Economic Consequences of Federal Aid and Subsidies to Southern Agriculture," *Southern Economic Journal,* 14 (July, 1947), 62-72.
Thompson, Warren S. "The Demographic Revolution in the United States," *The Annals of the American Academy of Political and Social Science,* 262 (March, 1949), 62-69.
Vance, Rupert B. "How Can the Southern Population Find Gainful Employment?" *Journal of Farm Economics,* 22 (February, 1940), 198-205.
────── in collaboration with Nadia Danilevsky. *All These People.* Chapel Hill: The University of North Carolina Press, 1945, Chaps. 9-20.
Welch, Frank J. "Some Economic and Social Implications of Agricultural Adjustments in the South," *Journal of Farm Economics,* 29 (February, 1947), 192-208.
Wood, Robert E. "Our New Frontier," *The Reader's Digest,* 53 (September, 1948), 17-20.

PUBLICATIONS OF SOUTHERN AGRICULTURAL EXPERIMENT STATIONS

Agricultural Progress in South Carolina 1947. Clemson Agricultural College cooperating with U. S. Dept. of Agri., Extension Service.
Alexander, William H. *Wartime Production and Transportation of Milk in the Shreveport Area of Louisiana.* La. Agri. Expt. Sta., Bul. 378, May, 1944.
Allred, Charles E., and Burnett, Jasper P. *Effect of Industrial Development on Agriculture.* Tenn. Agri. Expt. Sta., Rural Research Series, Monograph No. 97, November, 1939.
Alvord, Ben F.; Crosby, M. A.; and Schiffman, E. G. *Factors Influencing Alabama Agriculture.* Agri. Expt. Sta. of the Ala. Polytechnic Institute in cooperation with U. S. Dept. of Agri., Bur. of Agri. Econ., Bul. 250, April, 1941.
Atkins, S. W., and Mantle, C. C. *Farming Systems and Practices, Red Soil Area, Eastern Highland Rim, Tennessee, 1944.* Tenn. Agri. Expt. Sta., Rural Research Series, Monograph No. 200, June, 1946.
Aull, G. H., and Stepp, J. M. *The Postwar Economic Outlook in an Agricultural-Industrial Area.* S. C. Agri. Expt. Sta., Bul. 355, May, 1945.
Austin, Clarence P.; Cook, Hugh L.; Forster, G. W.; Ferrier, W. T.; Penny, N. M.; Farmer, L. E.; and Mahan, J. N. *Fruit and Vegetable Concentration Markets in North Carolina, South Carolina, Georgia, and Alabama.* S. C. Agri. Expt. Sta., Bul. 367, July, 1946.

Selected Bibliography

Barlow, Frank D., Jr. *An Economic Study of Peach Production in Louisiana.* La. Agri. Expt. Sta., Bul. No. 398, November, 1945.

Blackstone, J. Homer. *Cost of Producing Fluid Milk in Alabama.* Agri. Expt. Sta. of the Ala. Polytechnic Institute, Bul. No. 265, June, 1948.

Brann, W. Paul. *Industrial Development in an Agricultural State.* University of Arkansas, Bureau of Research, Information Series No. 4, January, 1947.

Butler, Charles P., and Crawford, D. E. *Farm Power Utilization and Cost on "Very Large" Farms in the South Carolina Piedmont.* S. C. Agri. Expt. Sta., Bul. 371, April, 1948.

———. *Economics of Tractor Farming in the Piedmont Area of South Carolina.* S. C. Agri. Expt. Sta., Bul. 377, Nov., 1948.

Campbell, John D. *Oklahoma Farmers' Experiences with Cotton Strippers.* Okla. Agri. Expt. Sta., Bul. No. B-324, Oct., 1948.

Christopher, R. C., and Roy, Kenneth B. *Cotton-Hog Farming on the Sand Mountain.* Agri. Expt. Sta. of the Ala. Polytechnic Institute, Circular No. 91, January, 1945.

Crowe, Grady B. *Mechanical Cotton Picker Operation in the Yazoo-Mississippi Delta: A Progress Report.* Miss. Agri. Expt. Sta. in cooperation with U. S. Dept. of Agri., Bur. of Agri. Econ., May, 1949.

Czarowitz, P. H., and Bonnen, C. A. *Information Basic to Farm Adjustments in the Rolling Plains Area of Texas.* Texas Agri. Expt. Sta., Bul. No. 617, Sept., 1942.

Danner, M. J.; Luebke, B. H.; and Raskopf, B. D. *Development and Present Importance of Nashville Livestock Market.* Tenn. Agri. Expt. Sta., Rural Research Series, Monograph No. 205, July, 1946.

Downen, M. L. *Seasonal Costs of Producing and Marketing Fluid Milk in Rutherford County, Tennessee, 1947-48.* Tenn. Agri. Expt. Sta., Rural Research Series, Monograph No. 242, April, 1949.

Dunlavy, Henry, and Parrott, I. M. *Mechanical Harvesting of Cotton.* Okla. Agri. Expt. Sta., Bul. No. 286, August, 1945.

Edwards, Allen D. *Population in Relation to Resources and Employment Opportunities in South Carolina.* S. C. Agri. Expt. Sta., Bul. 358, May, 1945.

A Farm Program for North Carolina. N. C. Agri. Ext. Service, July, 1948.

Fenske, Leo J., and Barlow, Frank D., Jr. *Tractors on Upland Farms in North Louisiana.* La. Agri. Expt. Sta. and U. S. Dept. of Agri., Bur. of Agri. Econ. cooperating, Bul. No. 399, November, 1945.

Forster, G. W. *Cropper Farming in the Coastal Plain.* N. C. Agri. Expt. Sta., Tech. Bul. No. 73, Sept., 1942.

Fulmer, J. L. *A Statistical Study of Agricultural and Related Trends in South Carolina.* S. C. Agri. Expt. Sta., Bul. 312, Oct., 1937.

Gabbard, L. P., and Jones, F. R. *Large-scale Cotton Production in Texas.* Texas Agri. Expt. Sta., Bul. No. 362, July, 1927.

Gaines, James P., and Crowe, Grady B. "Operating Costs of Tractors, Trucks, Trailers, and Combines Studied." *Mississippi Farm Research,* 12 (April, 1949), 6-7.

Gee, Wilson. *The Qualitative Nature of Rural Depopulation in Santuc Township, South Carolina 1900-1930.* S. C. Agri. Expt. Sta., Bul. 287, January, 1933.

Greene, R. E. L. *The Dairy Farm—Its Organization and Cost. 89 Farms Wholesaling Fluid Milk in the Raleigh-Durham and Greensboro–Winston-Salem Areas, 1941.* N. C. Agri. Expt. Sta., Bul. No. 345, June, 1944.

———; James, H. Brooks; and Dawson, C. G. *Farm Mechanization in the Piedmont.* N. C. Agri. Expt. Sta., Tech. Bul. 84, August, 1947.

Grigsby, Reid M., and Ballinger, Roy A. *The New Orleans Market for Fluid Milk.* La. Agri. Expt. Sta., Bul. No. 339, February, 1942.

Gull, P. W., and Adams, J. E. *Mechanical Production of Cotton.* Miss. Agri. Expt. Sta., Bul. 423, Sept., 1945.

Hitt, Homer L. *Recent Migration into and within the Upper Mississippi Delta of Louisiana.* La. Agri. Expt. Sta., Bul. 364, June, 1943.

Holcomb, E. J., and Aull, G. H. *Sharecroppers and Wage Laborers on Selected Farms in Two Counties in South Carolina.* S. C. Agri. Expt. Sta. in cooperation with the U. S. Dept. of Agri., Bur. of Agri. Econ., Bul. 328, June, 1940.

James, H. Brooks, and Barlow, Frank D., Jr., *Farm Mechanization: Power Costs and Production Requirements in the Northern Coastal Plains.* N. C. Agri. Expt. Sta., Bul. No. 348, December, 1944.

Johnson, Magnus B., and Allred, C. E. *Graphic Summary of Purebred Livestock, Tennessee and United States.* Tenn. Agri. Expt. Sta., Rural Research Series, Monograph No. 158, June, 1943.

Land Tenure in the Southwestern States, a Summary of Significant Findings of the Regional Land Tenure Research Project. Arkansas Agri. Expt. Sta. and Agri. Expt. Stations of Miss., La., Okla., and Texas cooperating; also Farm Foundation and U. S. Dept. of Agri., Bul. 482, Oct., 1948.

Lanham, Ben T., Jr., *Farm Power and Equipment Costs in Northern Alabama.* Agri. Expt. Sta. of the Alabama Polytechnic Institute, Bul. 260, March, 1947.

Lee, Alvin T. M., and Aull, George H. *Land Use and Soil Conservation in the Broad River Soil Conservation District of South Carolina.* S. C. Agri. Expt. Sta. in cooperation with U. S. Dept. of Agri., Bureau of Agri. Econ., Bul. 373, June, 1948.

Looking Forward in Oklahoma Agriculture. Published by Division of Agriculture, Oklahoma A. and M. College, Stillwater. Bul. No. B-299, June, 1946.

Luebke, B. H. *Changing Pattern of Hay Production in Tennessee.* Tenn. Agri. Expt. Sta., Rural Research Series, Monograph No. 234, May, 1948.

———. *Graphic Summary of Changes in Use of Cropland in Tennessee.* Tenn. Agri. Expt. Sta., Rural Research Series, Monograph No. 218, April, 1947.

———. *Trends in Livestock Production by Type of Farming Areas.* Tenn. Agri. Expt. Sta., Rural Research Series, Monograph No. 228, August, 1947.

———, and Mantle, C. C. *Changes in Milk Collection Situation, Knoxville Milk Shed, 1943 and 1944.* Tenn. Agri. Expt. Sta., Rural Research Series, Monograph No. 174, August, 1944.

McPherson, W. K. *A General Appraisal of the Livestock Industry in the Southeastern States.* Agri. Expt. Sta. of the Ala. Polytechnic Institute, Bul. 257, June, 1942.

McVay, Francis E. *Factory Meets Farm in North Carolina.* N. C. Agri. Expt. Sta., Tech. Bul. No. 83, October, 1947.

Magee, A. C.; Bonnen, C. A.; and Thibodeaux, B. H. *Information Basic to Farm Adjustments in the High Plains Area of Texas.* Texas Agri. Expt. Sta., Bul. No. 652, July, 1944.

Masters, Fred N., and Allred, Charles E. *Population Situation and Trends in Tennessee as a Whole.* Tenn. Agri. Expt. Sta., Rural Research Series, Monograph No. 166, March, 1944.

———, and Chambers, A. H. *Farm Machinery in Jonesboro Area, Washington County, Tennessee, 1943.* Tenn. Agri. Expt. Sta., Rural Research Series, Monograph No. 211, November, 1946.

Mayo, Selz C., and Hamilton, C. Horace. *Rural Population Problems in North Carolina.* N. C. Agri. Expt. Sta., Tech. Bul. No. 76, August, 1943.

Miley, D. Gray. *Commercial Agricultural Production and Marketing Methods and Facilities in Mississippi.* Miss. Agri. Expt. Sta., Bul. 394, Oct., 1943.

Motheral, Joe R. *Trends in the Texas Farm Population, 1947.* Texas Agri. Expt. Sta., Progress Report 1098, November, 1947.

Selected Bibliography

Nichols, Ralph R., and King, Morton B., Jr. *Social Effects of Government Land Purchase.* Miss. Agri. Expt. Sta., Bul. 390, June, 1943.

Parvin, D. W. *Development of the Dairy Industry in Mississippi.* Miss. Agri. Expt. Sta., Bul. 422, July, 1945.

―――. *Livestock Auctions in Mississippi.* Miss. Agri. Expt. Sta., Bul. 400, May, 1944.

Peterson, M. J., and Aull, G. H. *A Pattern of Agricultural Production in South Carolina after the War.* S. C. Agri. Expt. Sta., Bul. 356, April, 1945.

Raskopf, B. D., and Guilford, Margaret M. *Outside Markets for Poultry and Eggs Shipped from Tennessee and Knoxville Trade Area.* Tenn. Agri. Expt. Sta., Rural Research Series, Monograph No. 229, August, 1947.

Rowan, W. S.; Luebke, B. H.; and Raskopf, B. D. *Volume, Transportation and Use by Local Farmers—Knoxville Livestock Market.* Tenn. Agri. Expt. Sta., Rural Research Series, Monograph No. 203, June, 1946.

Slusher, M. W., and Mullins, Troy. *Mechanization of the Rice Harvest.* Ark. Agri. Expt. Sta. and U. S. Dept. of Agri., Bur. of Agri. Econ. cooperating, Report Series 11, August, 1948.

Smith, H. P., and Jones, D. L. *Mechanized Production of Cotton in Texas.* Texas Agri. Expt. Sta., Bulletin 704, Sept., 1948.

Smith, H. P.; Killough, D. T.; Byrom, M. H.; Scoates, D.; and Jones, D. L. *The Mechanical Harvesting of Cotton.* Texas Agri. Expt. Sta., Bul. No. 452, August, 1932.

Smith, H. P.; Killough, D. T.; and Jones, D. L. *Factors Affecting the Performance of Mechanical Cotton Harvesters (Stripper Type), Extractors and Cleaners.* Texas Agri. Expt. Sta., Bul. No. 686, December, 1946.

Smith, H. P.; Killough, D. T.; Jones, D. L.; and Byrom, M. H. *Mechanical Harvesting of Cotton as Affected by Varietal Characteristics and Other Factors.* Texas Agri. Expt. Sta., Bul. No. 580, Dec., 1939.

Stepp, J. M., and Plaxico, J. S. *The Labor Supply of a Rural Industry.* S. C. Agri. Expt. Sta., Bul. 376, July, 1948.

Tharp, Max M. *The Farm Tenure Situation in the Southeast.* S. C. Agri. Expt. Sta. in cooperation with the U. S. Dept. of Agri., Bul. 370, January, 1948.

Welch, Frank J. *Economic Problems in Mississippi and the South.* Miss. Agri. Expt. Sta., Special Circular 2, April, 1944.

―――. *The Plantation Land Tenure System in Mississippi.* Miss. Agri. Expt. Sta., Bul. 385, June, 1943.

―――, and Miley, D. Gray. *Mechanization of the Cotton Harvest.* Miss. Agri. Expt. Sta., Bul. 420, June, 1945.

Selected Bibliography

Whatley, Thomas J. *Significant Trends in Agriculture of Crockett County, Tennessee, 1879-1945.* Tenn. Agri. Expt. Sta., Rural Research Series, Monograph No. 230, September, 1947.

———. *Trends and Opportunities for Dairying in Haywood and Weakley Counties, Tennessee.* Tenn. Agri. Expt. Sta., Rural Research Series, Monograph No. 231, December, 1947.

Williams, B. O. *Occupational Mobility among Farmers;* Pt. I: *Mobility Patterns.* S. C. Expt. Sta., Bul. 296, June, 1934.

Government Publications

Anderson, Olav F. *Dairying in War and Peace.* U. S. Dept. of Agri., Bur. of Agri. Econ., F. M. 61, March, 1947.

Bachman, K. L.; Crowe, G. B.; and Goodman, K. V. *Peanuts in Southern Agriculture.* U. S. Dept. of Agri., Bur. of Agri. Econ., F. M. 65, 1947.

Bernert, Eleanor H. *Volume and Composition of Net Migration from the Rural-Farm Population, 1930-1940, for the United States, Major Geographic Divisions and States.* U. S. Dept. of Agri., Bur. of Agri. Econ., Mimeographed, January, 1944.

Brodell, A. P., and Cooper, M. R. *Number and Duty of Principal Farm Machines.* U. S. Dept. of Agri., Bur. of Agri. Econ., F. M. 46, November, 1944, pp. 26-39.

———, and Ewing, J. A. *Use of Tractor Power, Animal Power, and Hand Methods in Crop Production.* U. S. Dept. of Agri., Bur. of Agri. Econ., F. M. 69, July, 1948, pp. 9-28.

Bureau of the Census. "Internal Migration in the United States: April, 1940, to April, 1947," *Current Population Reports,* Series P-20, No. 14, April 15, 1948.

———. "Internal Migration in the United States: April, 1947, to April, 1948," *Current Population Reports,* Series P-20, No. 22, January 28, 1949.

Cooper, Martin R. *Production Costs and Returns.* U. S. Dept. of Agri., Bur. of Agri. Econ., June, 1939.

———; Barton, Glen T.; and Brodell, Albert P. *Progress of Farm Mechanization.* U. S. Dept. of Agri., Misc. Pub. No. 630, October, 1947.

Cotton. Hearings before the Subcommittee of the Committee on Agriculture, House of Representatives, Seventy-eighth Congress, Second Session, December 4 to 9., 1944.

Current Population Reports: Consumer Income. U. S. Dept. of Commerce, Bureau of the Census, Series P-60, No. 3, June, 1948.

Geographic Distribution of Construction in the United States 1939-1947. U. S. Dept. of Commerce, January, 1948.

Selected Bibliography

Graphic Summary of Farm Tenure in the United States: Cooperative Report. U. S. Dept. of Commerce and U. S. Dept. of Agriculture, 1948.

Johnson, Neil W. *Changes in Hay Production in War and Peace.* U. S. Dept. of Agri., Bur. of Agri. Econ., F. M. 47, March, 1945.

Johnson, Sherman E. *Changes in Farming.* U. S. Dept. of Agri., Bur. of Agri. Econ., F. M. 58, Revised, June, 1948.

———. *Should the South Shift to Livestock?* U. S. Dept. of Agri., Bur. of Agri. Econ., Mimeographed, July, 1941.

Labor in the South. U. S. Dept. of Labor, Bul. No. 898, 1947, pp. 1-55.

Langsford, E. L. *Changes in Cotton Production in War and Peace.* U. S. Dept. of Agri., Bur. of Agri. Econ., F. M. 45, Dec., 1944.

Long-range Agricultural Policy. A Study of Selected Trends and Factors Relating to the Long-range Prospect for American Agriculture for the Committee on Agriculture of the House of Representatives, Eightieth Congress, Second Session, March 10, 1948.

Mesick, D. O. *Farm Machinery.* U. S. Dept. of Agri., Bur. of Agri. Econ., Mimeographed, March, 1949, pp. 4-5.

Mullins, Troy. *Harvesting Cotton in the High Plains Area of Texas: Machine Versus Hand.* U. S. Dept. of Agri., Bur. of Agri. Econ., in cooperation with Texas Agri. Expt. Sta., Progress Report No. 952, August, 1945.

Raper, A. *Role of Agricultural Technology in Southern Social Change.* U. S. Dept. of Agri., Bur. of Agri. Econ., May, 1946.

Regional Adjustments to Meet War Impacts, U. S. Dept. of Agri., Oct., 1940, pp. 16-36.

Reuss, L. A.; Wooten, H. H.; and Marschner, F. J. *Inventory of Major Land Uses in the United States.* U. S. Dept. of Agri., Bur. of Agri. Econ., Misc. Pub. No. 663.

Schwartz, Charles F., and Graham, Robert E., Jr. "State Income Payments in 1947," *Survey of Current Business,* U. S. Dept. of Commerce, August, 1948, pp. 10-21.

Strand, Edwin G. *Soybean Production in War and Peace.* U. S. Dept. of Agri., Bur. of Agri. Econ., F. M. 50, Sept., 1945.

Study of the Agricultural and Economic Problems of the Cotton Belt. Hearings before Special Subcommittee on Cotton of the Committee on Agriculture, House of Representatives, Eightieth Congress, First Session, July 7 and 8, 1947.

Taylor, Carl C.; Ducoff, Louis J.; and Hagood, Margaret Jarman. *Trends in the Tenure Status of Farm Workers in the United States since 1880.* U. S. Dept. of Agri., Bur. of Agri. Econ., July, 1948.

Thibodeaux, B. H. *Factors of Economic Importance in Southern Agriculture.* U. S. Dept. of Agri., Bur. of Agri. Econ., Sept., 1939.

SOURCES OF STATISTICAL DATA

Agricultural Statistics, 1940, 1944, 1946, and 1947. U. S. Dept. of Agriculture.

Annual Estimates of the Farm Population, by States, 1920-1940. U. S. Dept. of Agri., Bur. of Agri. Econ., Mimeographed, February, 1944.

Bernert, Eleanor H. *County-variation in Net Migration from the Rural-Farm Population, 1930-40.* U. S. Dept. of Agri., Bur. of Agri. Econ., Mimeographed, December, 1944.

Cash Receipts from Farming by States and Commodities, Calendar Years 1924-44. U. S. Dept. of Agri., Bur. of Agri. Econ., Jan., 1946.

Census of Agriculture, 1945. Reprints from Vol. II. *Age, Residence, Years on Farm, and Work off Farm.* U. S. Dept. of Commerce, Bur. of the Census, Chap. IV.

———. *Color and Tenure of Farm Operator.* U. S. Dept. of Commerce, Bur. of the Census, Chap. III.

———. *Farms and Farm Property.* U. S. Dept. of Commerce, Bur. of the Census, Chap. I.

———. *Farm Facilities, Roads, and Farm Machinery.* U. S. Dept. of Commerce, Bur. of the Census, Chap. VI.

———. *Farm Population and Farm Labor.* U. S. Dept. of Commerce, Bur. of the Census, Chap. V.

———. *Field Crops and Vegetables.* U. S. Dept. of Commerce, Bur. of the Census, Chap. VIII.

———. *Livestock and Livestock Products.* U. S. Dept. of Commerce, Bur. of the Census, Chap. VII.

Census of Agriculture, 1945. *Multiple-unit Operations.* U. S. Dept. of Commerce, Bur. of the Census, 1947.

Cotton Acreage, Yield, and Production, 1866-1938, by States; and Related Data. U. S. Dept. of Agri., Sept., 1940.

Crops and Markets. U. S. Dept. of Agri., Vol. 19, February, 1942, pp. 33 and 40.

The Farm Income Situation. U. S. Dept. of Agri., Bur. of Agri. Econ., FIS Nos. 73, 99, and 100.

Farm Population, Estimates, United States and Major Geographic Divisions, 1940-1947; States, 1940-1945. U. S. Dept. of Agri., Bur. of Agri. Econ., August, 1947.

Farm Population Estimates, January, 1948. U. S. Dept. of Agri., Bur. of Agri. Econ., June, 1948.

Selected Bibliography

Farm Production and Disposition of Chickens and Eggs, 1925-1937; Chickens on Farms, January 1, 1925-1938, by States. U. S. Dept. of Agri., Bur. of Agri. Econ., December, 1938.

Farm Production, Farm Disposition, and Value of Cotton and Cottonseed, and Related Data, 1928-44, by States. U. S. Dept. of Agri., Bur. of Agri. Econ., Oct., 1945.

Livestock on Farms, January 1, 1867-1935: Revised Estimates, Number, Value per Head, Total Value, by States and Divisions. U. S. Dept. of Agri., Bur. of Agri. Econ., Jan., 1938.

Livestock on Farms Jan. 1. U. S. Dept. of Agri., Crop Reporting Board, Feb., 1948.

Livestock and Poultry on Farms January 1, Number, Value per Head, and Total Value: Livestock and Poultry by Classes, Revised Estimates, 1940-1945, by States. U. S. Dept. of Agri., Bur. of Agri. Econ., February, 1947.

Meat Animals: Farm Production and Income, 1924-44, Revised Estimates by States. U. S. Dept. of Agri., Bur. of Agri. Econ., Sept., 1947.

National Income Supplement to Survey of Current Business. U. S. Dept. of Commerce, July, 1947.

Peanuts: Acreage, Yield per Acre, Production, Farm Disposition, and Value, 1909-45, by States, and Areas for the United States. U. S. Dept. of Agri., Bur. of Agri. Econ., March, 1948.

Sixteenth Census of the United States, 1940. *Population;* Vol. I, *Number of Inhabitants.* U. S. Dept. of Commerce, Bur. of the Census, 1942.

———. *Population;* Vol. II, *Characteristics of the Population.* U. S. Dept. of Commerce, Bur. of the Census, 1943.

Statistical Abstract of the United States, 1940 and 1946. U. S. Dept. of Commerce.

Statistics on Cotton and Related Data. U. S. Dept. of Agri., Bur. of Agri. Econ., Dec., 1939.

Tobaccos of the United States: Acreage, Yield per Acre, Production, Price, and Value; By States, 1866-1945 and by Types and Classes, 1919-1945. U. S. Dept. of Agri., Bur. of Agri. Econ., CS-30, July, 1948.

Index

Index

A.A.A. programs, classes of farmers affected by, 146; conservation, aspects of, 146, 173-74; effects of, 4, 80, 136, 138-39, 144-46, 174; and experiment station research, 146, 189; flexibility in, 182; incentive payments of, 146; safeguards for future programs, 182; and yield effects of Soil Conservation Service compared, 146, 174. *See also* Agricultural progress

Agricultural education, 3, 183-86

Agricultural policy. *See under* Agricultural progress

Agricultural progress: agricultural adjustments, subsidies for, 183; agricultural research, dissemination and application of, 189-90; conditions for future progress, 168, 179-90; cotton acreage, decline in, 170; cotton acreage adjustments, flexibility in, 179, 182; cotton acreage limitations, 179-83; economic structure of South, changes in, 178; effects of, 152-53, 156-57; factors influencing, 170-78; farm income changes, 177-78; farming career, inducements to qualified persons, 183-86; farm labor program, 186-87; farm population, decline in, 18, 38-40, 133, 174; government loans to prospective capable farmers, 183-86; market organization for products competitive with cotton, 183; national land use policy, 187-88; number of farms, reduction in, 19, 40-41, 172; number of tractors, increase in, 17, 36-38, 69n, 170; pasture increase, 10-11, 31-32; sharecroppers, decline in, 74-76, 171; soil conservation programs, 144-46, 173-74; tenancy, decline in, 74-75, 172; urbanization, increase in, 123-29, 175-76; yields, increase in, 7, 24, 26-27, 173. *See also* A.A.A. programs, Business conditions, *and* World War II

Agricultural relief, agitation for, 3

Agricultural research, 189-90

Aull, G. H., 77, 81

Barton, Glen T., 61

Binders, grain, 67

Birth rates. *See* Reproduction rates

Black, John D., 158

Boll weevil, 3-4, 136

Brodell, Albert T., 61

Brunner, Edmund de S., 129, 133n

Business conditions, and agriculture, 157-58; carry-over of cotton related to, 180; and city growth, 113; effect on off-farm work, 124; farm migration, relation to, 20-21; and ratio of milk cows to all cattle, 14, 35; relation to agricultural surpluses and income, 180-81; relation to farm purchases, 76

Cash farm receipts, shifts in sources of, 21-22, 42-44; sources by states, leading ones summarized, 46; sources given by dollar volume and rank by states, 44-46; specialty enterprises, dollar volume for leading states, 46-47; trends in, 21-22, 42-44, 149-50, 177. *See also* Farm income *and* Per capita cash farm receipts

Cattle, density comparisons of Cotton Belt and 38 other states, 58-59; increase by regions compared to 38 other states, 55-57; increase in, 12-13, 33-34; number in different regions as ratio to 38 other

230 *Index*

states, 57-58; number per farm and trends in, by regions, 50-53; ratio to cropland and trends in, by regions, 53-55; recent changes in, 15, 34; rise in relative cash farm receipts from, 21-22, 43; trend in number per farm in Cotton Belt compared to 38 other states, 58-59

Chickens, changes in, 14-15, 33-34; changes in relative cash farm receipts, 21-22, 43; density comparisons of Cotton Belt and 38 other states, 58-59; increase by regions compared to 38 other states, 55-57; number in different regions as ratio to 38 other states, 57-58; number per farm and trends in, by regions, 50-53; ratio to cropland and trends in, by regions, 53-55; trend in eggs per hen, U. S. average, 16

Cities, employment characteristics in Cotton Belt cities compared to those of large northern cities, 116-17; facilities provided for industrial growth by, 107; factors in rapid growth of, 113-15; and farm labor, educational level of, 132-33; and farm migration, 129; growth, most rapid periods of, 113; growth and economic status of farm population, 108; growth and pattern of agriculture, 108, 129; industrial growth and demand for raw materials, 107; listed, 114-15; as markets for perishable agricultural products, 125; and part-time employment for farm labor, 123-25; population supply, sources of, 118, 175; prospects for further growth, 117; reproduction rate of, 118; size of, related to average per capita income, 134n; size of, related to demand for milk, eggs, and fresh fruits and vegetables, 125; and surplus farm population, 118, 123, 133, 175. *See also* Urban centers *and* Urban population

Coffee County, Alabama, 4

Combines, 67-69

Committee on industrialization of the South, forecasts: of labor displacement by cotton picker and flame cultivator, 71, 80, 102, 106; of labor displacement by tractors, 71, 80; of number of tractors in 1965, 70

Cooper, Martin R., 60n, 61, 76n, 143

Corn, 8-9, 27-30

Cotton, cash farm receipts, relative loss in, 21, 42-43; cyclical crops of, 5; effects of 1948 crop, 5, 7; enterprises replacing, 42-44, 169-70; income, relative decline in, 20, 169; salability of, 82; trends in 1948, 30. *See also* Cotton stripper *and* Mechanical cotton picker

Cotton acreage, declines in, 5, 24; decrease, effect of, 10, 170; government loans and 1949 expansion of, 181-82; and number of tractors, 171; per farm, trend in, 136-38, 173; program, 179-83

Cotton Belt regions: cash farm receipts, 21, 42-46, 170; cropland use, 48-50, 53-55; cotton, 24-25, 29-30, 43-44, 63-66, 136-38, 170; cotton farms, 29-30, 40-42, 135-36, 139-42, 147; farm organization, 47-48, 50-53, 172-73; farm population, 38-40, 122-23, 139-41, 147; government payments per capita, 150-52; income payments, 161-63; livestock, 33-35, 55-59; livestock products, 36-37, 125-29; number of farms, 40-42; non-cotton crops, 27, 30, 125-27; output per worker in agriculture, 154-57; pasture, 11, 31-32, 47; per capita cash farm receipts, 150-57; per capita income payments, 159-61; population, 122-23, 125-29, 161-62; sharecroppers, 74-75; size of farms, 41, 47; tractors, 36-38, 54-55, 63-69, 72-75, 143-44, 171; workstock, 38, 51-55, 141-44

Cotton carry-over, 179-80

Cotton farms, age distribution of operators, 129-33, 177; conditions affecting, review of, 135-36; decline in, 41-42, 135; effect of decline in, upon farm population, 140-41, 147; maximum number since 1920, 41-42, 135; and number of tractors, 80; and number of workstock, 141-42, 147; trend in size of, 136-38, 173

Cotton harvest, by machine in 1946,

Index

102n, 104; and mechanical picker in Delta, analysis of, 87-106; Mexican cotton pickers, 83, 87; migratory cotton pickers, 83, 141n; picker, rate of, 97-98, 104; prospects for picker in, 103-6; snapped, 85; snapping defined, 83n; stripper, importance of, 85; stripper, rate of, 83-84, 97; West Texas stripper analyzed, 82-87. *See also* Cotton stripper *and* Mechanical cotton picker

Cotton mechanization. *See under* Mechanization

Cotton picker. *See* Mechanical cotton picker

Cotton production, areas of, 24-25; decline in, 24; and flame cultivation, 98n; importance of, in California, 25-27; interregional trends, 25-26; irrigated areas, 25-27; labor requirements, trends in, 61-62; mechanization of, 63-67; per farm, trend in, 136-38, 173; technological improvements in, compared to those in wheat and corn, 61-62, 79; trends in, 5, 24; turning point in, 5

Cotton stripper, analysis relative to, 82-87, 103-6; acreage performance compared to mechanical picker, 97-98; conditions favoring, 83, 85-87; effect of, on Cotton Belt's agriculture, 97-103; and cotton harvest in West Texas, 85, 104; details of operation, 83-84; effect on farm consolidation, 101; effect on farm size, 101; effect on labor requirements of production operations, 98-100; farmers' models of, 83; grade loss from, 84; gin equipment for, 83; and hand-snapping, 85; and hand-worker ratio, 84, 97; introduction in West Texas, 83; investment in, 104n; labor displacement from, 102; and labor saving in cotton harvest, 98-100; number in operation, 106n; patents issued for, 82-83; and size of cotton crop, 83, 86; and supply of labor, 85-87; and waste loss from, 84; and weather conditions, 86-87. *See also* Mechanical cotton picker

Cotton yield, increase in, 7, 24, 26-27, 80, 144, 173

Cows. *See* Livestock *and* Milk cows

Crop yields, effect of A.A.A. conservation programs upon, 144-46, 174; effect of Soil Conservation Service programs upon, 144-46, 174; factors affecting increase, 7, 80, 144; general increase of, in United States, 60; increase in cotton yields, 6-7, 24-27, 173; increase related to decrease in sharecroppers, 76-79; of tractor farms and non-tractor farms compared, 70

Cropland, 8, 10, 41, 47-50

Crowe, Grady B., 90, 91, 92n, 93, 97, 98n, 101n, 102n, 104n, 105

Dairy products, 15-16, 21-23, 36-37, 43

Danielson, G. B., 98n

Delta states, defined, 24n. *See also* Cotton Belt regions

Diversification, 3. *See also* Agricultural progress

Eastern cotton states, defined, 7n, 24n. *See also* Cotton Belt regions

Economic conditions. *See* Business conditions

Education, agricultural, 3, 183, 185; of migrants, 133

Efficiency, disparity in Cotton Belt with rest of United States, 156-57, 167; effect of combines, 67-69; increase of crop yield, U. S. average, 60; increase of labor, 60-62, 79; increase of land, U. S. average, 60; increase of livestock and livestock products, U. S. average, 16; and per capita cash farm receipts, 154-57; related to training program for labor, 187. *See also* Mechanization *and* Tractors

Eggs, increase in output per hen, U. S. average, 16; production related to changes in total population, 126-29; trends in, 15-16, 21-22, 36-37, 43

Electricity, 17

Extensive crops, acreage per farm and trends by regions, 47-49; definition of, 47n; proportion of cropland in and trends by regions, 48-50

Farm income, from cotton and cottonseed, decline in relative importance of, 19-20, 169-70; and income payments of Cotton Belt related, 158; and national income payments related, 157-58; trends in distribution of, 19-20, 169-70. *See also* Cash farm receipts

Farm labor, disparity in output per worker, 156-57, 167; displacement by mechanical cotton picker and flame cultivator, 71, 80, 102, 106; displacement by tractors, 71, 80; efficiency of, increase in, 60-61; farm wage rates and price of cotton related, 76-77; hand-worker ratio to cotton stripper, 84, 97, 104; hand-worker ratio to mechanical cotton picker, 97, 104; and high industrial wages, 4; and mechanization, estimated effect on cotton labor requirements, 97-100; Mexican cotton pickers, 83, 87; migratory cotton pickers, 83, 87, 141n; output per worker, trends in, 154-56; requirements of corn, cotton, and wheat since 1800, 61-62; requirements of jobs in cotton production, estimated effects of mechanization, 97-100. *See also* Farm wages

Farm loans. *See* Government loans

Farm machinery, flexibility of price response to price level changes, 92, 94n; price inflexibility of, compared to farm wages, 100; number on farms and trends in, 67-69; suggested price policy for deflation period, 95-97. *See also* Mechanization *and* Tractors

Farm operators and owners, age distribution of, 129-33, 177; compensation from farming, 184; and education, 133-34, 183-84; factors favoring purchase of farms, 76; inducements to ownership, 133, 134, 177, 183-86

Farm population, changes in, 17-18, 38-40, 174-75; effects of decrease in, 18, 133; forecast of, 119-21; and growth of urban centers, 118, 133, 175; and industrialization, 108, 174-75; and housing shortage, 18; and migration, 17-18, 38-40, 129-33; net reproduction rates of, 118-19; recovery of war losses of, 18, 39-40; relative growth in three Cotton Belt reigons, 122; and resources, 18, 133

Farm power. *See* Electricity, Trucks, Tractors, *and* Workstock

Farm returns, intangibles, 184; related to educational level, 184-85. *See also* Cash farm receipts *and* Farm income.

Farms. *See* Cotton farms, Number of farms, *and* Size of farm

Farm wages, and price of cotton, 76-79; and snapping of cotton, 83, 86; and stripper operation, 86-87; relationship of hand picking rates of cotton to costs of operating mechanical cotton picker, 89, 91, 96; terms of exchange for farm machinery, 100. *See also* Farm labor

Feed supply, 9-10, 27-30, 171

Fertilizer increase, 16-17, 173

Flame cultivator, conclusions relative to, 98n; labor displacement by, 71, 80, 102; reduction in cotton production requirements, 99

Forster, G. W., 144n

Gin equipment, adaptations to stripper-harvested cotton, 83; experiments with mechanically harvested cotton, 97n; installations for mechanically harvested cotton, rate of, 97n

Government loans, to capable prospective farmers, 133, 134, 177, 185-86; effect on cotton acreage in 1949, 181-82

Government programs. *See* A.A.A. programs

Graham, Robert E., Jr., 164

Grain sorghums, 9, 27-30

Greene, R. E. L., 70, 144n

Hogs, changes in cotton regions compared to changes in 38 other states, 55-56; changes in relative cash farm receipts, 21-22, 43; density comparisons of Cotton Belt and 38 other states, 58-59; number in cotton regions as ratio to 38 other states,

Index

57-58; number per farm and trends by regions, 50-53; output per sow, U. S. average, 16; ratio to cropland and trends in, by regions, 53-55; recent changes in, 15, 34; trends in, 11-13, 33-34, 58-59

Holcomb, E. J., 77, 81

Income. *See* Farm income, Farm wages *and* Industrial wages

Income payments, disparity of, in Cotton Belt regions, 161-62; and farm income, 157-58; gains of Cotton Belt, 161-63; and population ratios compared by regions, 161-62; postwar, 163-66. *See also* Per capita income payments

Industrialization in the South, factors in, 163-65; factors in shift of industrial axis, 166-67; postwar expansion of, 165-66; progress of, 163-65; relation to agricultural progress, 168, 178; trend in, 165, 166-67

Industrial wages, effect of high wages on farm labor, 4; effect of World War II upon, 163; gains in South and United States compared, 163

Intensive crops, acreage per farm and trends by regions, 47-49; definition of, 47n; percentage of cropland in, and trends by regions, 48-50

Johnson, Sherman E., 16n, 60n, 154n

Labor. *See* Farm labor, Farm wages, *and* Industrial wages

Labor training program, for city migrants, 186; for farm labor, 187; relation to agricultural productivity, 187

Land, A.A.A. programs and quality of, 80; increase in acreage per farm, 19, 41, 47; increase in efficiency of, 60; quality of and crop yields, 80; urbanization and value of, 129

Langsford, E. L., 24, 25n, 26, 98-99

Lanham, Ben T., Jr., 69n, 144n

Lespedeza hay, 8-10, 27-30, 144

Lime, 16-17

Livestock, changes by cotton regions compared to 38 other states, 55-57; complicating factors in analysis of, 11-12; density comparisons of Cotton Belt and 38 other states, 58-59; gain in income position of, 19-20; increase in production per animal, U. S. average, 16; number in cotton regions as ratio to 38 other states, 57-58; number per farm and trends in, by regions, 50-53; pasture expansion related to, 11, 31-32; recent changes in, 15, 34; trends in cash farm receipts, 21-22, 42-43; trends in, 11-15, 32-36, 53-55, 58-59

Livestock products, 15-16, 19-23, 36-37, 42-44

Loans. *See* Government loans

McVay, Francis E., 123, 124n

Mechanical cotton picker, and acreage performance of stripper compared, 97-98; analysis relative to, 87-106; conditions influencing operation of, 87, 103-4; cost components, shift in relative importance of, 91; cost items, trends in, 90; costs at different yield and cotton prices, assumptions in computation of, 93-94; and costs of hand-picking compared, 89, 91-92; costs of operation itemized, 89, 91; cotton harvesting, rate of, 88-89, 91, 92n, 105; effect of, on Cotton Belt's agriculture, 97-103; grade loss, 89, 90, 91, 97n; and hand-worker ratio, 97-98; introduction in Mississippi Delta, 87; investments in picker and tractor, 89n, 104n; and labor displacement in Cotton Belt, 102; and labor displacement in the Mississippi Delta, 101; and labor requirements in production operations, 98-100; and labor saving in cotton harvest, 98-100; on large farms, 92n, 101n; number in operation, 102n, 106, 106n; operation of, 87-88; overhead charges, assumptions in calculation of, 89n, 90; performance rates required for three cotton yield and price assumptions, 95; price of cotton, analysis of effects of, 92-97; on small farms, 100; yield of cotton, analysis of effects of, 92-97; yield of cotton and price effects, conclusions relative to, 95-97. *See also* Cotton stripper

Mechanization, of the cotton harvest, 82-106; effect on labor requirements of jobs in cotton farming, 98-100; effect on Southern agriculture, 69-81, 97-106; increase in number of tractors, 17, 36-38, 69n, 80, 170; increase in tractor-drawn machinery, 67-69; labor displacement, forecast of, 70-71, 80, 101-102; and long-run decrease in labor requirements of corn, cotton, and wheat, 60-62; of production operations in corn, cotton, and small grains, extent of and trend in, 63-66; reasons for slow progress in Southeast, 66. *See also*. Cotton stripper, Mechanical cotton picker, *and* Tractors

Medium intensive crops, acreage per farm and trends by regions, 47-49; definition of, 48n; proportion of cropland in and trends by regions, 48-50

Mexican labor, 83, 87

Migration, and age distribution of farm operators, 129-32; age distribution of migrants, 129; and city growth, 118, 123; and educational level related, 133; effect on agriculture, 129-33; of farm population, 17-18, 38-40, 176-77; from farms, harmful effects of, 133-34, 177; and industrialization, 108, 174-75; to local urban centers, 123, 175; and net reproduction rates, 118-19, 176-77; new axis of, 123n; patterns of, 123, 129, 133, 175; and prospective adjustments in agriculture, 132-34; and training program for city-migrants, 86; and urban growth, 118, 175; and World War II, 17-18, 38-40, 123

Miley, D. Gray, 88, 90, 91, 93, 101, 102, 103, 105

Milk, increase in quantity produced and sold, 16, 36-37; quantity sold related to non-farm population growth, 125-26

Milk cows, 12-15, 34-35

Mullins, Troy, 85, 86n

Number of farms, related to number of tractors, 73, 136, 172; trends in, 19, 40-41, 172. *See also* Cotton farms *and* Size of farm

Oats, 8-9, 28-30

Off-farm work, 123-25

Oklahoma-Texas region. *See* Cotton Belt regions

Operators. *See* Farm operators

Output per worker in agriculture, disparity between Cotton Belt and rest of United States, 156-57, 167; and per capita cash farm income, 156-57, 167; trend in, 154-56. *See also* Efficiency

Owners. *See* Farm operators and owners

Pasture, increase in acreage of, 10-11, 31-32; percentage increase in types of pasture other than woodland, 11, 32; proportion classified as woodland, 11, 32

Peanuts, 8-9, 21-22, 28-31, 42-43

Per capita cash farm receipts, conclusions relative to, 150, 159, 167; disparity in, 150-52, 167, 177-78; effect on efficiency in Southern agriculture, 154-57; effect on progressive changes in Southern agriculture, 152-54; factors influencing, 152-54; farm population decrease related to, 152-54; and farm price increases, 152-54; government payments by regions compared, 150-52, 167, 178; increases in Cotton Belt compared to rest of the United States, 150-51; trends in, by regions, 150-52, 177. *See also* Cash farm receipts

Per capita income payments, conclusions relative to, 159, 167; disparity of Cotton Belt regions in, 160-61; trends in, 159-60. *See also* Income payments

Population, balance between categories of, 121, 133; projection forecasts for major categories, 119-21; ratio to demand for eggs, 126-29; ratio between Oklahoma-Texas and rest of United States, trend in, 161. *See also* Farm population,

Rural-nonfarm population, *and* Urban population

Productivity. *See* Efficiency *and* Output per worker in agriculture

Raper, A., 97n

Reproduction rates, 118-19

Richmond Times-Dispatch, 166-67

Rural-nonfarm population, projection forecasts of, 119-21; relative growth in three Cotton Belt regions, 122-23

Rust brothers, 82, 102. *See also* Mechanical cotton picker

Schwartz, Charles F., 164

Sharecroppers, decline of, 74-75, 171; effect of decline on Southern Agriculture, 75; margin of profitableness with hired labor, 76-79, 171-72; and mechanization, 72, 76, 79-81, 136, 171-72; number of, related to factors favorable to ownership, 76. *See also* Tenants

Sheep, stock, 35-36, 56-58

Size of farm, in Cotton Belt regions compared, 48-49, 172; and crop intensity, trends in, 47-48; increase in, 19, 41; and mechanical cotton harvesting, 101; probable adjustments in, 133-34; shift in, by states, 41n; trends in acreage and production of cotton per farm, 136-38, 173; trends in number of livestock per farm, 50-53; workstock per farm, decline in, 51-53

Smith, T. Lynn, 119n

Soil Conservation Service, 144-46, 147-48, 174

Stripper. *See* Cotton stripper

Subsistence farming, 21

Taylor, Carl C., 75n, 79n

Tenants, age distribution of, trends in, 129-32; decline of, 75, 76, 171. *See also* Sharecroppers

Texas-Oklahoma region. *See* Cotton Belt regions

Tharp, Max M., 75n

Thompson, Warren S., 118-19

Tobacco, 7-8, 21-22, 42-43, 124

Tractor-drawn equipment, in corn, cotton, and small grain production by regions, 63-66; reasons for slow progress of use of, in cotton production in Southeast, 65-66; trends in number on farms, 67-69. *See also* Cotton stripper, Mechanical cotton picker, *and* Tractors

Tractors, advantages of, 71-72; and capacity use, 70; and cropland ratio, trends in, 54-55; and cropland ratio in Cotton Belt compared to rest of United States, 17, 37, 170; disadvantages of, 72; farming operations in corn, cotton, and small grain production, trends in use of, 63-66; farm organization and management, problems posed by, 69-70, 171; and feed increase, 10, 171; labor displacement, forecast of, 70-71, 80; labor requirements in cotton production, estimated effect on, 99; and non-cotton farms, increase in, 72-75, 80, 136, 147, 171; number, increase of, 17, 36-38, 69n, 80, 170; number in South, forecast of, 70-71, 80; ownership, inducements to, 71-72, 170-71; and sharecroppers, 72, 76, 79-81, 136, 171-72; size of farm, effect on efficient use of, 70; and Southern agriculture, effect on, 69-81; tractor-drawn machines, trends in, 67-69; and workstock combinations on cost of power, 69; and workstock decrease, 38, 142, 171; and workstock displacement, 69-70, 143-44

Truck crops, 21-22, 42-44. *See also* Vegetables harvested for sale

Trucks, 17

T.V.A., 163

United States (exclusive of Cotton Belt): income payments and population ratios in, compared to Cotton Belt regions, 161-62; livestock increase in, compared to that of Cotton Belt, 55-59; per capita cash farm receipts in—and efficiency related, 154-57; factors related to, 152-54; compared to those of Cotton Belt, 150-51, 159; conclusions relative to, 153, 167—per capita government payments in, related to Cotton Belt regions, 150-52; per capita income payments in—compared to Cotton Belt regions, 160-61; conclusions relative to, 159, 167—productivity per worker in agriculture in, 154-57

Upper Piedmont, 131n, 132, 183

Urban centers, defined, 110n; and demand for farm products, 133-34; economic services of, 107; growth related to agriculture, 107-8; important urban counties making most rapid growth, 110, 112; location of important urban counties, 110-11. *See also* Cities *and* Urban population

Urbanization, and economic progress, 107; effect on farm land values, 129; effects on agriculture, 123-29, 175; and industrial growth, 107; and off-farm work, 123-25; summary of effects of, 133-34. *See also* Cities *and* Urban population

Urban population, defined, 108n; and farm population ratios, 109-10, 175; farm and rural-nonfarm populations by regions, relative growths compared to, 122-23; forecasts of, 119-21; growth in Cotton Belt compared to rest of United States, 109-10; milk and vegetables, demand for related to growth of, 125-27; and perishable farm products, 125, 129, 133-34

Vegetables harvested for sale, factors in demand for, 107-8, 125; relationship of demand to growth of nonfarm population, 125-27; trends in, 8-10, 21-22, 28-30, 42-44

Wages. *See* Farm wages *and* Industrial wages

Warren, G. F., 185

Welch, Frank J., 88, 90, 91, 93, 101, 102, 103, 105

West Texas, 82-87, 100, 102, 103-4, 131n, 141

Wheat, 8-10, 21-22, 28-30, 43-44

Workstock, decline in, 10, 36-38; decrease in cropland ratio, by regions, 53-55; displacement per farm by tractors, 143-44; effect of decline on feed supply, 10, 171; and number of cotton farms, relationship between, 141-42, 147; number per farm, decline in, 51-53; and tractor combinations, effect on costs, 69; and tractor cropland ratios, trends in compared, 54-55; and tractor increase, 38, 142, 171; and tractor ratio in Alabama, 144n; underutilization caused by tractors, 69. *See also* Tractors

World War II, and city growth, 113; effect on South's industrial pattern, 163-65; expansion in peanut production, 30-31; increase in farm ownership, 76; increase in livestock on farms, 33-34; net migration effects, 176-77; pattern of migration, 123; price rise on per capita cash farm receipts, 152-54; reduction of farm population pressure, 7, 17-18, 38-40, 139, 174; reduction of surplus farm labor, 4; rise of crude birth rates, 118-19; rise of industrial wages, 163

Yields. *See* Crop yields

www.ingramcontent.com/pod-product-compliance
Lightning Source LLC
Chambersburg PA
CBHW021359290426
44108CB00010B/314